Mourning Sex

This is a book about the exhilaration and the catastrophe of embodiment. Analyzing different instances of injured bodies, Phelan considers what sustained attention to the affective force of trauma might yield for critical theory. Advocating what she calls "performative writing", Phelan creates an extraordinary fusion of critical and creative thinking which erodes the distinction between art and theory, fact and fiction.

The bodies she examines here include Christ's, as represented in Caravaggio's painting *The Incredulity of St Thomas*; Anita Hill's and Clarence Thomas's bodies as they were performed during the senate hearings; the disinterred body of the Rose Theatre; exemplary bodies reconstructed through psychoanalytic talking cures; and the filmic bodies created by Tom Joslin, Mark Massi, and Peter Friedman in *Silverlake Life: The View From Here*.

This new work by the highly acclaimed author of *Unmarked* makes a stunning advance in performance theory in dialogue with psycho-analysis, queer theory, and cultural studies.

Peggy Phelan is Chair of the Department of Performance Studies, Tisch School of the Arts, New York University.

Mourning Sex

Performing Public Memories

Peggy Phelan

London and New York

First published 1997
by Routledge
11 New Fetter Lane, London EC4P 4EE

Simultaneously published in the USA and Canada
by Routledge
29 West 35th Street, New York, NY 10001

Typeset in 10 on 12 point Palatino by
Florencetype Ltd, Stoodleigh, Devon

Printed and bound in Great Britain by
Butler & Tanner, Frome, Somerset

British Library Cataloguing in Publication Data
A catalogue record for this book is available from the British Library

Library of Congress Cataloguing in Publication Data
Phelan, Peggy.
   Mourning sex: performing public memories / Peggy Phelan.
      p. cm.
   Includes bibliographical references and index.

   1. Psychic trauma. 2. Loss (Psychology). 3. Grief.
4. Psychoanalysis and culture. 5. Bereavement – Psychological
aspects – Cross cultural studies. I. Title.
BF175.5.P75P48 1997
155.9'37 – dc20   96-9345
                                                         CIP

ISBN   0–415–14758–1(hbk)
ISBN   0–415–14759–X(pbk)

For the Cure
by Love

Contents

Figures

Acknowledgments

I was fortunate to be a Fellow at the University of California-Irvine, Humanities Research Institute, under the direction of Mark Rose, in the spring of 1993. As a participant in the "Choreographing History" seminar, convened by Susan Foster, I have benefitted from conversations with other colleagues in residence, especially Randy Martin, Mark Franko, Sally Ness, Marta Saviligiano, Heidi Gilpin, Linda Tomko, and Lena Hamergren. Debby Massey made my life and times in Irvine infinitely more pleasant and I remain grateful to Chris Aschan, Sauni Hayes, and all the staff for their efficiency, good will, and most especially, for the gift of the garlic press.

The Australian National University of Canberra, Australia, hosted me for several months in 1995 under the auspices of their Humanities Research Centre. I am grateful to Graeme Clarke, Iain McCalman, and their staff for providing me with space, a computer, and a tranquil environment in which to write.

My colleagues at the Tisch School of the Arts, New York University, continue to provoke and stimulate my thinking. As department chair I have had the sobering experience of appreciating retrospectively what it actually takes to make it possible for faculty members to write. The people who have made it possible for me to write this include: Joe Simmons, Todd Rinehart, Jackie Allen, Assistant Dean Peggy Wreen, Dean Mary Schmidt Campbell, my students, and my faculty colleagues in Performance Studies.

I am grateful to Christina Duffy, Carolyn Shapiro, Branislav Jakovljevic, and Kirsten Stammer Fury for their many hours of research assistance, correspondence, and interest. Kirsten has been especially helpful to me in preparing the bibliography, acquiring permissions, and attempting to keep me more or less sane in the final months of this project. Branislav helped me with the copy editing and indexed the book. Their collective intelligence and good grace gives me great confidence in the future of progressive critical thought.

Jane Malmo has been an ideal editor: scrupulous without causing excessive humiliation. Her astute reading of both Renaissance anatomy and psychoanalysis has influenced and clarified the argument developed here. I am grateful for her meticulous attention to my sentences.

Sections of the Anna O chapter appeared in a different form in Susan Foster's edited anthology, *Corporealities* (Indiana University Press, 1995). "Dying Man With A Movie Camera" appeared in *GLQ* in 1995. And "Playing Dead in Stone" appeared in Elin Diamond's anthology, *Performance and Cultural Politics* (Routledge, 1996). I am also grateful to all concerned for granting permission to reproduce the visual art in this book, especially John Burrell for his architectural drawings and the people at Art and Commerce who handle the work of Robert Mapplethorpe. Isabela Basombrio, with whom I made the photographs that cover this book, taught me to be less afraid of color.

Teresa Brennan read an early version of this book and encouraged me to be bolder. Talia Rodgers has been extremely accommodating and generous in her response to all of my requests. Sophie Powell and Diane Stafford were efficient and attentive to the challenges of the book's production. Jody Greene, Susan Bennett, Peta Tait, and Jane Bennett have been sustaining correspondents who encouraged me throughout this long process. Robert Sember has been a loving critic of my work and person. I am grateful to each of them for their attention to this project.

I learn something important in every conversation I have with Lynda Hart: her love and intelligence have had a large influence on my work and life.

Books always cost things far beyond what a single author can pay. I have had to ask my family and most cherished interlocuters to forgive my many disappearances as I took myself from them in order to pay attention to this book. The accounts can never be balanced. This book is not a compensation but it is an elaboration of the decisions I made. Thank you each again for your generous forgiveness.

The deaths of Rena Grant, Danitra Vance, Jay Dorff, Martin Worman, and James Amankulor have been part of the woof in which I wove this writing. The one who drowned made me cry. After a long, dry time, a brown fly touched with the wings of an angel made me laugh. Queen listened beyond all sounding. Private debts. Public records. Thank you each for all.

the gods   the goods: the best we could

1

Introduction: this book's body

I once had a beautiful book with a shiny red vinyl cover. The book's title I cannot remember, something along the lines of "The Wonder of Science" or "Science for Children" or "Science and Other Mysteries." The book had gorgeously detailed illustrations of the interior of thermometers and maps of how clouds formed. It was a fascinating book and I read it with a kind of unbounded thirst. I did not read according to the law of genre but I somehow knew that this particular book was different from my other favorite book, *Old Peter's Russian Fairy Tales*, a big gold-covered worn book with fabulous colored drawings of witches and cauldrons, and different still from the flat beige encyclopedia with small black and white diagrams of machines. What I loved about the red science book was its exhilaration, its sense of true wonder. This wonder was of a different sort from the "let's pretend" of most fairy tales and the secure facts of the encyclopedia.

The red book was also an alluring tactile object – its cover could handle my peanut butter and jelly coated fingers, and on the last page there was a pop-up anatomy of a man that I quickly demolished. I don't remember why I tore it out, probably because I could. I liked to feel my strength in those days, and paper was a foe I could master. I remember looking at the hole I had made with great pride. I showed it to my sister, laughing about how this outline was a much better anatomy of a man than the one with red ink and blue veins provided by the book publishers. My sister did not understand my delight but she indulged me anyway and asked if I wanted to make another pop-up model. I did not, but I lacked the words then to tell her why.

Maybe it has taken me all these years to find the words to explain why I thought the loss of the pop-up model revealed the anatomy of the body more fully than the drawing. (Maybe such a claim will locate us more securely in the law of this genre: introduction to a critical book). The body's anatomy was the primary wonder of the wonder of science because it could not be represented without tearing the body open.

When the body was opened, science rushed in. Anatomy established an interiority to the body that transformed representation itself (and was itself predicated on changes in representational technologies – most notably perspective). Even within the genre of science-for-5-year-olds, anatomy demanded and merited a form of representation denied to clouds and thermometers. The pop-up model was one way to signal this difference in representation.

Tearing out the pop-up art and refusing science's comprehensible mysteries, I created a gouged page that held the hole where the body once was. Finding myself now faced with the task of introducing this book, I want to say that that gesture was my first piece of performance art. It was an act whose primary goal was to enact the disappearance of the manifest visual object. Performance and theatre are instances of enactments predicated on their own disappearance. Like a detective's chalk rendering of a murdered body, the demolished pop-up page illustrated the outline of a body in a state of arrested movement. The book now presented the shadow of a man lying down in a pale white casket, a man's outline asleep in the page's proscenium stage, a chiselled tracing of a body that I had forcefully and gleefully evicted from my red book. I wanted the outline of that body, its paper ghost, much more than I wanted the illustrated body.

If this was my first piece of performance art, an "if" that has a certain pedagogical virtue for me now, it was also my first sense of the deep relationship between bodies and holes, and between performance and the phantasmatical. I loved that red book in part because it illustrated something about what haunted me even then, the ghostly mysteries of what we cannot see. Theatre, of course, has had a long romance with ghosts and it would not be too much to say that the theatricality of spiritualism, parapsychology, and other ghostly (pseudo)sciences owes something to theatre's conviction that it can make manifest what cannot be seen. From the ghost of Hamlet's father to the ghost in the machine of contemporary theatre's special effects, Western theatre has had a sustained conversation with the incorporeal. The specific weight given to the physical sets and settings of theatrical performances create a kind of mausoleum, a space designed to summon the phantasmatical charge of the immaterial.

As our current cultural moment is buffeted on one side by the claims of virtual reality and electronic presence, and on the other by a politicized and commodified spirituality (from Christian fundamentalism to new age gurus), it behooves us to think more seriously about what theatre and performance have to teach us about the possibilities and perils of summoning the incorporeal. To what end are we seeking an escape from bodies? What are we mourning when we flee the catastrophe and exhilaration of embodiment?

Live performance and theatre ("art with real bodies") persist despite an economy of reproduction that makes them seem illogical and certainly a poor investment.[1] The many reasons for this persistence exceed the content of this book. But it may well be that theatre and performance respond to a psychic need to rehearse for loss, and especially for death. Billed as rehearsal, performance and theatre have a special relation to art as memorial. We are currently ensnared by what D.A. Miller has called "morbidity culture," and theatre and performance have especially potent lessons for those interested in reassessing our relations to mourning, grief, and loss (Miller 1990).

As I attempted to make clear in *Unmarked*, one of the deepest challenges of writing about performance is that the object of one's meditation, the performance itself, disappears. In this sense, performance theory and criticism are instances of writing history. Performance theory and criticism have tended to respond to the loss of the object by adapting a primarily conservative and conserving method. Writing about performance has largely been dedicated to describing in exhaustive detail the mise-en-scène, the physical gestures, the voice, the score, the action of the performance event. This dedication stems from the knowledge that the reader may not have seen the event and therefore the critic must record it. This urge to record has given rise to an odd situation in which some of the most radical and troubling art of our cultural moment has inspired some of the most conservative (and even reactionary) critical commentary. The desire to preserve and represent the performance event is a desire we should resist. For what one otherwise preserves is an illustrated corpse, a pop-up anatomical drawing that stands in for the thing that one most wants to save, the embodied performance.

I am investigating, in *Mourning Sex*, the possibility that something substantial can be made from the outline left after the body has disappeared. My hunch is that the affective outline of what we've lost might bring us closer to the bodies we want still to touch than the restored illustration can. Or at least the hollow of the outline might allow us to understand more deeply why we long to hold bodies that are gone.

Performance and theatre make manifest something both more than and less than "the body." And yet the acts made visible in theatre and performance are acts that we attribute over and over again to bodies, often immaterial and phantasmatic ones. (This conflation of act and body is much the same conflation that Judith Butler has articulated in relationship to gendered performances and gender identities – we tend to read gestures as expressions of "authentic" selves, performances as identities.[2] In the days ahead it will be increasingly difficult to insist on the distinction between acts of creation and identities. We are more and more only what we make, what we do. And those who are unable to make or do will have a harder time dramatizing their value. This difficulty, for me, is a source of a different grief than the one I am trying to live with here.)

The enactment of invocation and disappearance undertaken by performance and theatre is precisely the drama of corporeality itself. At once a consolidated fleshly form and an eroding, decomposing formlessness, the body beckons us and resists our attempts to remake it. This resistant beckoning was the lure for this writing, a writing toward and against bodies who die.

I

The title *Mourning Sex* is meant to respond to the end of a certain possibility opened up by what social historians and fast-typing journalists have called the "sexual revolution." It never seemed to me that the "revolutionary" part of the sexual revolution stemmed entirely from the act, the performance of corporeal choreography that it denominated. Viewed from the sidelines where those too young to participate are always consigned to observe, the revolutionary aspect of the sexual revolution seemed to come from the self-consciously forged relationship between desire and act, between will and body, that made apparent a new social, psychic, and political relationship to making itself. The making in "making love" marks an allegiance to nothing more and nothing less than the force of the desire to make something in the present tense. The particular making enacted through sex, with sex, and in sex, quickly bleeds from the thing itself into social, psychic, and political making more broadly, more publicly, imagined. If people could copulate without coercion (an "if" that remains primarily phantasmatic for many women), if people could touch without the restraining influences of orthodox social codes (even while rapidly establishing new orthodoxies), how might making love and having sex become revolutionary acts? What language would be made in this making? What death? These latter questions, realized through the spectacle of the "liberation" of sexual acts, opened up a way of thinking that transformed social politics. Sex was in every way necessary to that opening but what was opened exceeded physical sexual acts.

The possibilities opened up by the sexual revolution, we have been told, have been foreclosed by the onslaught of AIDS. This claim is both shockingly inaccurate and deceptively true. The reasons for the foreclosure of those possibilities are many and AIDS is, among other things, a *tabula rasa* for the projections of multiple myths. But I am not interested here in providing another interpretation of the last thirty years of U.S. cultural, sexual, political and social history. I am concerned rather with how we perform our mourning, how we recover from the trauma of loss. I find that the most compelling explanations for the intricate working through of mourning come from psychoanalytic theory. This theory accounts for the affective force of the sexual and psychic remaking that surviving loss entails. As we go about making new sexual sexualities in the technologies and misprisions of "safe(r) sex" we also mourn the loss of the "liberation" (however phantasmatical) that stands behind this remaking.

One of the propositions informing this argument is one that I cannot prove but nonetheless find generative. What psychoanalysis makes clear is that the experience of loss is one of the central repetitions of subjectivity. It may well be that just as linguists have argued that syntax is "hard-wired" into the brain which allows infants to discern that specific sounds are language bits, perhaps the syntax of loss is hard-wired into the psyche which structures our encounters with the world. Severed from the placenta and cast from the womb, we enter the world as an amputated body whose being will be determined by the very mortality of that body. Prior to recognizing the specific content of an affective grief, perhaps the human subject is born ready to mourn. Perhaps a psychic syntax of mourning is in place before the subject learns specific vocabularies of grief. Without such a syntax, the subject might be overwhelmed and find life-as-loss unbearable.

The psyche has no material form and yet in describing it we tend often to give it a body. From the mystic writing pad to the ghost in the microprocessor, we have attempted to speak of the psyche as a body, however phantasmatical. We talk about the psyche as something subject to wounds, to tears, to traumas. We believe it can be made healthy. We treat it, in short, as a body.

Throughout *Mourning Sex* I rely on "trauma" as a way to understand injuries to both body and psyche. Psychoanalysis gives us the idea that trauma is simultaneously untouchable and remarkably unattached to, untouching of, what surrounds it. Often trauma is not recognized until well after it has happened, in part because it is a complete, contained event. Trauma's potency comes in part from how well it is contained. When I say trauma is untouchable, I mean that it cannot be represented. The symbolic cannot carry it: trauma makes a tear in the symbolic network itself.[3]

I begin with a fairy tale – a parable of sorts about the trauma of the loss of language's direct communicative function – because I am trying to forge a different formal relation between the critical thinker and reader; I am trying to suggest a different way of reading critical commentary. The emphasis throughout is on movement as a political, intellectual, physical, and psychic force. The movements of the voices in *Mourning Sex* are integral to the movement of the argument.

II

THE ADVENTURES OF WORDS

Once upon a time words were magnificent laborers. Climbing in and out of obscure mines they hauled sharply pointed quarry from interior shadows to the bright light of the town square. The words rode around on beautiful little tracks called sentences, that snaked in and out of places no one knew how to visit otherwise. People came to admire, to find solace in, to love these sturdy words and all they carefully and skillfully carried.

After a while, people began to rely on words for all kinds of things that had little to do with information and labor as such, and the words, efficient little beasts, seemed happy enough to try anything. People began to touch the words, to swallow them, to spit them out. They began to toss them tentatively back and forth and unhinge them from their burdens and wagons. They began to play with the words. Much to everyone's surprise it seemed that the more one asked words to do the more extraordinary and expansive they became. They made shapes and forms that dazzled all who beheld them. They danced and made a wondrous music. They circulated in the expanse of sky echoing the elegance of geese flying in formation.

Soon those people who could throw and catch words the best began putting on shows. These experts quickly took up specialties: those who cared primarily about the beauty and expressive power of the words became known as artists; those who found ways to make the words consoling and inspiring became known as healers; and those who became expert at using words to inspire social action became politicians. Children and lovers would often sneak up the hill late at night and go to the wagons where the words slumbered. Tentatively they would touch the words, imitating the gestures and sounds they saw the specialists create in public. The words were drowsy and sleepy but they did not mind the secret touching.

Then one day a terrible accident occurred. No one really knows what caused it. But suddenly the words that had hitherto soared and swooned sank like stones. They became dull immobile balls. Theories of the whys and hows abound and thousands offered stultifyingly dull diagnoses. (Stultifying because they were offered in dead letters.) At first, I personally suspected the words were just exhausted. They were sick of everyone believing so much in them. It was hard to be the object of faith, trust, love, for so many people. The words had been asked to carry everyone's histories and dreams. One day they simply refused the caressing hands of the artists, the tired promises of the healers, the dreamy lies of the politicians. The words fell apart, split, in the users' bodies. The words would not carry any of the things the people implored them to, dreamed they might, imagined they once had. As the words cleaved into obstinate fragments, the users' bodies became scattered, nervous, symptomatic. The buildings trembled, the bakeries crumbled their buns, the banks counted their change. The breaking words broke the people's bodies.

After the words stopped their dances, some other noise, not exactly poetry, not exactly music, filled the air. It was a kind of clawing sound: as if the words themselves were shimmying up a brick vine-covered edifice whose structure the people sensed but could not see. The words slid and gasped, huffed and puffed, boasted and buckled, trying to reach the very top of the sky's light. As I listened to them hoist themselves up and away from the tracks and wagons, straining beyond the reach of the artists, the hopes of the healers, the exhortations of the politicians, I began to realize that my theory of their exhaustion was ridiculous.

The only other time I saw such a desperate exertion, heard such an otherworldly clamor to escape, was when a lover fled my embrace with a thrust of adrenaline that left us each panting and shaking for several years. Like my lover, the words were fleeing because they had been horribly misrecognized. We had made the mistake of loving them the way teenagers love music: not for the sound itself but for the postures the music allowed us to take under its cover: the slouch, the wriggle, the scream, the ache, the joy, the question. We forgot to love the words the harder way: not "for themselves," since they were supremely for us, but for the more-in-them-than-themselves that made it possible for them to create something we could never control, the more-in-them that made it possible for them to travel to places whose topography we could never map. Misrecognized like my lover, the words rang and clanged toward a grammar of light and left us panting in the dark silence of desire's endless call.

Of course this is also a ridiculous theory.

But what can I do? I have heard the words leave. They flew right out of my body, out of my ear, out of my mouth. I tried to hold on but they were so much stronger than I. It's only fairy tales now: truth is what we can make from what we've missed.

The words climbed believing that, once up, their labors would end. While they were exhausted and beaten, the words were inspired to this heroic exertion because they were propelling themselves. They were not in the hands, on the tongues, in the limbs of people: this was words' own sojourn. The few hearty words that did make it to the top of the sky's remotest light threw their heads back, laughed, and then with suicidal ecstasy plummeted down an interior lattice that hung like a net at the lip of the sky's tunneling light. As they fell, I could see the end of each sentence I had ever wanted to compose obliterate itself in a completely silent fireworks display: a sizzling *z* turning into a cascading comet, a radiating *a* embracing the man in the moon, a keening k nestling into a cloud. *Z A K*, Zacharia and they all fell down.

Listening to the silence, composure gone, I was at first embarrassed by my sudden feebleness, by my loss of command. For I had become one of the word smiths who put on shows and had developed what I thought was an intimate relation with words. But because I know, for reasons that far exceed the content of this book, when I am soundly defeated, I left the words blinking in a grammar of light that is beyond me. I dedicated myself to learning to love this other strange music, this scratchy, jumpy noise that filled the sky after the words exploded. This book is the result of that surrender. It is written in loss, with words all too conscious of what they are unable to convey.

Keening carries tears better than argument. Despite the extensive attempt to revise, to suture, to replace the holes with something whole, much of the writing here functions as gravestone marking, in gray pallor and chiseled syllables, the ruins of braver, fuller, stronger, livelier words.

Apologies offered and the plunge taken: wet behind the ears we begin. Again.

III

RESISTANCE AND THE POEM

"The sign begins by repeating itself," repeated Jacques Derrida in the front of the room. White hair, grave voice: the serious dedication of this speaker unnerves me. Derrida in English teaching a poem by Paul Celan in German in Irvine, California, spring 1993. On the way to his lecture, I pass a small tent perched on Irvine's concrete campus. Asian-American students are holding a hunger strike to protest the lack of an Asian-American Studies Department at a university that has the largest Asian-American student population in the United States. Each day, the protesters change the heavily graffittied calendar that sits next to their tent. The numbers pile up as the days and the words disappear. This particular day, Derrida introduces us to one of Celan's most celebrated poems.

Ashglory behind
your shaken-knotted
hands at the threeway.

Pontic erstwhile: here,
a drop,
on
the drowned rudder blade,
deep
in the petrified oath,
it roars up.

(On the vertical
breathrope, in those days,
higher than above,
between two painknots,
  while
the glossy
Tartarmoon climbed up
  to us,
I dug myself into you and
  into you.)

Ash-
glory behind
your threeway
hands.
The cast-in-front-of-you,
  from
the East, terrible.

Nobody
bears witness for the
witness.

ASCHENGLORIE hinter
deinen erschüttert-verknoteten
Händen am Dreiweg

Pontisches Einstmals: hier,
ein Tropfen,
auf
dem ertrunkenen Ruderblatt,
tief
im versteinerten Schwur,
rauscht es auf.

(Auf dem senkrechten
Atemseil, damals,
höher als oben,
zwischen zwei Schmerzknoten,
  während
der blanke
Tatarenmond zu uns
  heraufklomm,
grub ich mich in dich und
  in dich.)

Aschen-
glorie hinter
euch Dreiweg-
Händen.
Das vor euch, vom Osten
  her, Hin-
gewürfelte, furchtbar.

Niemand
zeugt für den
Zeugen.

(Celan 1995: 177)

I have heard Derrida lecture many times and I recognize something
unusual in his voice as he reads this poem. Derrida's forte is a speech
of precise touch.[4] He taps on the silent black-on-white words until the
colors bleed across the page and the words reveal the blood beneath
their skin (sometimes Derrida tries to clean up the mess by employing
test tubes of etymological lineage). But with this Celan poem something
else happens. Derrida cannot stop tapping. He cannot find the blood in
Celan's ash. He produces xeroxes of translations: from German to French
to English, from German to English to French. The threeway knot is

getting tighter, and I begin to wonder how Derrida ties his impeccably blue ties. He explains why "I burrow into you and into you" is a better translation of *grub ich mich in dich und in dich* than "I dug myself into you and into you." He begins to read the poem again. Still no blood. He leaves the poem to the side for a moment and tries to blow life into Celan's autobiography. The camps. Escape. Exile. Love. Words. Suicide. Derrida finds a noose in Celan's two painknots. The vertical breathrope chokes. We all dangle from it. The poem watches us, unimpressed.

I am fascinated by Derrida's ministrations. I have never before witnessed this reader clutch at a word. Today, though, the poem spurns him and we cannot move. A terrible panic floods me: we will be suspended forever outside this poem, unable to leave it alone, unable to embrace it. My hands are useless; I cannot even do my rote Bartleby copying. My hands do not want to be "shaken-knotted/ at the threeway" conjunction between Derrida, Celan, and myself. Triangulated and impassive, I am unable to enter the poem. Something in it stops me.

Then Derrida's voice changes. He approaches the poem from another entry point. I now hear Derrida plunging into the bloody tongue of his own desire to hear, to respond, to witness Celan's inert ash. Instead of tapping on the poem, Derrida now taps delicately on his own aspiration to witness. Humble before Celan's poem, Derrida is performing an ethics of death and resignation that is not a defeat but nonetheless yields to the harsh unanswerability of Celan's ash. Derrida has heard the words' vanishing and lets the empty wagons roll down the hills: *Clack Click Clack Zac Splat and we all lie down.*

Cast as witness to what is not there, the reader cannot rest anywhere within the space of the poem's unbearable stillness. The formal relation of address that usually adheres between reader and poem collapses. The formlessness of the poem's ash, the remains that stand *as* remains rather than body, cannot be assimilated into a mute object of the reader's contemplation. The poem insists on mediation, on translation, and triangulation. Derrida provides us three languages in which to discover Celan's three-way knot, but my two hands cannot touch that hot ash. In response to the three-way knot, I triangulate my relationship to Celan by mediating it through Derrida's reading. But these efforts to triangulate are futile attempts to make a form for what Celan insists is formlessness itself. The horror of the poem's steady excavation of its cavernous center, "Nobody/bears witness for the/witness," comes from recognizing that the ash that arrests us has, is, no-body. The haunting remains of the Holocaust bear mute witness to our inability to make a form from, and thereby a way to survive, that anonymous and formless ash.

Later in my rented room in Irvine, I read Michael Hamburger's translations of Celan and see him return over and over to the same scene, the same chronicle of a suicide foretold. When I dream that night, I enter a world in which Celan is translated into Hindi, Japanese, Korean, Chinese, and the University of California-Irvine founds the first Asian-American Studies Department devoted to German poetry of the Holocaust.

Haunted by Derrida's reading, the slow fade toward and away from the mute ash of Celan's poem, I recall Merleau-Ponty's spiraling question about the language of philosophy:

> Hence it is a question whether philosophy as reconquest of brute or wild being can be accompanied by the resources of an eloquent language, or whether or not it would be necessary for philosophy to use language in a way that takes from it its power of immediacy or direct signification in order to make it equal to what philosophy wishes all the same to say.
>
> (Merleau-Ponty 1968: 102–3)

Such a question acknowledges the limitations of direct signification as a means to capture brute or wild being. Philosophy's own resourceful language cannot capture that and must perhaps risk "poetry." But not a poetry of seductive Shakespearean sonnets, the long marching timbres of Tennyson, the cool elegance of Stevens, the agonizing precision of Dickinson. The poetry that philosophy's exhaustion produces is catastrophic. Paul Celan's writing performs some of the consequences of that catastrophe.

This catastrophic language touches a kind of madness, not a psychosis exactly, not quite a neurosis. A self-conscious language that is in danger of becoming ensnared by its own narcissism. Paranoia speaks the eloquent language of brute fear; sometimes one cannot name the source of paranoia, sometimes the source is so well known that naming becomes superfluous, redundant. (Just as the signifier of the beloved breeds endearments so too do the sources of paranoia proliferate.) Paranoia is a defense against connection; it multiplies potential connections so feverishly any single one becomes impossible.

Contemporary theory's paranoia animates the ash of critical writing, transforms it into a landscape composed of thousands of horizontal breathropes. These prose ropes slap the page like jump ropes sweeping concrete. Its nervous mutating catastrophic reach propels what I call performative writing. Performative writing is different from personal criticism or autobiographical essay, although it owes a lot to both genres. Performative writing is an attempt to find a form for "what philosophy wishes all the same to say." Rather than describing the performance event in "direct signification," a task I believe to be impossible and not terrifically interesting, I want this writing to enact the affective force of the performance event again, as it plays itself out in an ongoing temporality made vivid by the psychic process of distortion (repression, fantasy, and the general hubbub of the individual and collective unconscious), and made narrow by the muscular force of political repression in all its mutative violence. The events I discuss here sound differently in the writing of them than in the "experiencing" of them, and it is the urgent call of that difference that I am hoping to amplify here. Performative writing is solicitous of affect even while it is nervous and tentative about the consequences of that solicitation. Alternately bold and coy, manipulative and unconscious, this writing points both to itself and to the "scenes" that motivate it. These scenes are fashioned and distorted in an attempt to say "what philosophy wishes all the same to say."

To name this "performative writing" is redundant since all good critical writing enacts something in excess of the thing that motivates it. But I am invoking that redundancy here because I want to mark the mimetic echo of what I "wish all the same to say." (I want you to hear my wish as well as my miss.) The mimicry that motivates much of the writing here is an imitation that knows both that it is too late and that it is "off," that in the very energy of its imaginative making it destroys what it most wants to save. In that mistake, I hope to find something else, something itself worthy of a generative knowing, even if the something else is only another mistake that demands to be remade, repeated.

Mimicry, I am more and more certain, is the fundamental performance of this cultural moment.[5] At the heart of mimicry is a fear that the match will not hold and the "the thing itself" (you, me, love, art) will disappear before we can reproduce it. So we hurl ourselves headlong toward copy machines, computers, newspapers, cloning labs. The clichés (among other things) of critical prose are themselves symptoms (among other things) of this long longed for assurance that we are saying something that someone might some day hear. I want less to describe and preserve performances than to enact and mimic the losses that beat away within them. In this mimicry, loss itself helps transform the repetitive force of trauma and might bring about a way to overcome it.

IV

QUEER DEATHS: THEATRE AND THE DRAMA OF EXPIRING BODIES

In his remarkable essay on *Antigone*, Jacques Lacan has suggested that tragic theatre is a place of play between two deaths.[6] Sophocles' tragedy, Lacan argues, suspends Antigone in "the zone between life and death" (Lacan 1992: 280). After Creon sentences Antigone to a stone vault, Antigone, while not dead, "is eliminated from the world of the living." While Antigone initially suggests that her death will be welcome, an end to her misery, neither Sophocles nor Lacan let such a wish be realized. Tragic theatre embodies the agonizing force of existence-as-rehearsal. In such a world, nothing ever happens once, not even death. The characters in Sophocles' play discover that what is truly tragic about death is that they survive it, at least once, only to realize that having survived it once they will have to face it again. Creon's late lamentation, "The pains that men will take to come to pain!" (Sophocles 1977: 236) is an oblique way of indicating both the immensity of the dying these characters do coming to death, and the immense pain the spectator feels watching each of them rehearse that same rehearsal, one after the other.

Sophocles's play is a meditation on the ways in which dying reproduces and multiplies death. Two brothers stab each other; one, an enemy of the state, is denied burial rights; the other, a defender of the state, is given full military honors and proper burial rights. One brother is killed once as a man by his brother; the other brother is killed twice, once as a man by his brother, the second time as a traitorous corpse by his King. Two sisters are asked to accept the distinction between the treatment of their brothers' remains; one finds she can and the other finds she cannot. Ismene tells Antigone that she wants to live and will not disobey Creon's dictate. "I beg the dead/to forgive me, but I am helpless: I must yield/ To those in authority" (p. 188). For Antigone, such a yielding betrays the sibling bond. In speaking about their bond to their dead brother Polyneices, Ismene and Antigone are also speaking about the living bond between them as sisters. In asking Ismene if she is willing to die for Polyneices, Antigone is also asking Ismene if she is willing to die for her. When Ismene admits she is not, Antigone effectively stops loving her. Ismene refuses to say that her love for Antigone extends beyond life and so Antigone sees no reason to sustain it in life. Refusing to assist Antigone in the burial of their brother's remains, Ismene attempts to cut her losses and to choose life over death. But instead she becomes absorbed in the terrible economy of death, an accelerating multiplication which tragic theatre dramatizes through the problem of what remains. Having heard Ismene's refusal, Antigone tells her, "It is the dead, / Not the living who make the longest demands: We die forever . . ." (p. 188). And rarely in tragic theatre does anyone die singly. (Think of *Hamlet*, *Macbeth*, *Richard III*. . . .) Antigone has died to her sister and to the world of the social in defying Creon. Banished from that world and sentenced to her stone vault, Antigone dies there a second time – but this time by her own hand. No longer subject to Creon's law, Antigone becomes her own subject by remaining, in her loyalty to her brother's remains, beyond the reach of the King.

Just as Polyneices is the cipher through which Ismene and Antigone discover the limits of the sibling bond, Antigone is the cipher through which Creon and Haimon discover the limits of the father–son bond.[7] In asking the King to change his mind about Polyneices' burial, Haimon essentially asks his father to abandon the part that he has taken up as inflexible King. Haimon asks his father to die to that version of himself on behalf of the love that he feels for his son. In essence, Haimon asks Creon to die a little as a King in order to love a little more as a father. Repeating what Ismene has said in response to her sister in the scene rehearsed in the Prologue, Creon says no to his son. Forced to confront the limit of his father's love, Haimon then lets his allegiance to him die. He goes to Antigone in her stone vault and finds her dead body. Too late to embrace Antigone in life, he turns his sword first toward his father, who has also come to Antigone's vault too late, but his sword misses. Foiled, Haimon then turns his sword into his own body. Having broken open Antigone's crypt, in time only to touch the stone cold bone of her suicided body, Haimon's suicide achieves its heroic dimension *as* imitation. Mimicking Antigone's radical choice, Haimon's suicide is captivating because it is a copy, an act, a piece of theatre. This is theatre that carries the force of the real, which is to say, this is theatre that rehearses deaths. Tragic theatre dramatizes the impossibility of an isolated death: fear death by copying.

Carrying his dead son back to the city, Creon claims that he himself is now a dead man. But in that utterance he proves he still has breath. Eurydice, hearing of her (second) son's death, kills herself, repeating the act that Antigone and Haimon had done before her. When the Messenger gives this news to Creon, who is still holding Haimon's corpse in his hands, he responds, "I was dead and your words are death again" (p. 236).

For Lacan, Antigone is sublime because she is the central image that leads us into *ate*, that domain between two deaths that is tragic theatre's province. Antigone stills the play's motion with her suffering and illustrates that tragedy is about truth rather than event (Lacan 1992: 265). For Lacan, the truth that tragedy exposes is the criminality of the mother's desire as it locates itself "beyond" the law of the father.

Whereas for Freud, Oedipus is the problem, for Lacan, it is Jocasta. As an heir of that incestuous union, Antigone has a particularly intense relation to proper social rituals. Unable to control the events that led to her conception, she has dedicated herself to controlling the events that lead to her death. Unfortunately, the economy of the signifier never balances things quite so evenly.

The symbolic is structured by words and reveals their "unsurpassable consequence" (Lacan 1992: 278). Polyneices' death leaves two different forms of remains: the physical corpse of his body and the remains of his name. Regardless of the content of his actions, regardless of his death, her brother's name remains a signifying force for Antigone. Having emerged from the same womb, formed from the same parents, related to the same (name of the) father, Antigone and Polyneices are forever bound to one another. Thus, for Lacan, Antigone's "splendor" derives from her courageous acknowledgment of the bond of the signifier, a bond that begins prior to conception and continues after death.

The problem with Lacan's argument is that it passes over the equally unsurpassable consequence of the structural and biological relation between Ismene and Antigone. For surely if her bond to her brother remains an indestructible, unwavering allegiance, why is Antigone so quick to cease her relation to her sister Ismene? It is not enough to say merely that because men carry the name of the father longer than women Antigone's allegiance to her brother outlasts her loyalty to her sister, for this overlooks too much. Antigone's speedy abandonment of Ismene is the consequence of a Sophoclean–Oedipal blindness. From within this logic, the allegiance that might pass between women cannot be dramatized theatrically or psychoanalytically, that it cannot be imagined? In other words, is it the incestuous desire of the mother that is criminal, as Lacan argues (Lacan 1992: 283), or is it that women's desire for anyone or anything always already (re)produces death within the masculine Imaginary? Insofar as the paternal metaphor is stabilizing, does it not arrest and freeze women's desire on the father and make her desire that which stabilizes the symbolic? Should her desire move from that rock, the whole edifice crumbles. Polyneices and Antigone reproduce the static suffering of tragedy: their bond extends beyond the law of the father represented by Creon and repeats the Oedipal tragedy which gave them first life. This is the tragedy of desire within the paternal symbolic.

But *Antigone* suggests, while not realizing, another way to play this drama. The phallic signifier which iterates sexual difference cannot carry the desire of two women for each other. As Antigone chooses to honor Polyneices, she also chooses to cut her bond with Ismene. Cast firmly in an Oedipal tragedy, Antigone and Ismene nonetheless point to a different form of theatre sisters might one day invent. Such a theatre would be more precise than Sophocles's or Lacan's about the distinction between desire and love. One of the reasons the phallic signifier cannot carry the desire two women feel for each other is because that desire tends to look too much like soral love. This has had both advantages and disadvantages for lesbians engaged in staging a new theatre of desire.

As an art form whose primary function is to meditate on the threshold that heralds between-ness, theatre encourages a specific and intense cathetic response in those who define themselves as liminal tricksters, socially disenfranchised, sexually aberrant, addicted, and otherwise queerly alienated from the law of the father. Queers are queer because we recognize that we have survived our own deaths. The Law of the Social has already repudiated us, spit us out, banished us, jailed us, and otherwise quarantined us from the cultural imagination it is so anxious to keep clean, pristine, well guarded. But, as Foucault has so convincingly demonstrated, those on the margins become the focal point for the center's self-definition and thus cannot ever be entirely eliminated. Queers ghost the cultural imagination and thereby foster the illusion that reality is non-phantasmatic, that death is what happens later and never now.[8] Queers who survive the death accorded them by the Law of the Social and go on to create another life, dream continually of another social space, one we help bring into being by reciting those dreams out loud.

Such recitations are themselves doubly performative. As theatrical performances, they stage the phantasmatic becoming indicative. That is, as the "as if" of the phantasm takes a place on a stage larger than the architecture of a single imagination, it carries the remains of a collective reality, however illusionary or material such remains may be. These recitations are also performatives in the linguistic sense, for in their very public articulation they create a promise. The speech act "we promise," is an exemplary performative in J.L. Austin's sense. In dedicating myself here to my dream of performative writing I risk the strange economy of every promise. In making this writing a promise, I admit that the thing itself is forever deferred. Much of what I am trying to articulate here exists only in a zone patrolled by regulative syntax, proper footnotes, blushing italics. In nominating performative writing as a way to intervene in the deadly asperities of contemporary thinking, I realize I am also reciting redundancy, flirting with a new marketing ploy, re-naming something that has existed for a very long time with little or no fanfare. Yet I risk those things (and others more painful to list) because I want to promise that there is a way to move even within the stone vaults to which too many of us have been banished. I want to promise it rather than prove it. I may be wrong and we'll be frozen forever on cold rocks. But I may not be wrong (which is different from being right) and to dream of dancing while whiling away the hours in the waiting room is better than some other alternatives I can think of.

Performative writing enacts the death of the "we" that we think we are before we begin to write. A statement of allegiance to the radicality of unknowing who we are becoming, this writing pushes against the ideology of knowledge as a progressive movement forever approaching a completed end-point. Performative writing is set against the normative ideology that insists that we die once in an expository, teleologically driven future.

I want to protect my body and the bodies of those I love from the cool violence of (my own) rationality. "The danger is that the disaster should acquire meaning instead of body" (Blanchot 1986: 41). When writing about the disaster of death it is easy to substitute interpretations for traumas. In that substitution, the trauma is tamed by the interpretative frame and peeled away from the raw "unthought" energy of the body. The unworded is sentenced to meaning. I am trying here to hear the body and its symptomatic utterance, that which always remains its most intimate echo, even while admitting that my hearing is pre-determined by the interpretative frame that limits any encounter with bodies. In the act of making this book public, giving you this body of work, I remove the illusion of the authenticity of the possessive that usually escorts bodies into sentences (his, hers, theirs, mine, yours) and render that possession phantasmatic. (I cannot write "my body" anymore than you can read yours.) Thus this book is necessarily a piece of theatre, a staging of an encounter that may or may not take place between two characters I might name "me" and "you." These two are the necessary fictions that structure the form of address in which the body of this work is composed. One character is framed by the architecture of this book's proscenium stage; the other is framed by the phantasms that we construct as I write (while re-reading) and you read (perhaps with pen in hand already re-writing this prose). The degree to which I can sustain my belief in a "me" and a "you" is the degree to which I can generate points fixed enough to keep writing. What you must generate to keep reading remains your affair.

The phantasmatic is always operative within the codes of the rational. Without according space to the phantasmatical, we have tended to take on faith the coherence of rationality itself. This (false) coherence leads to a repression of the force of the incoherence of affect itself. By soliciting the phantasmatic so openly here I realize that I have perhaps lost a certain authority as authentic scribe. But I hope I have at least pointed to another possibility within critical theory, one that has remained largely untouched to date. The method here *is* troubling and is not offered in the spirit of a "solution." A record of what is and is not possible within the genre of critical commentary, *Mourning Sex* illustrates the drama of our present tense – we are past the diagnosis, but not yet in the future tense of the cure. Attempting to write with and toward a theatre of affect, I sometimes found it necessary to invoke critical fictions and factual phantasms. This co-mingling places some of this argument in a liminal space that I hope retains some of the performative force of transformation itself. Part of the liminality of this space stems from its proximity to the subject of death. The only way to solicit and survive the deaths summoned in these pages is to admit that death is not entirely biological, nor entirely cultural (Derrida 1993: 42). Like thought and affect, death is a bewildering mixture of facts and phantasms.

V

"TOUCH ME NOT," OR, TRAUMAS OF THE BOOK

Maybe bodies come to be "ours" when we recognize them as traumatic. Sensing they need a foothold, we take them in to us. Sooner or later, we are burrowing into them. The holes in them help us feel attached. But that attachment is also what motivates the catastrophe and curative lure of touch.

> You grabbed my fist so hard
> My body stopped falling, my head
> about a half-inch from the floor.
>
> Later that night I lay you
> open on your bed. I pushed you.
> As you fell
>
> toward the center of your throat
> crying with the weight of my insistence
> you opened further. With the fist
>
> you caught in the middle
> of your fall I held you
> there a half-inch from ripping
> and drank your tears like beer.

Beginning with Caravaggio's astounding painting *The Incredulity of St. Thomas* (1601), this book asks what kind of body remains after death. What should be done with the remains of (redeeming) bodies? Portraying Christ as he pilots Thomas' finger into the center of his wound, Caravaggio's painting expertly exposes the main themes and questions of this book: what does it mean to have a killing touch? a redemptive touch? How does a man-to-man penetrating touch caress femininity? What is it to observe, to witness, the shattering of the body? And how is that shattering perceived if it is primarily violent? primarily sexual? primarily racist? primarily artistic? primarily sacred? primarily curative?

The treatment that informs self-help and recovery groups is derived from "the talking cure" of psychoanalysis. Josef Breuer's case history of Anna O., the inventor of the talking cure, is the subject of Chapter 3. Before the talking began, and often throughout their sessions, Anna O. assured herself of Breuer's attention by taking his hands. When she held his hands, she was able to speak. Her hysterical symptoms involved periodic blindness and temporary paralysis. I am interested in the relation, admittedly long buried, between a "talking cure" launched by the security of a listening touch, and death, a traumatic event in part because it (seems to) prohibits touch. I am interested in how Anna O.'s body seeks to rehearse its death, by fainting, falling unconscious, and dreaming, but above all, by transferring death's touch from her body to her father's.

Crucial to this transference is movement itself. My reading of Anna O.'s case history is cast as a performance of interpretation by someone more skilled in movement than I. The narrator of this chapter is a ballerina who encounters psychoanalysis by way of her broken hip. Unable to return to her usual role in the corps de ballet, she studies the sudden paralysis of Anna O.'s leg, a stutter step that began the parade of psychoanalytic case histories which march along in different disguises in *Mourning Sex*.

We bury more than bodies. The dry ground in which our fingers burrow sometimes touch the bones of buildings. In London in 1989, the Rose Theatre, home of Christopher Marlowe's plays, surfaced during an excavation and touched the skin of the contemporary city. Live actors jumped in the hole, the legendary pit, and argued that the theatre remains must be saved. Politicians charged with the decision to salvage or bury the Rose quickly transformed the building into a body. They debated, for a surprisingly long time, whether or not the theatre was living or dead. In this debate the theatre remains became a body defined, graphically, as a hole. In "Uncovered rectums: disinterring the Rose Theatre," I register some of the reverberations of the trauma unearthed by the excavation of the Rose.

The public outcry over the Rose helps us understand a bit more clearly the outcry generated in the U.S. when Anita Hill accused Clarence Thomas of sexual harassment in 1991. The Thomas–Hill hearings dramatized a particularly dense set of anxieties around race, violence, and sexuality that simultaneously fascinate and thwart the symptomatic acting out of the contemporary cultural unconscious. In "Bloody nose, loose noose: hearing Anita Hill and Clarence Thomas," I read the various discourses of "evidence" that are both provoked and prohibited by sexual trauma. Arguing that there is a profound incompatibility between the logic of evidence demanded by law, and the logic of sexuality that interprets trauma, abuse, and violence, I suggest that we need a new language, a new means of measuring sexual injury.

One of those new languages might be melodrama. Chapter 6 uses the structure of melodrama to forge an interpretation of distortion in art and criminal trials. When four members of the Los Angeles' police department pummeled Rodney King, whose skull shattered? When the news agencies played and replayed the video tape of that beating, alternating with the video chorus of the beating of Reginald Denny after the first trial of the police officers, what trauma were they attempting to master? Whose history were they seeking to repeat? And as we watched the videos in our customary televisual stupor what were we screening? What were we burying? From whose home, whose streets, were we escaping? The density and complexity of the cultural unconscious's response to the verdict of innocent makes it impossible to pretend one can provide an adequate interpretation of civic unrest in thirty or forty pages. The narrative of "riot" produces its own imperatives, and the media thrives on its own version of melodrama. "Shattered skulls: Rodney King and Holbein's *The Ambassadors*" is composed as a media/ted melodrama in which the protagonist uses Holbein's painting as a way to interpret shattered skulls, skulls that cannot be contained by the frame of painting, television, or critical melodrama. The excess produced by the shattered skull is the engine that drives the critical performance that comes several years too late for both the protagonist and her creator.

Moving then from public traumas to a more personal one, but absorbing the lessons of form and structure learned from these spectacles, "Failed live(r)s: whatever happened to her public grief? in memory of Rena Grant (1959–1992)," is a case history of a patient called Echo who grieves over the death of her colleague, Rena Grant, a critic and assistant professor at the time of her death. Staged as a performance of repetition, citation, and copying, this chapter attempts to understand the present tense of grief for young white women who carry the burden of reproduction.

Finally, "Infected eyes: Dying Man With A Movie Camera, *Silverlake Life: The View From Here*" returns to the catastrophe of the end of touch that death brings. *Silverlake Life* is a video diary of Tom Joslin's and Mark Massi's daily struggle with AIDS and a record of their living and dying in contemporary Los Angeles. At once a meditation on the borders that separate life from death, and a consideration of the psychic equations between an ever dwindling physical body and an ever expansive celluloid body, *Silverlake Life* attempts to create a cinema for the dead. In that creation, a different order of time is suggested, one that allows us, at last, to learn a richer vocabulary for the present tense.

Each of the chapters in this book is focused on a particular body part. I am attempting to compose a critical anatomy for a phantasmatic body. This body is incomplete but it is, emphatically, a body with organs. The critical bodies we make are as symptomatic as the bodies with which we create them. *Mourning Sex* studies a wounded torso, a paralyzed leg, a failed liver, a bleeding nose, a grave-like rectum, a shattered skull, an infected eye. Unlike the perfect blue-red body of my childhood anatomy book that I was compelled to banish, this body's flaws I hope will keep you with it. Cobbled together from the bits I found in the abandoned wagons of formerly working words, I hope this clanky cranky body goes some way toward rethinking the connection between language and death, as Paul Celan, Martin Heidegger, and Jacques Derrida (among many others) have encouraged us to do. "The essential connection between death and language flashes up before us, but remains still unthought" (Heidegger 1971: 107). The stillness of those remains are what I am attempting to animate here.

> while
> the glossy
> Tartarmoon climbed up to us
> I dug myself into you and into you

VI

THEATRE, WRITING, AND THE PAGE SET

In theatre, as in psychoanalysis, the dramatic encounter occurs in a physical set that is at once materially specific and theatrical – (a) set apart from "reality." This makes spatial arrangements on stage and in the analytic encounter particularly precarious, tentative, unstable – liquid rather than solid. The fluidity of this spatial architecture is instructive for writing too. *Mourning Sex* aspires to the blue print more than to the bound book, to the imagined plan more than the actual fact. And yet, I also want you to find these arguments persuasive, if not exactly "right." I hope that they might be seen as a gesture toward creating a more imaginatively generous way of conducting critical inquiries into the things that keep us moving toward and away from our deaths.

When I was younger I traveled to archives full of the thrilling dreams common to any intrepid explorer. In one archive I visited, a building that housed the blue prints for thousands of buildings never built, I found a text composed by an anonymous woman architect. Cast somewhere between blue print and love letter, her writing was surrounded by fabulous drawings of a luscious phantasmatic body. I copy her words but leave you to compose the images of her dreams:

Scars

> *If I were an architect, an architect in love, I would redesign my body. Mail you blue prints. Redraw. I'd move my blood lines to make rivers in places you would like to swim. I'd use my muscles to shore up hills; I'd use my ribs to pile bridges from here to there (delicate little bridges that would sail above my heart). I'd paint the interior of my skin with birds and light; my breasts would be two small mountains you would sleep between; my feet the boats upon which you flow through time; my eyes the mirror you most deeply crave; my two mouths the music that wakes you to a city you've always wanted to call home.*

The critic in me could read this text, elaborate its essentialisms, mediate its mystifications, point out the slender pivot of its initial "if," assess its alliances with music, maternity, and home, but the rest of me prefers to give it to you unprotected. Another fragile dream of a not-yet built body still beckoning for image. In the spirit of this never-made but phantasmatically weighty body, I offer you this print. Embodied, embloodied, worded, unworded. Blues played on a horn I have never touched: *querida, lover, darling, dear. Beep bop seep sap and we weep all the way down.*

NOTES

1 This paragraph is a condensed version of some of the argument of my book, *Unmarked* (1993). See it for full elaboration.
2 See Butler (1994).
3 The single best and most comprehensive discussion of trauma I have read is Caruth (1994).
4 I am grateful to Mark Scott for numerous conversations over many years about a speech of touch.
5 See Diamond (1993) for an excellent discussion of the distinction between mimesis and mimicry.
6 'The Essence of Tragedy: A Commentary on Sophocles's *Antigone*,' in Lacan (1992: 243–90).
7 Interrogating the Other can only be accomplished through the Other's stand-in. See the next chapter, 'Whole wounds: bodies at the vanishing point,' for the elaboration of this argument.
8 For a discussion of how lesbians haunt the cultural imaginary see Hart (1993). For a different attempt to explain the relation between queer death and performance see Hart and Phelan (1995).

2

Whole wounds: bodies at the vanishing point

At the end of *Minima Moralia*, Theodor Adorno concludes:

> The only philosophy which can be responsibly practiced in the face of despair is the attempt to contemplate all things as they would present themselves from the standpoint of redemption.... The question of the reality or unreality of redemption itself hardly matters.

> (1974: 247)

Adorno is concerned with the dialectical ability of thought to unthink the concepts that produce it. Writing in 1944, in an age in which despair is a reasonable response to the horror of the world, Adorno suggests that philosophy contemplate all things from "the standpoint of redemption" because such a contemplation upsets, if only temporarily, the stability of despair. Lifting despair, if only for a moment, can change one's perspective, dialectically, on what one contemplates.

In our own age of despair, the project of contemplating redemption seems to me increasingly unfathomable. And yet that very unfathomableness beckons me like a lure. The lure for me is almost always an image. What does it look like from the standpoint of redemption if you are the Redeemer? If you are in despair? The history of Western art (which is an iconic history of the economy of Christianity, and especially Roman Catholicism), contains hundreds of thousands of images of the Redemption, but I was overtaken by Caravaggio's extraordinarily theatrical painting of 1601, *The Incredulity of St. Thomas*. I am interested in Caravaggio's complex staging of redemptive faith but I am even more fascinated by his ideas about painting bodies after the (re)invention of the vanishing point.

Put simply, the vanishing point was derived from a theory of optics based on the illusion that parallel lines converge at a point in the distance. The painter placed that convergence at the optical center of his or her composition; that became known as the vanishing point. The vanishing point gained depth and significance because it presupposed

a parallel point outside the frame called the viewing point. The construction of spectatorial space outside the frame was as crucial to the
development of visual art as the composition inside the frame.

Symmetry, balance, scale, depth, and relation were achieved not by
accurately measuring the height and width of a building or a person
and copying that height and width within the painting, but rather by
having the building or person line up in a symmetrical relation to the
vanishing point. The hole in the painting, the vanishing point itself,
became the foundation for the new aesthetic based on perspective.[1] As
Samuel Edgerton has observed,

> After 1425 the new linear perspective rules became increasingly indis-
> pensable to artists. ... [T]he artist started the picture with a central
> dot, representing the vanishing point, and constructed the perspective
> of his picture with little or no recourse to complexities of ground plan
> or elevation.
>
> (Edgerton 1975: 132)

The "indispensability" of perspective also supported a new fascination with interiority more generally. For the Foucault of *The Order of
Things: An Archaeology of the Human Sciences* (1970), the discovery of such
interiority marked the origin of the Classical episteme; and with that
discovery, Foucault argues, the human subject became, perforce, "a theological conception." Commentators on Foucault have concentrated on
the extraordinary passage at the end of *The Order of Things*, in which
he argues that if the arrangements of knowledge that constitute our
current age were to disappear, as the arrangements that constituted the
Classical Age disappeared at the end of the eighteenth century, then
one can wager that man "would be erased, like a face drawn in sand
at the edge of the sea" (1970: 387). Emphasizing this apocalyptic, even
sensationalist passage, commentators have argued that Foucault's
conception of the human subject is, quintessentially, a historical one.[2]
But this characterization of Foucault's project misses the structure of
belief which organizes Foucault's argument.

When Foucault argues that the human subject becomes a theological
concept in the Classical Age, he means, among other things, that
"man" is a construction of a belief system in the same way that "God"
is a construction of one belief system, and "Allah," "Buddha," and
"Krishna" are constructions of other belief systems. Just as it is possible
to trace the historical ascendance and devaluation of Mary within Roman
Catholicism, for example, so it is possible to analyze the centrality and
marginality of "man" in the history of thought. Foucault's own historical project, then, is a profoundly theological investigation, a complex
analysis of the belief system that produces both God-terms (the state,
the institution, the King) and those who become subject to those terms.

To put it slightly differently, Foucault seeks to ascertain how certain subjects at certain times (the history of power-knowledge) find verbs ("technologies") to move objects (the sick, the criminal, the insane, in short, all those subjects too weak to control verbs). Thus, Foucault's *oeuvre* is also a theory of the Theos of The Word. Foucault's archaeological history is a rolling away of the rock that has obscured the fundamental logical corpus of an epistemic system we call the order of things.

At the heart of Foucault's excavation of the Classical episteme is a profound belief in the power of the stand-in, the decoy that can effectively substitute for the real.[3] In orthodox Christianity, Christ the son stands in for God the father; in language, the signifier stands in for the signified; in perspective, the vanishing point stands in for the illusionary convergence of parallel lines. Thus the stand-in itself is not only a tool in the construction of "man" as a theological concept, but it too is a theological concept. The foundation of the epistemology of the stand-in is the vanishing point: the hole that launches the illusion of perspective underlies the Classical Age's ordering system.

Foucault begins his re-animation of the logic of the Classical Age with an extended analysis of Velasquez's extraordinary painting, *Las Meninas* (1646) (Figure 1). At once a standard self-portrait of the painter painting in his studio and a complex meditation upon representation "as pure form" (1970: 16), Velasquez's painting positions the spectator in a "slender line of reciprocal visibility" that in turn "embraces a whole complex network of uncertainties, exchanges, feints" (ibid.: 4). That network pivots on the mirror on the far wall of the painting, in the exact center of *Las Meninas*. Reflecting and deflecting the image of King Philip IV and his wife, Queen Mariana, whose double portrait Velasquez is painting, the mirror turns the picture into a complex meta-painting: a painting about painting people who are simultaneously the subjects and intended viewers of the work.[4]

The mirror creates a triangle in which the spectator beholds the King and Queen from the exterior of the painting, but from exactly the same spot in which the King and Queen pose for the canvas that Velasquez is composing in the painting-within-the-painting. Thus, Velasquez's self-portrait places the painter himself "at the threshold of two incompatible visibilities" (ibid.). Unable to see both his painting and his model, the painter must become momentarily blind to one in order to grasp the other. This blindness forges the illusion of depth, giving the flat canvas a foreground and background and establishing a horizontal axis across the surface. This illusionary depth in turn creates two optical centers of the painting: the mirror at the back that reflects the image of the King and Queen who are in the center of the painting-within-the painting; and the Infanta Margarita who stands in the center of the scene that

Figure 1 Velasquez, *Las Meninas* (1646). Copyright The Prado Gallery. Reproduced with permission.

reveals the painter's studio. This double center allows Velasquez to substitute one form of in/visibility for another, to trade them back and forth, thereby giving the still canvas a sense of dynamic motion. The movement of the spectators' eyes must cross the two fictions established by the painting-within-the-painting and by the painting.[5]

In using the mirror this way Velasquez's painting creates two paradoxical statements. One: the mirror is pure surface; yet once painted at the vanishing point of the painting, it becomes the anchor that gives the flat canvas its illusionary depth. Two: the King and Queen are absolute monarchs; yet their image cannot be rendered except as reflected in the gaze of their subjects. In order to be seen, the King and Queen require the theatrical props that support them in their roles: dogs, maids, courtiers, children, artists. The paradox of power concentrated in the ruling couple renders them simultaneously the subject and object of the drama of representation itself. This is the doubleness that Velasquez's painting captures.

Las Meninas, in Foucault's argument, issues from the discovery that the human subject's "depth" isolates him from God. This isolation dramatizes the human subject's doubt about his or her position within the order of things more generally. Foucault's thesis that the Classical Age creates human subjects who *become* theological concepts (a becoming made possible through reciprocal logic and the economy of substitution), also requires that theological concepts become human subjects. Thus, the Classical Age required stories dramatizing God becoming man *and* of man becoming God. The epistemology that Foucault discovers in the Classical Age is above all a theatrical order of things, an order based on transformation and substitution. Crucial to the invention of a theatrical epistemology is perspective, for it is a technology that supports the economy of substitution that drives Western theatre itself.

Perspective is a theatrical technology and a technology of theatre. Parallel lines do not meet, yet the vanishing point makes it look as if they do. The "as if," the illusionary indicative that theatre animates, allows for the construction of depth, for the "invention" of physical interiority and psychic subjectivity. Once established optically, physical interiority becomes the subject of a new science, anatomy, and eventually psychic interiority gives rise to the invention of another new science, psychoanalysis, or as North Americans like to say "depth psychology." These sciences, in turn, produce critical technologies that provide the frameworks for my reading of Caravaggio's *The Incredulity of St. Thomas*.

The Biblical story from which Caravaggio takes his drama is worth rehearsing, for if Caravaggio was a strict adherent to the laws of perspective, he was far less orthodox in his interpretation of Scripture. The Gospel according to St John tells how Christ's best friend, the prostitute Mary of Magdalene, goes to the tomb where he had been laid two days before. A large rock had been placed over the entrance to the cave where he had been buried. When Mary arrives, she finds that the rock has been rolled away. Frightened, she flees and returns with the apostles Peter and Simon Peter. They all enter the tomb but do not find Christ's body. The shroud in which they wrapped his dead body is there but the body itself is gone. The men are bewildered and leave the tomb. Mary stays outside the empty sepulcher, weeping. Two angels appear and tell Mary that the body that died lives again. Then Christ himself appears to Mary and says, "Touch me not." He tells her to tell the disciples that she has seen him. The following week, Christ appears to the disciples. But Thomas is not among them and when he hears the news later he simply does not believe the report. He thinks his friends have seen a phantom, not an angel. He thinks the body has been moved or hidden or stolen or. . . . And with that special form of bravado common to white male skeptics, Thomas says he'll believe Christ is resurrected only when he puts his hand in the wound of Christ's living body. "Except I shall see in his hands the print of the nails, and . . . thrust my hands into his side, I will not believe" (John 20: 25).

Eight days later Jesus meets Thomas. Thomas now claims he believes in the resurrection since he can see the living Christ standing there before him. But Christ now doubts Thomas' proclamation of his new found faith. "Reach hither thy finger and behold my hands; and reach hither thy hand and thrust it into my side; and be not faithless, but believing" (John 20: 27). The aftermath of the redeemer doubting Thomas' repudiation of his doubt is the moment Caravaggio gives us (Figure 2).

There is a hole in the delicate tissue of faith which takes at least two to sustain. Christ takes the hand of a suddenly reluctant but still intensely curious and somewhat ashamed Thomas (he is ashamed because his curiosity has outmuscled his faith and he knows he must abandon his posture of bravado in the presence of a corporeal Christ). Holding his wrist, Christ pilots Thomas' fingers into the wound beneath his nipple. Thomas' brow is furrowed; the two apostles who look on also raise their furrowed brows. These creviced foreheads echo the creviced folds of Christ's wound. Plunging his fingers into the wound, Thomas enters the interior cavity of Christ's body. Opening his body to the curious fingers of an incredulous man, yielding his body to Thomas' quest for evidence and proof, Christ is witnessed as the redeemer.

Just as Velasquez employs "two incompatible visibilities" in *Las Meninas*, Caravaggio discovers two incompatible propositions in the story of the redemption. The surface reading of the story is that Thomas doubts; but Caravaggio insists that Christ also doubts. Caravaggio's painting opens up a series of questions that exceed the particular narrative drama of the painting itself but could not be prompted without the particularities of that drama. Caravaggio's Christ is uncertain who he is after the resurrection, and especially who he is in relation to the men with whom he had shared a history and with whom he had tried to forge a collective body. Cast as the ultimate stand-in, Christ had already given his body to the script, a script that had him say the words, "This is my body, take and eat," in an effort to dissolve the boundary between a divine body and a fallen one.

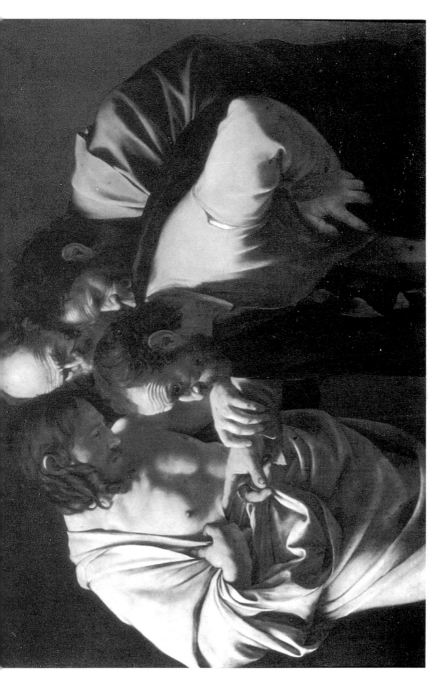

Figure 2 Caravaggio, *The Incredulity of St Thomas*. Copyright the Superintendency for Artistic and Cultural Heritage of Florence, Pistoia, and Prato. Reproduced with permission.

What does it take to dissolve the boundaries between bodies? If death is not that dissolving process, what is? If Christ is "the son of God made man" until his death, who is he eight days after his resurrection? Is he an apparition? An angel? If he can be said to be "living" after his resurrection, what gives him life if his wounded body lacks blood? Is the resurrected body "pure representation," always in circulation and forever repeating its appearances? These questions are more than theological ones; for Caravaggio they are painterly questions. Should Christ's wound bleed? Should he place red paint at the lip of Christ's open orifice? Has Caravaggio depicted a drama of corporeal penetration that does not touch the bloody borders between two (hol-y) bodies?

The theological argument about the nature of the body of Christ after the resurrection pivots on the question of touch. Thomas Aquinas, for example, argues that if a body can be touched, it is a corruptible body. In the garden of Gethsemane before the Passion, Christ says "Touch me not."[6] He repeats this injunction to Mary Magdalene when he appears to her at the lip of the sepulcher. But after his resurrection, he says to Thomas "touch me." Having given up all his blood for salvation, Christ, logic would indicate, should have no more blood left. If he is a bloodless body is he still "the son of God made man?" Thomas Aquinas' solution to the problem of whether or not Christ's resurrected body contained blood presages the aesthetic quandary intensified by the technology of perspective. Trying to negotiate between the doctrine of the incorruptible and therefore bloodless body of Christ on the one hand, and the evidence of Christ's blood that many Church leaders had declared "authentic" holy relics on the other, Thomas Aquinas cleverly lets painting solve the apparent contradiction. "This [blood] did not flow from Christ's side, but is said to have poured forth from images of Christ when they were struck" (Aquinas 1976: 3, 54, 3).[7] If painting allows for the illusion of interiority and depth it should not surprise us that such a perspective turns paintings quite literally into bodies, and bloody ones at that. I am not making an historical claim here. Thomas Aquinas was writing well before the invention of perspective. Perspective makes literal a certain kind of interiority that has long circulated around the aura of the painted image. Perhaps perspective was a response to the belief that painting must gain interiority if it were to carry human bodies.

The lack of blood at the lip of Christ's wound in Caravaggio's painting makes us somewhat uncertain about the status of "corporeal" penetration that the painting so dramatically stages. Uncertainty about the ontology of Christ's body heightens uncertainty about Christ as a dramatic, theological character. Did Christ believe he was truly loved, not only by the apostles, but by God? What would it take to accept such love "on faith"? Perhaps the lesson of the redemption is that to the degree to which Jesus was a man, he doubted he was loved. Perhaps he needed Thomas' fingers to slit open the scripted words in order to make him believe the part he played in his father's script was "real."

The question of love is the question of the painting – and I suppose to some degree the question of the Bible as love story. Luce Irigaray, our great interpreter of surfaces and cavities, has suggested that "The typical sentence produced by a woman is: Do you love me?" (Irigaray 1993: 134). Insofar as Caravaggio's painting can be said to be a speech act, a drama of interrogation, this is the question the two central bodies ask one other. Such a question must go beyond the surface: it must be a question forever welling up within one's own body, and a question infinitely more difficult for the subject to recognize within the body of the other. (This is why touch is always necessary in the love relation and why non-consensual touch is so distortingly violent. It is also why the "essentialisms" that hood virtually all discussions of the body are so persistent. Even though we know very well how hideously bodies lie, we want to retain some faith in the authenticity of the body's gestures.) "Do you love me?" is a social question, a question of relation. It is fundamentally a question of perspective, of where one is in relation to the other, to the painting, to the beloved. "Do you love me?" is a question that can come into being only if the other is cast as a witness, an auditor, who will testify to the authenticity of the interrogation as pure form, as that which is forever in question. "Do you love me?" is an elaboration of the questions "Do you see me?" and "Do you hear me?" and these three questions constitute the trinity of Western theatre, a set of technologies designed to ask what it means to be, and to make, embodied form from that which is not Present. (Behind these three questions is the question "Will you die for me?" and this is the question Sophocles' *Antigone* and the Redemption each try in their different ways to stage.)

Western theatre is itself predicated on the belief that there is an audience, an other willing to be cast in the role of auditor. The "act" at the heart of theatre making is the leap of faith that someone (that ideal spectator some call "God") will indeed see, hear, and love those brave enough to admit that this is the movement that keeps us from our deaths (or at least from permanently dark houses). The psychic problem raised by theatre is that it remains a perpetual rehearsal. The one for whom the theatre maker makes the piece never arrives for the performance. ("Nobody/bears witness for the/witness"). This is why theatre remains an art rather than a cure.

In this waiting, this rehearsal and masquerade, theatre is feminine. Like other feminine forms in patriarchal cultures, theatre is seen as something that needs control, even policing. The persistent anti-theatrical prejudice that accompanies theatre – from the anxiety about cross dressing in the Renaissance to the furor over the National Endowment for the Arts' funding decisions now – is one manifestation of a general widespread anxiety about femininity and effeminacy. This debate worries that femininity will spread, that works of art will contaminate and infect their viewers who will imitate what they see on stage.[8] This same sense of scandal haunts the reception of Caravaggio's works.

Caravaggio's painting gives the feminine question to (the body of) Christ who asks, "Do you love me Thomas?" He asks Thomas not so much to know his answer – Thomas has already denied his doubt and reaffirmed his faith and love verbally – but rather because he can only rehearse the question he most wants to ask the Other (God the father) with someone other-than that Other (in this case, Thomas is other-than God). The depth of the drama of the human body is made literal in Caravaggio's painting: the hole in the body is the physical mark of the separation between one and the Other. That hole stands as beckoning lure and unbreachable threshold.

All of our deepest questions are addressed to interlocutors who are not here, who cannot hear us. (If we could have a ready response our questions would not be "deep" – what makes them deep is their unanswerability.) Theatre is the arena in which the form and fury of the question is most consistently staged. Characters on-stage stand in for primary others who are not there, and this is one reason why the heroes of Western modern theatre, Beckett, Genet, and Artaud, are so thoroughly "theological" theatre makers. It is also why one so often feels behind the time one is in. The past happened when we were not looking and the future is always coming too soon. The one to whom we ache to speak is always the one who has already left and even as we speak to the others who are with us now we anticipate that later they will be the ones for whom we look after they too have left. And they will leave because they sense our distraction, our looking over their shoulder, under their skin, in the hidden orifices of their most intimate cavities for someone, something, else.

Caravaggio's painting also can be read as an allegory of the transference enacted in psychoanalysis, itself a mini-theatre. When it is working right, psychoanalysis is a carefully directed collaborative form of acting out. Within the psychoanalytic encounter, the analyst and the patient interrogate one another as a way of repeating, and thereby potentially reversing, the question put to the primary Other who never answered or answers. The quality of the psychoanalytic cure depends on the effectiveness of the performance of the stand-ins. Therefore the overall proposition of Adorno's rational redemption is that, since despair tells us so well how unlikely it is that the stand-in would have the substance of the real, then the dialectic necessity of thought requires that we consider that the stand-in is indeed as substantial as the real. In order to test that mental operation, we must also contend with the psychic, political, aesthetic and ideological consequences of the stand-in in a world that has lost the aura of the real.

Within the arc of resemblance and mimesis that perspective inaugurates, the stand-in stands in for a real that, like God and the Other, forever eludes us. The point is not so much to "find" the Other, but rather to play the drama in such a way that the stand-ins come to reveal that *the kernel of the drama of the Other is that the Other is always a stand-in*. In this sense, Thomas is Christ's God at least as much as Christ is Thomas' – for in the drama of intrasubjectivity (here heralded by bodily penetration and literal introjection) they are each one another's Other. In the two figures we confront the two incompatible propositions that perspective gives us: that we are framed, arrested in an illusion, a theatre of substantiation, and that the authenticity of our most intimate theatre can only become truly real through the agency of a stand-in. The 'proof' of Christ's resurrection cannot be authenticated by God: Thomas must play this other part.

Eight days after his resurrection, eleven days after his death, Christ puts Thomas' finger in his wound. There is something deeply scandalous in this scene, and the scandal only gets more radical as one looks more closely. The care with which Caravaggio paints Christ's robe spilling out beneath Thomas' penetrating finger serves to highlight the femininity of Christ; the robe is rendered with the diaphanous folds so characteristic of sixteenth- and seventeenth-century depictions of the clothes worn by the Virgin. While in keeping with the spirit of Caravaggio's earlier work that emphasized the double gender of the mythological god, Bacchus, Caravaggio is making a bolder claim in *The Incredulity*. Caravaggio forces us to see that for a man to penetrate the body of another man (and here again it is helpful to recall that the Resurrection, whatever else its theological significance, is the defining moment of Christ "as a man") another hole (a hole other than the mouth and anus, a hole for the Other) is required.[9] This is also what is required for linear perspective, for the eye to penetrate an interior space.

The remarkable foreshortening of the bodies in *The Incredulity* underlines again that there is a hole in perspective, a philosophy of the limit of the body in representation. Not then portraits of full bodies, but bodies amputated, castrated, by the drama in which they find themselves, caught between the living and the dead, captured between the flat surface of the canvas and the "depth" of the body's interiority. The vanishing point also underlines the hole in the viewer's body: it points to what painting, and corporeal vision itself, cannot show, cannot see.

In the piercing intimacy of the exchange between Thomas and Christ, Caravaggio cannot forget to record the attitude of the two apostles who witness the exchange. (Bodily acts are rarely absolutely private.) It is useful to think of the two apostles in the interior scene of the painting as surrogates for the spectator that Caravaggio's painting anticipates outside the frame. The four heads placed "in a concentrated diamond in the center of the canvas" (Hibbard 1983: 168) serve as internal focalizers of the drama. The spectator looks at everyone looking and looks to see what they see. The arching folds of the apostles' foreheads capture the characteristic posture of the partially-uncomprehending spectator; as witnesses to this re-giving, the apostles' bodies imitate the opening flesh of the skin that gives. Moreover, the upward arch of their brows balances the descending arch of Christ's robe. The lighting emphasizes their foreheads and brows while obscuring the eyes themselves. Hungry for an eye to return our regard, we find that a further movement in the allegory of the painting occurs.

The expression on the apostles' faces dramatizes the uneasiness of our relation to the painting's allure. For whatever else Caravaggio's painting can be said to be "about," it is fundamentally a drama of what it is to look at bodily penetration. Such looking is at once captivating and repelling. Perspective, from the Latin, means "looking through" and Caravaggio asks us to look through the painting of Christ's body that he offers. Caravaggio allegorizes perspective by displaying a body at the limit of the gaze. *The Incredulity*'s spectator, dizzy with the force of the image of penetration (an image that penetrates the viewer's own eye), attempts to find a gaze that will meet hers in a space outside of that wound. Deprived of a reciprocal regard, the viewer transforms Christ's wound into that returning eye. Given the symmetrical correspondence between the vanishing point and the viewing point, the logic of the scene suggests that the spectator's own eye is penetrated, that the painting, as it were, pokes the spectator in the eye, and thereby pierces the I who possesses a look, the I who is in the act of looking. "The self-possession of the viewing subject has built into it therefore, the principle of its own annihilation: annihilation of the subject as center is a condition of the very moment of the look" (Bryson 1988: 91). In order to continue to gaze at Caravaggio's mesmerizing painting, the spectator must blindly sustain the injury that the painting's logic inflicts. The spectator must, as it were, forgive Caravaggio's faithful rendering of perspective's logic. In order to look at what is painted, the viewer must overlook the hole. The symmetrical axis created by the painting's vanishing point and the viewer's viewing point mirrors the symmetry of Caravaggio's rendering of the narrative situation: Christ and Thomas bound by the body of doubt between them. Like those two, the viewer is cast in the role of both doubter and redeemer (of doubting redeemer). The painting insists on the reciprocity of these two positions. In Adorno's terms, the dialectical movement of the painting transforms Christ into doubting Thomas and Thomas into Christ's redeemer. That movement is repeated as the viewer moves toward and away from the surface of Caravaggio's canvas, and as the symmetry of the vanishing points and viewing points invites the viewer to transform Christ's wound into the source of a returning regard. In the performance of these transformations, Caravaggio suggests that reciprocity itself might be redemptive. Moreover, in looking at the penetrated orifice, the viewer begins to sense what a body unbounded by skin might feel like.

The wound in Christ's body opens up to an interiority that painting cannot expose. The absolute limit of the look is underscored here: even at the moment that heralds and "proves" the narrative endpoint of Redemption, the physical body nonetheless remains partially inaccessible to vision. The redemption of painting, Caravaggio seems to imply, requires, as does Thomas' doubt, that painting go *through* the body, to penetrate its interiority and to display that. But such a penetration cannot happen without a cutting, a tearing, a wounding, of painting's skin. The dramatic symmetry of Caravaggio's painting, its precise reciprocity and balance, creates a bizarre ricochet effect. Just as the eye of the spectator is led in toward the center of Christ's wound, so too does the painting send the spectator's eye out and off the canvas itself. The dramatic staging of the proof of Christ's resurrection is a proof that brings us, at once, too close to life and too close to death. If this scene of penetration is on the side of life, it is equally on the side of death. The painting's movement toward and away from the center of the hole mimics the motion we make toward and away from our own deaths. The suspension of that approach and retreat creates the stillness of the painting itself. Since both motions are solicited by the painting, it seems as if the painting has no time, no narrative advance or retreat. It is as if time itself were held in Christ's wound. Like the story of the boy who stopped the flood by putting his finger in the dike, Thomas' finger stoppers time and keeps the vitality of time's flowing blood bottled up in the wound of a liminal body. What the painting freezes is the terrible stillness of looking at a body that is neither living nor dead, neither Christ nor the artist's model, an insatiable looking that is the living eye's search for the image (the still image) of its own death. Since we are emphatically not redeemed, we call this body paint. We revere it and love it and look at it again and again because, unlike God, painting has and is a body we can touch.

Caravaggio's painting holds the viewer's eye in the vanishing depth of the image of a wounded body. That image serves as a mirror capable of reflecting the eye's own longing to be arrested, to be still, to be done with looking, to be held. High art seems to promise that such a coming to the eye's still core, its orbicular closure, will be beautiful, sublimely redemptive. High art promises that the eye will be arrested by the searing ache of its own gorgeous creation. Pornography and "low" art make the opposite promise: that the fulfillment of the eye's ravenous desire to see will be abjecting and degrading, that the very end of looking will render the body as pure hole, bottomless wound. In Caravaggio's painting and in the spectacular penetrations of the body given to us in photographic porn, we are made to see that there is an injury, a wound, a hole, that makes all we see incomplete, partial, painful. Michael Fried remarks that as painting approaches realism it creates

> an implied affront to seeing – a stunning, or worse, a wounding of seeing – that leads me to imagine that the definitive realist painting would be one that the viewer literally could not bear to look at: as if at its most extreme, or at this extreme, the enterprise of realism required an effacing of seeing in the act of looking. . . . What confronts us . . . is an image at once painful to look at (so piercingly does it threaten our visual defenses) and all but impossible, hence painful *to look away from* (so keen is our craving for precisely the confirmation of our own bodily reality), and that it is above all the conflictedness of our situation that grips and excruciates and in the end virtually stupefies us before the picture.
>
> (Fried 1987: 65).

But it is not for nothing that Caravaggio's "wounding" of the look finds its most passionate expression in the penetration of the wound in Christ's body. What "grips and excruciates and in the end virtually stupefies" me in relation to Caravaggio's *The Incredulity* is that what might be most redemptive in the Redemption is the endlessness of the body's transformations. Perhaps death is not an end at all. The dynamic propulsion of the look's movement enacted by Caravaggio's painting might be one way to rehearse for the "still life" still ahead of us. If we now ask painting to hold the bodies we can no longer touch, perhaps then looking at and touching painting will truly save us from death, from the cessation of touch.

Rendered purely compositional, the human body undergoes a fascinating and shifting montage within the stillness of perspectival painting. Body parts, even in the most surgically realistic portrait, become other parts as the viewer's eye touches their surfaces. The visible hole the vanishing point gives us activates our attention to the holes we do not see. Thomas' penetrating finger allows us to see Christ's wound as a sort of stand-in, a substitute for a masculine vagina which is itself a substitute for something that the painting cannot show us: a penetrated anus. High art must wait for Robert Mapplethorpe to find the elaboration of that image.[10]

Composed with the calm surety of sculpture, Mapplethorpe's *Lou* exposes photography's devotion to documentation as a service exercise and insists that it find a more artistically sublime and psychically radical ambition. Mapplethorpe wants to push the camera to illuminate the male body's underexposed secrets. Cropping the head of his model, Mapplethorpe shows us a portrait of a man that the camera cannot fully capture. Rather than demonstrating yet again how skillfully the camera stops and arrests the model in a little death, Mapplethorpe's *Lou* points to the possibility of a scene, an act, capable of arresting and stopping the otherwise-endlessly dilating eye of the camera's aperture. This camera's eye finds its own still spot, its own little death, at the tip of a penetrated penis.

What is surprising about Mapplethorpe's photograph is that even while the camera reaches a kind of stopping point, it carries with it every virtue and every banality of the documentary desire of portraiture. Lou's hair follicles are so closely recorded it is almost as if the image suggests that hairs themselves penetrate skin in much the way the finger penetrates the penis in the center of the image. Moreover, the finely delineated veins of his arm and hand work to suggest the idea that "being erect" is a performance that requires reciprocal holding, even in explicitly auto-erotic undertakings. The tunneling veins are discernible as forms beneath the skin because of the way in which they bulge with photographic light (the very "blood" of the image).

Mapplethorpe, like Caravaggio, wants to tear open the flat surface of photographic perspective. He wants the image to tear open the paper of the print and become a sculptural object. He wants his spectator to want to hold his photograph with the same calculated desire with which the model in *Lou* holds his penis. Thus, the drama of penetration central to Caravaggio's narrative is staged by Mapplethorpe across the lip of the frame, between the spectator and, uncannily, not "the model" but rather the image of a kind of inverted penetration. (The arm that holds the penis looks a bit like an inverted penis.) Not the usual photograph of the pornographic penis, endlessly hard and endlessly penetrating, Mapplethorpe's *Lou* exposes the penis as it is penetrated. The fanning fingers frame that moment when the model pilots his own finger into his penis; Mapplethorpe spreads the light between the model's fingers in the way a pornographer might spread the buttocks, and then stops that light at the point of penetration. *Lou* condenses and consolidates photography's theory and performance of the vanishing point.

There is something perverse at work in perspective: some form of looking away that gets activated by the structure of the vanishing point. Saint Augustine argued that perversion was the willful looking away from God. Lacan has suggested that perversion is most visible within the intersubjective experience, within the identification with the other (Lacan 1991: 215). What distinguishes perversion from other forms of

Figure 3 Robert Mapplethorpe, *Lou, N.Y.C., 1978*. Copyright 1978 The estate of Robert Mapplethorpe. Reproduced with permission.

neuroses is the structure of disavowal, captured in the expression, "I know very well, but just the same." In *The Incredulity* Caravaggio gives us a painting in which we can see orthodox Christianity's disavowal of the dynamic and shifting positions of Thomas and Christ. Christ doubts that he is Christ and uses Thomas to assure him that he is the redeemer. What makes the painting performative, an act of doing, is that the spectator, like Christ and Thomas, must shift their position in order to look at the painting: the viewer must move both toward and away from Christ's wound – must look at it and look away from it. Thus, the painting's subjectivity resides in the movement that the viewer must undertake in order to see it.

If the reciprocal identifications between Thomas and Christ can be understood to be perverse, perspective fosters the spectator's perversion. We know this is a flat canvas, but just the same, we want it to have depth enough to hold the interiority of the bodies it displays. Perversion can be understood to be the refusal to remain oneself in the drama of the other's doubt, a refusal almost always born of desire, if not love. Painting a scene in which Christ abandons his own role as redeemer and takes up the role of doubting Thomas, Caravaggio perverts the relation that orthodox Christianity argues adheres between God and man. For Caravaggio, Christ transforms Thomas into his God because he needs him in order to learn who he is. (This is one explanation for the invention of any god.) In that transformation, Christ "redeems" Thomas – but only because Thomas redeemed him by expressing, by embodying, Christ's own doubt. The expression of that doubt motivates the scene Caravaggio gives us, even while the narrative force of the scene insists that it is proof, not doubt, that the story gives us. Perversion is the disavowal of singular perspective in favor of mutative, transforming identifications. Identifications that penetrate the skin-ego and cause it to turn away from itself, cause it to doubt its own boundaries and limits, constitute what we might call the theatre of perversions. If perspective establishes a route for the eye to move through, it also at the same time establishes perversion: for just as surely as Caravaggio's painting draws us in and makes us want to look at the divine, it also throws us out and prompts us to turn away from the image.

In Freud's theories of male homosexuality, perhaps best illustrated in his analysis of Schreber, erotic desire involves one man imagining himself to be in the passive "feminine" position so that another man may penetrate his anus.[11] What Caravaggio's painting helps us discover is that the vanishing point of vision, the hole into which the eye cannot penetrate, stands in for another deeper hole in the ground of vision's own body. The eye can be slit open like a dilating vagina. But this opening distracts us from the opening which truly captivates and repels the sexual desire at the heart of visual pleasure within the always-already masculine Imaginary.[12] Painting the slit in the male body, a slit that raises the question of the (passive, penetrable) feminine, both points to and leaves obscure the masculine anus. The obsessive focus on the naked body of women that fuels both high art and pornography is itself a stand-in, a substitute for the perhaps-more-fervently-desired image of a penetrable male body. In other words, the desire to create an image of a penetrable man is often accomplished by passing *through*, looking through, the bodies of women. High art's and pornography's continual exposition of the possibility of men's penetration of women's bodies via "the male gaze" is contingent upon the unmarked possibility of men's penetration of the bodies of men.

In moving then from the logic of substitution to an economy of psychic displacement we see again that substitutive logic is never politically or psychically neutral. Freud's contention that the sexual instinct is independent of the sexual object suggests that the art of erotic life is an endless performance of sublimation.

> The sexual instinct . . . places extraordinarily large amounts of force at the disposal of civilized activity, and it does this in virtue of its especially marked characteristic of being able to displace its aim without materially diminishing in intensity. This capacity to exchange its originally sexual aim for another one which is no longer sexual but which is psychically related to the first aim, is called the capacity for sublimation.
>
> (Freud 1908: 87)

Displacing the sexual aim is part of the cultural work that high art undertakes.

In Caravaggio's painting, the dynamic propulsion that forces the viewer to transform the wound into an eye that stares back is a rehearsal for the larger displacement that the erotic performance of the painting undertakes. The eye we make from the wound is an eye that is slit open, an eye the viewer seeks in order to constitute herself as an "I." Sublimating the feminine into the body of Christ, Caravaggio simultaneously conceals and reveals the "perversity" of Thomas' and Christ's erotic touching. This "perversion" is itself sublimated into a scene of high theological drama in which the co-mingling of bodies is transformed into the narrative of redemption. The implicit sado-masochism of the scene is sublimated into an illustration of divine love: this is and is not a portrait of painful penetration; this is and is not a portrait of redemptive love in which Christ's body is a resurrected body between two deaths. Given the reciprocal logic of Caravaggio's painting, such a reading also suggests the divinity of the sacrifice rendered within s/m sexual performances. What is "offered up" in these sexual performances is perhaps the desire to lay down one's body for the other and the equally spectacular desire to solicit and to accept such a sacrifice. S/m performances are perhaps testaments to the desire to discover that (little) deaths are never still, never quite over, never exchanges which expire. The stillness of the little death, like the stillness of Caravaggio's painting, holds the seemingly endless oscillation toward and away from the body of the other, toward and away from death, toward and away from the still frame of some phantasmatic square bed, square canvas, square coffin, which frames the desire to move, to give and to take some love we cannot touch and cannot stop trying to touch.

But even as I transform the wound in Christ's body into an eye, I also blind myself to the truest terror of the painting and the story that lies behind it. When his friends and mother go to look for Christ in the tomb, it is empty. The form, the skeleton, the very corpse that held Christ's body is gone. The interiority of the tomb will not yield the form they seek. Nobody is there. The failure of the body to remain a solid set of remains is underscored by Caravaggio's painting as it encourages the viewer to transform the wound into an eye. This transformation reflects the changing and seemingly endless slipping away from us that the dying do. Not even the dead will hold still: they do not leave us all at once, which would be horribly violent but clear. They fall away from us piece by piece until we cannot bear the withering decomposition of their form of relation to us. It is the lack of form, the lack of anything to hold onto in death, that inspires the drama of love that can offer us only bodies with holes in them. The radical formlessness of the beloved's body (its utter failure to remain static) creates the wild terror of Caravaggio's painting.

For beneath the skin of this theory I am trying to drape across this painting there is yet another hole we may fall through. Caravaggio's painting captures the suffering of flesh. These men take form, are composed, as forms of painted skin. The way the shoulders are exposed in the rip of the garments, the way the foreheads of the apostles crease and rise, the way Thomas' finger seems so preternaturally large, the way the wrist of Thomas is stitched into the hand of Christ, the way the wound gives, all suggest the ways in which the skin suffers as it tries to contain the form of drama in which we love. Such dramas exceed the elasticity of skin; the skin cannot hold all we ask it to contain. Skin lacks the depth, the interiority, we want it to give us. If skin would give us this depth we might actually have proof that we do have such interiority, that the precarious feelings, dreams, phantasms, inner speech that we call subjectivity is real, that it can be embodied, enclosed in skin's own form. But this is precisely what skin, as surface covering, cannot offer us. Hence we suffer our skins and our skins suffer us. Perspective itself, the transformation of the flat surface into an illusionary deep space, fosters our desire for our skin to have depth.

Lacan, writing about Freud's dream of Irma's injection, locates this suffering in the phantasmatic cave of Freud's vision of Irma's open mouth, wounded and oozing:

> the flesh in as much as it is suffering, is formless, in as much as its form in itself is something that provokes anxiety. Specter of anxiety, identification of anxiety, the final revelation of *you are this – You are this, which is so far from you, this which is the ultimate formlessness*.
>
> (Lacan 1988: 154–5; Lacan's emphasis).

The paradox of Caravaggio's painting lies precisely here: in the narrative "proof" of Christ's embodiment Caravaggio paints the radical disembodiment of human love and subjectivity. Recording the narrative "proof" of Christ as (eternally) living body, Caravaggio's painting gives us a wounded, bloodless body. An arrested frozen image, Caravaggio's Christ makes vivid the terror of embodiment. Irma's throat, which oozes and vibrates across the screen of Freud's dream, is disconcertingly alive. Her throat contains a formlessness that cannot be fixed or mastered by any of her doctors. It is furiously mutative. But it lives beyond its own skin, it becomes the phantasm of Freud's dream. As a wound that oozes, Irma's throat proves her skin will not contain her.

In placing Irma's throat next to Caravaggio's rendering of Christ's wound I am trying to suggest two different terrors that embodiment holds: Irma's oozing throat has too much substance; Christ's bloodless wound has too little. Together, they point to a formlessness that haunts the psychic experience of embodiment itself.

Withholding an image of blood at the lip of Christ's wound, Caravaggio forces the spectator to confront the possibility that there is no interior form to the body at all. Just as the interior cave could not yield Christ's corpse to those who loved him, so might it be that the flesh we crave as confirmation of our forms cannot do anything but turn us forever out even as we burrow into and into the holes we find there. "You are this, which is so far from you . . ." This endless looking for an interior beneath the surface of the bodies and images with which we are forever ensnared is the catastrophe of living (in) skin. Skinned alive, our bodies are sentenced to find a form that might hold our love, a form that might hold our deaths. The promise of that constantly-deferred final sentence, exuberant sky writing, why's own writing, is what keeps us performing repeated acts of looking, repeated acts of loving. They must be repeated because they cannot be sustained. The radical formlessness and apparent endlessness of our vision, of our sexuality, of our dying, makes it impossible to still these things and declare them "still lives." The impossibility of declaring or deciding what constitutes our habits of looking, of making love, of dying, leads us to occupy ourselves with re-naming and repeating our attempts to contain these things. Caravaggio's painting and the performance of looking that it inspires, illustrates our deep desire to give form to the endless attempt to move toward and away from dying.

NOTES

1 The vanishing point also served a crucial role in the long debate about whether or not painting was a liberal or a mechanical art. Insofar as it was derived from mathematics and geometry, the vanishing point situated painting in league with science. Protected by the status of science, painting became "a high art" – economically, politically, historically.
2 Poirier (1981) is the best reading of Foucault's apocalyptic passage that I have read.
3 The very momentum of this economy of substitution renders "the real" an unstable category.
4 In contemporary theatre, the work of Anna Deavere Smith does much the same thing. She interviews people, uses their speech as the "content" of her theatre pieces, and invites her interviewees to the performance.
5 There are actually three crossings in the painting. Velasquez and the courtier in the doorway create a third diagonal axis in the visual field.
6 See Anzieu (1989) for a further elaboration of the psychoanalytic dimensions of this encounter.
7 Presumably these images of Christ were so ravishing, and the desire of viewers to touch an embodied Christ so extraordinary, viewers were prompted to "strike" the images.
8 One of the best post-Barrish readings of the anti-theatrical prejudice in the Renaissance is Laura Levine's *Men in Women's Clothing* (1994). On the NEA see my "Money Talks" (1990) and "Money Talks, Again" (1991).
9 It needs to be a wound because the emphasis of redemption is on Christ's suffering and sacrifice.
10 David Hickey has written a sharp, but alas brief, comparison of Mapplethorpe and Caravaggio. See Hickey (1993).
11 Freud's argument is quite complex and I must apologize for this foreshortened and therefore distorting treatment. But see Freud, "Psychoanalytic Notes on an Autobiographical Account of a Case of Paranoia (Dementia Paranoides)" (1911), *Standard Edition*, 12, 1958.
12 For a full exposition of how the Symbolic is the product of the male Imaginary see Hart (1993).

3

Immobile legs, stalled words: psychoanalysis and moving deaths

I

I have had a long and, if I may say so myself, distinguished career as a member of the corps de ballet in the New York City Ballet, or NYCB as we call it. We had been entrusted with preserving the works of George Balanchine, without a doubt the master choreographer of this century. Even as a young girl I longed to dance – before I had ever seen a ballet. I cannot explain this deep urge in me. It just is. Or perhaps was. But I get ahead of myself, like James Joyce's Lily. "Lily was so busy she was literally run off her feet." Joyce's daughter was a dancer, and surely he learned from her how peculiarly the feet flee the body after a long dance. Anyway, I had devoted my life to dance and it is my greatest happiness to feel I have been able to interpret accurately and passionately some of the movements Balanchine had imagined.

Most of my colleagues at NYCB viewed their work in the corps as a kind of advanced apprenticeship, a necessary stepping stone toward their real goal, which was to become a principal dancer. I myself, however, was content to remain a member of the corps. I have certain physical limitations (I am not as tall as the ideal ballerina needs to be), but more importantly, I am not dedicated enough to put my body through the disciplined work, especially in relation to the precise technique of dancing on pointe, that cannot be side-stepped by any aspiring principal.

I was happy to make a relatively anonymous contribution to Balanchine's expansive vision. My ex-husband liked this in me and often remarked that I was one of the few remaining women who understood the value of subsuming individual ambition for a larger collective purpose. To my distress I soon found it much easier to give myself fully to the work of Balanchine than to my marriage; I believed in the vision of Mr B wholeheartedly but discovered I could not sustain the faith needed for marriage.

But I digress. I do not want to burden you with the details of my personal life. Rather, I would like to tell a different story altogether, one that I hope will play some small part in opening a long deferred conversation between dancers and cultural theorists, more particularly, those interested in psychoanalysis and questions of the feminine body. For reasons that I hope will be apparent a bit further on, I find it necessary to frame my entry point into the conversation by making some mention of the events that led to my interest in the relationship between dance and psychoanalysis.

Once I realized that my marriage was ending and that I would not be on the same career path as most of the corps, I found that I had a small amount of time and psychic freedom to pursue certain questions that had surfaced from time to time in my life but that I had always put aside to dedicate myself entirely to the dance. I found, for example, that I had a certain appetite for finance and a rather surprising interest in science, especially kinesiology. Moreover, I became interested in risk–gain ratios and found myself calculating what the percentages of injuring knees, hips, and ankles would be in relation to the number of hours the troupe rehearsed, divided by the number of hours we performed. I made charts to include travel time via airplanes, and compared these with charts of travel time and crime statistics on the New York subway. I realized that all my years counting at the barre and doing various exercises had given me a deeply intimate kinship with numbers. I had come to order my habits of thinking in relation to numbers and found that I had a strange facility for understanding the ways in which they could be combined and divided. It seemed to me that numbers had an inner logic, a sort of affinity for certain other numbers, that I found comforting. Numbers seemed to be a kind of music that extended from dance into a richly layered world whose movements I wanted to graph, to plot, to lay out – as if on an enormous clock that everyone in the whole world could see. This rather late and large ambition threw me at first.

My ex-husband was (actually is) something of a computer wizard and some of the calmest times we had together were spent choreographing numbers across a computer screen. After we divorced, I became almost obsessive about creating a fantastical virtual ballet on the computer. My efforts in this regard were made all the more pleasurable by the possibility of imagining movement as pure form. It was only later that I realized my passion for computers was a way of grieving. Having felt the deep pain of realizing that my marriage was a mis-step, I was in danger of losing my way everywhere. I had devoted most of my life to placing one foot in front of the other, and suddenly I was profoundly unsure about where to step. As my feet tapped away under my chair and my fingers typed on the keys, I began to feel that the lack of direction in my feet might be cured by the mapping my fingers were making on the keyboard. I was transferring the hesitation in my feet to the plotting of my calmer hands. A strange form of grieving perhaps but for me a helpful one.

After a while I came to realize that my computer plans could not be realized. I simply did not know enough about the deep structure of statistics and computation to do what I most wanted to do – develop a computerized version of Balanchine's elegant ballets. I dreamt that if

I could learn these skills I might bring the beauty of Balanchine to an audience who had never heard of him or seen his work.

I went to the NYCB directors and explained my vision. They were supportive but in a vague, immaterial way. I wanted them to fund my study at the Courant Institute of Mathematics at New York University where my ex-husband's best friend was a professor. He had assured me that the Institute would admit me as a special student. Unfortunately, the tuition there was considerably more than I could afford and since I would not be enrolled in a degree program I was not eligible for financial aid. The ballet directors were not forthcoming with the fees however and I could not bring myself to push the matter beyond my broad hint. I knew and respected that the NYCB had to devote itself to preserving Balanchine's real ballets first and foremost and while I thought my project in virtual ballet was certainly compatible with that mission I also knew it would take several years and promised only uncertain results.

*Despite my intellectual acceptance of the directors' decision, I grew depressed and somewhat despondent during rehearsals. I had been a member of the corps for twelve years and it was increasingly difficult for me to maintain my initial enthusiasm for practice. I spent about six months in this inattentive condition. Then one evening during a sparsely attended performance of **Mozartiana** at Lincoln Center (it was sparsely attended because there was a snow storm and I was thinking about how I might plot the risk–injury ratio of audiences from Manhattan versus New Jersey) when I extended my right leg in the air above my waist, as I had done thousands upon thousands of times before, I heard my hip crack.*

After the bone was set and I was in the hospital recovering, I thought about the ironies of my injury. I had been plotting the probabilities of injuries for about three years. I wondered if I had somehow known in advance that I would break my hip. Was my statistical frenzy an elaborate form of self-explanation, self-justification? I also considered the irony of my injury occurring during a performance of **Mozartiana**. While Balanchine choreographed it he spoke often of the death of Mozart and the kind of smooth order his music represented (perfect integers). Tchaikovsky's Suite No. 4 sets Mozart's piano pieces for an orchestra, and Balanchine used Tchaikovsky's score to illustrate how music could be seen and dance could be heard. As the music builds on the principal drive of the piano, so too did the corps elaborate the central drama of the four principals. Balanchine privately referred to the role of his principal dancer in one sequence as a dance for "the angel of death." Publicly, the sequence is called "Prayer." The simplicity of Balanchine's choreography in **Mozartiana** struck me as his most spiritually searching work; it was my personal favorite. But if you asked me what it was "about," I could not say. It was more of a feeling than anything else for me – a feeling of searching, of longing.

As I lay in the hospital bed, I tried to hear my own longing. While my injury was extraordinarily painful and I dreaded being immobile, I had to admit that somewhere part of my spirit felt liberated. I was out of the corps for at least eight months, possibly a year. I had reasonable amounts of insurance and on the third day of my convalescence the ballet directors came in and rather sheepishly told me they had paid the fees for Courant. I was to be the first injured ballerina to enroll in the prestigious institute.

But as is so often the case in human affairs, when I arrived at Courant I was immediately overwhelmed. I had been essentially self-taught. I could not decipher any of the language in which these professors spoke. They were on a planet so remote that I knew that what I needed to join them there was beyond whatever resources I had or even wanted to summon. Professional mathematicians seemed so different *from professional dancers that I began to think my plan utterly mad, impossible.*

This became clear after the fifth lecture of the "Introduction to Statistics" course. The course was so large it was held in the psychology building which had large lecture theatres. The course was designed for social scientists. The professors at Courant told me quite frankly that it was the easiest of all their course offerings and that it would ground me in the basic language of computation necessary for instruction in "higher" mathematical forms. At the end of the fifth lecture, however, I was totally lost. I could not find an entry point despite my most heroic efforts to concentrate. I sat there in the lecture hall dejectedly, waiting for the pain in my hip to subside. Absentmindedly, I began doodling with some numbers on my notepad and did not notice for some time that a new class had begun, something having to do with psychology. By the time I began to listen I could feel the force of Providence re-setting my bones. This, after all, was what I had been moving toward, but as in the best choreography, I never would have guessed where I would wind up from where I had started.

The lecture was being given by a young, apparently serious but not especially talented, lecturer. She seemed at times quite over her head. I liked that. Suddenly I did not feel as if I were the only one at sea. I actually could follow most of what she said. I rushed to the book store and began reading voraciously. This class was going to answer all the questions I did not even know were "mine."

What follows is a long version of my interpretation of the lecturer's remarks. She is not a dancer, but most of what she said was so applicable to dance that I have, with her permission, entwined our thoughts. I asked her if I could use her name since so much of the work is hers but she insisted that all teachers want this kind of collaboration to happen. She prefers to remain an unmarked presence in my text.

II

In the inaugural text of classical psychoanalysis, Josef Breuer's and Sigmund Freud's 1895 *Studies on Hysteria,* a remarkable amount of attention is given to bodies, and to body parts, that will not or cannot move. The first of the five case histories collected in *Studies,* Breuer's account of his treatment of Anna O., and the last, Freud's account of his treatment of Elisabeth von R., contain especially fascinating and often overlooked notions of the relationship between the body and truth, the body and time, and the body and language. Here, we would like to recast the usual critical approach to *Studies on Hysteria* that accents the invention of the *talking* cure, and review another hope for a psychical cure that these early case histories also express. This cure had as its foundation a deep faith in the "truth" of bodily performances.

The psychoanalytic session, at least as it was conceived in these early case histories, involved the acting out, the performative elaboration, of the symptom. While the case histories chart several different notions of performance – ventriloquism, imitation, "possession" – we will concentrate here on the ideas of dance and movement that inform *Studies.* Following the lead of Freud and Breuer, we will be concerned with paralytic feet and eloquent thighs, and with the transfers enacted in psychic and physical movements and "obstructions."

Dragging feet, feet with sharp cramps, feet that swell and limp, feet that are suddenly too heavy to move, feet that support legs frozen in contractions, give *Studies on Hysteria* a strange rhythm and rocky gait. It is on the basis of these aching feet that psychoanalysis proposes a new reproductive system for the female body (all five of the case histories are of women). In Breuer's analysis of Bertha Pappenheim, whom he names Anna O., "when the first of her chronic symptoms disappeared," the contracture of her right leg, the psychoanalytic method was born:

> These findings – that in the case of this patient the hysterical phenomena disappeared as soon as the event which had given rise to them was reproduced in her hypnosis – made it possible to arrive at a therapeutic technical procedure which left nothing to be desired in its logical consistency and systematic application.
>
> (Freud and Breuer 1895: 35)

Returning suppleness and motion to Anna O.'s right leg enables both Anna O. and psychoanalysis itself to "take a great step forward" (ibid.). In the disappearance of the contraction in the right leg, the technique "which left nothing to be desired" was born.[1]

The birth of psychoanalysis requires the re-production and re-presentation of the "event" which triggered the contraction of Anna O.'s rightleg. In that re-enactment psychic and physical movement are restored. The psychoanalytic reproduction of the symptomatic body requires two people. In these early histories, the patient and the doctor connect both physically and psychically. Freud eventually theorized the psychical contact in the transference and counter-transference. In *Studies*, however, the physical contact between the doctor and the patient is instrumental to the cure. "But she would never begin to talk until she had satisfied herself of my identity by carefully feeling my hands" (1895: 30). Peter Swales has documented that when Freud told Sandor Ferenczi about his early years as an analyst he admitted that when he ana-lyzed Frau Cäcilie M., whose history is documented in *Studies*, "he had even lain on the floor, sometimes for hours at a time accompanying [her] through hysterical crises" (Swales 1986: 50). For both doctors, although for different reasons, the physical cure presented too many risks. Psychoanalysis moved away from embracing the body and refined the talking cure. A technique that depended too heavily upon touch was a huge risk for an epistemological revolution whose visionary leader was determined to be, above all, scientific. *Studies*, almost unwittingly, realizes two different approaches to the cure – and the psychoanalytic movement followed the one that left the body untouched.

Like blind men first learning Braille, the fingers of Freud and Breuer press and prod the somatic utterances of their patients' hysterical bodies.[2] The doctors apply mental and/or physical pressure to the indecipherable bodily signifier, the symptom, until it "joins in the con-versation." Different body parts of the patient join the doctor in an ongoing conversation whose subject is no longer strictly speaking "her" body but is rather "their body," the body being made and manipulated in their discursive and physical interaction. In his history of Elisabeth von R., Freud describes this technique which "left nothing to be desired":

> [H]er painful legs[3] began to 'join in the conversation' during our analyses. . . . If . . . by a question or by pressure upon her head I called up a memory, a sensation of pain would make its first appearance, and this was usually so sharp that the patient would give a start and put her hand to the spot. The pain that was thus aroused would persist so long as she was under the influence of the memory; it would reach its climax when she was in the act of telling me the essential and decisive part of what she had to communicate, and with the last word it would disappear. I came in time to use such pains as a compass to guide me; if she stopped talking but admitted that she still had a pain, I knew she had not told me everything, and insisted on her continuing her story till the pain had been talked away. Not until then did I arouse a fresh memory.[4]

(1895: 148)

The "arousal" of a fresh memory reproduces a fresh body, one newly made in the somatic and verbal performance Freud and Elisabeth enact. Putting his hand on her head causes pressure to build; her hand flies to a different body part which is then verbally massaged. Freud transforms Elisabeth's leg's contribution to the conversation into a truth-meter, a somatic lie-detector.[5] Although Freud doubts his patient's verbal starts and stops, her narrative's beginnings and endings, for him her thigh does not lie.[6]

In *Studies*, Freud and Breuer tried to find the history of the symptom. Their search for history has led many scholars to use a kind of short-hand in describing the relation between history and hysteria: hysteria is a disease that is the consequence of a jumbled narrative, an incoherent autobiography, a failure of historical accounts.[7] But it would be more accurate to say that hysteria is the disease through which psycho-analysis imagines a history of the symptom and the patient discovers that her body's history must be spoken. The imposition of narrative order, an imposition rehearsed when the doctor composes his account, imposes psychic order on the body.[8] What is profoundly startling to realize, however, is that the body does not contain such an order independent of this narrative imposition. Psychoanalysis suggests that the body's "truth" does not organize itself narratologically or chrono-logically. The body does not experience the world in the way that consciousness does: the aim of psychoanalysis is to find a way to suture the body into time's order (time's truth is its order).[9] The equally logical task of suturing consciousness to bodily "truth" remains outside the official domains of mainstream science, and thrives in new age philos-ophy and alternative medicine.

Dance can be said to be the elaboration of possible temporalities for the body that are interpreted in movement; and psychoanalysis can be said to be the elaboration of possible narratives for the body that are interpreted (or displaced) in the body's symptom. Dance frames the body performing movement in time and space. While it is true that bodies usually manage to move in time and space, dancing *consciously* performs the body's discovery of its temporal and spatial dimensions. For many dancers, of course, dancing is timing. Lacking a good sense of timing, some people abandon dancing.

> *I feel an overwhelming need to interrupt the partnering that I am doing here. The following few paragraphs constitute my solo writing. Perhaps I have secretly longed to be a principal dancer and have been renouncing that desire all this time. So much of my past is lost to me now. Anyway:*

When I began to dance Balanchine's ballets as a teenager I entered his system of time. I became one of a number of bodies he wanted to move, and my body became for him a type of number. While Balanchine generated his numbers from the music, I generated mine from the measure of my limbs' movements. Looking back I can now see that Balanchine's choreography cured a certain fear of being lost that I sometimes had before I fully became a dancer. On those rare occasions when I did not practice or rehearse for a day or two, I would remember that vague feeling of drift that I had experienced prior to my training. It was as if I could not find a place to land, a way to be in the world. Dancing gave me that place, that way of counting. With a broken hip I was in danger of losing a certain mental equilibrium. As I read the psychoanalytic case histories over and over I would listen to Mozart as a way to keep my body in the time to which it had grown accustomed.

Soon I began to see aspects of my own past in these histories that inspired me to revise my relation to my training. This absorption with my past startled me, for dancers are disciplined to think in the present tense exclusively – to be fully in the moment. Remembrance is replaced by "reconstruction," a present performance of dances that have been re-scored in notation practices that are only now becoming common ways to preserve dance.

Freud's favorite word for psychoanalysis was reconstruction. I began to see a deep similarity between the process of reassembling the movements that constitute dance and the psychic remembering and working through of psychoanalysis. While ballet is dedicated to "beauty," psychoanalysis is dedicated to "health." But both practices are very close.

Physical movement and psychic transference allow for a revision of the body's relation to its own past. Psychic transference is the work accomplished in the actual analysis itself and

*then repeated in the analyst's act of composing
and publishing the case history. Breuer's record
of Anna O.'s cure re-enacts the process by
which his discursive interpretation "surmounts"
the questions raised by her body. However, in
the translation of the somatic symptom into the
discursive cure, another movement occurs. In
addition to moving simply and elegantly from
the logic of the symptom to the logic of discourse,
the body makes another move. It dances.
Something central to the vitality of the body
cannot be contained by even the most exhaustive psychoanalytic cure.*

*For my lecturer this "something" is the irre-
ducible symptom of femininity itself. Jacqueline
Rose argues that "hysteria is assimilated to a
body as site of the feminine, outside discourse,
silent finally, or at best, 'dancing'" (Rose 1989:
28). But Rose and my lecturer seem to assume
that talking is better than dancing, that language
is more expressive than somatic utterances. I
myself cannot accept this assumption. Moreover,
the argument about hysteria and femininity
neglects the question of what Breuer and
Balanchine wanted to cure in their own bodies.
Breuer's copious note-taking and Balanchine's
breath-taking choreography answered some need
in them that had little to do with the women
upon whose bodies they sought to pose their
deepest questions.*

*Like dancers and choreographers, Freud and
Breuer admitted that the body can express things
that consciousness and its discursive formations
cannot. Within psychoanalysis, these bodily
expressions are called symptoms. Symptoms
are somatic expressions which signal the work
of repression; they are the bodily place holders
for material that consciousness cannot fully
absorb. Symptoms are condensed indexes of a
not-yet-consciously-narrativized event. Therefore, symptoms can only occur in the present
tense; once the event finds a past tense, the
symptom (temporarily) disappears.[10] Within the
terms of psychoanalysis, bodies are symptomatic;*

some symptoms are dangerous, but most are not. Although we tend to think of a symptom as a pathology, we will use the word here in the genuine psychoanalytic sense, to refer to bodily expressions not yet interpreted.

From a dancer's point of view the symptom is one way of understanding a movement phrase. Movement phrases are somatic expressions that are condensed versions of particular techniques. They consolidate a specific physical gesture in the dance even while pointing to the broader movement vocabulary from which the phrase is derived. Likewise, the symptom registers a particular "something" that the body can only perform symptomatically (a cough, a paralyzed arm), while also pointing to something that eludes conscious narration. In dance, the exclusions of movement choices, which are fundamental to establishing the technique from which the phrase emerges, function in a way similar to the repressions of the unconscious: they are as vital to the legibility of the movement phrase itself as symptoms are to the legibility of a particular subjectivity. A failed movement phrase, in my case, a broken hip, might be an expression of some dis-join that my body must dis-play precisely because I cannot name it. (Some injuries of course are the result of bad choreography: if everyone in the troupe keeps breaking bones perhaps it is the choreography that needs to be re-set.)

Psychoanalysis is the performance in which the doctor and the patient interpret a symptom that gives the body temporal coherence. Part of the burden of establishing temporal order for the body, for both dancing and psychoanalysis, often falls to narrative since one of the things that narrative generates is temporal order. But even without narrative, dance organizes its movement across a temporal schema often carried by music. And in this sense, dance, like psychoanalysis, helps join the body to time. But just as the proliferation of dance styles throughout history and across cultures implicitly suggests the enormous

*range of temporal possibilities within movement
performances, so too do the interpretations of
the symptom emerge from historically and
culturally specific meanings and values.
Psychoanalytic symptoms and their interpretations are subject to historical, political, and
cultural pressures. We can see that certain
diseases, for example hysteria at the turn of the
century and depression now, achieve a kind of
cultural currency that instigates a change in
the technique of the cure. Thus the technique
of the talking cure surmounts the technique of
hypnosis, and the techniques of pharmacology,
especially Prozac, have surmounted the talking
cure.*

*But again, I get ahead of myself. In the inter-
ests of clarity I here move offstage until the end
of our collaborative analysis of the first case
histories of psychoanalysis. The corps will come
back, as bodies always do.*

III

The first symptoms Anna O. and Elisabeth von R. developed were
sympathetically reproduced somatizations of their fathers' pain. These
symptoms were the result of a kind of stilling kinesthetic empathy: each
woman became partially paralyzed. The somatic symptoms were
motivated by the daughters' desire to show love for their fathers by
lending them their own bodies. If they could transfer the pain in their
fathers' bodies into their own, they believed that they could help
their fathers live. When the somatic symptom (paralysis) failed to keep the
father alive, new more dangerous hysterical symptoms emerged.

Anna O.'s paralysis was a mimetic response to her father's stillness. As
he lay in bed struggling to breathe and as she anticipated his final loss of
breath in the stillness of death, she herself became spectacularly still.[11]
Through paralysis Anna O. attempted to sacrifice her own youthful
active body to the stillness encroaching upon her father's. If the stillness
could have another body on which to alight, if the stage could be larger,
perhaps the stillness would not have to engulf her father's body so
completely that he would expire.

Anna O.'s cough, her breath's stutter step, began the night she heard
the dance music playing. "She began coughing for the first time when
once, as she was sitting at her father's bedside, she heard the sound
of dance music coming from a neighbouring house, felt a sudden wish

to be there, and was overcome with self-reproaches. Thereafter, throughout the whole length of her illness she reacted to any markedly rhythmical music with a *tussis nervosa* [nervous cough]" (Freud and Breuer 1895: 40). So let us set the stage: she hears the music playing while she sits near her father's bed. He is dying. She is watching. She is watching and not dying. Outside, dance music is playing. Her foot starts tapping involuntarily. She stills it. Sharp intake of breath, a slight, hastily silenced cough. All she wants to do, all she wants to do, is dance. The rhythm of the music is infecting her body. Her blood picks up a little speed; she's remembering the two step. And her romance with her father is that she cannot live without him. She is her father's daughter. His girl. The apple of his eye. She is going to nurse him back to life. She will tell him nursery rhymes, fairy tales. ("He joked with her in English, Na, how are you, Miss Bertha?"[12] Na, how are you, Papa? Papa don't die. Papa Pappenheim ...) The music playing inside and outside her body. In the still of the night. ... Time is the bed and Then and Now are breathing in and out and you are one of the ones there waking, waking with a stretch joining Then and Now. Mourning the loss of him and of her body's dance. ... Laid out there, stiff in the sheet of time, he sleeps. And she stifles her cough. Finding her mourning breath.

In concluding his analysis, Breuer returned to Anna O.'s desire to dance and noted, "The patient could not understand how it was that dance music made her cough; such a construction is too meaningless to have been deliberate. (It seemed very likely to me, incidentally, that each of her twinges of conscience brought on one of her regular spasms of the glottis and that the motor impulses which she felt – for she was very fond of dancing – transformed the spasm into a *tussis nervosa*)" (ibid.: 43–4).[13] By coughing instead of dancing, Anna O. changed the beat of desire within her body. Her timing, one could say, is off.

Breuer's respect for the "meaningless" connection between dance music and coughing is remarkable. The very triviality of dance music produced both the desire to dance (to escape the deadly seriousness of her father's illness) and the repression of this desire (dancing is inappropriate because of the gravity of the father's illness). Anna O.'s body registered the damping of her desire through the dis-ease of the cough. In the face of her father's impending death, marked by his audible struggle to breathe (he suffered from a sub-pleural abscess), a daughter with a conscience trained to "twinge" could not permit herself to dance and also could not deny her desire to dance. Her cough signaled her body's effort to renounce her conscious renunciation of dancing. Her resistance to renunciation creates the conflict that gives life to the symptom. "Overcome with self-reproaches," her body was caught in the space between sitting and dancing, between moving and watching, between exhaling and inhaling, between living and dying; gulping air in and pushing it out at the same time, she coughed, again and again.

Registering her somatic and temporal unmooring, the cough stood in for a larger uncertainty about how to move after the law of the father has been shaken, rendered mortal. Her psyche was "stuck in time" and to get her moving, Breuer and Anna returned to the events of the past:

> A year had now passed since she had been separated from her father and had taken to her bed, and from this time on her condition became clearer and was systematized in a very peculiar manner. . . . [N]ow she lived like the rest of us, in the winter of 1881–2, whereas [under daily hypnosis . . .] she lived in the winter of 1880–1. . . . She was carried back to the previous year with such intensity that in the new house she hallucinated her old room, so when she wanted to go to the door she knocked up against the stove which stood in the same relation to the window as did the door in the old room. . . . But this transfer into the past did not take place in a general or indefinite manner; she lived through the previous winter day by day. I should have only been able to *suspect* that this was happening, had it not been that every evening during the hypnosis she talked through whatever it was that had excited her on the same day in 1881, and had it not been that a private diary kept by her mother in 1881 confirmed beyond a doubt the occurrence of the underlying events.[14] This reliving of the past year continued till the illness came to its final close in June, 1882.
>
> (Freud and Breuer 1895: 33; Breuer's emphasis)

Anna O.'s submission to the flow of time thus became for her a betrayal of her father. For she had promised him she could not live without him. What was unbearable to Anna O., as to most survivors, was that she had already survived the trauma that she had dreaded for so long. Anna O. placed herself back in 1880 with Breuer as witness and repeated the birth of her first set of somatic ("failed") symptoms. She wanted Breuer to assure her that she did everything she could possibly do to avert the trauma of her father's death. She described, in meticulous detail, the advent of each symptom. For example, she noted the 108 times she failed to notice that someone entered the room in which she was; off in her "private theatre" she was selectively deaf to someone's entry. The first time that this selective deafness occurred, the visitor was her father. In recounting each of these symptoms, Anna O. "relived" them in the presence of Breuer and thereby transformed her private theatre, the intimate space of her psychic secrets, into a social space. More particularly, she described the advent of her symptoms in the exact order in which they occurred; if she made an error in the chronology she had to begin all over again. By lining her symptoms up in the past, she could use their narrative order as a way of getting past them. (One can only wonder at the tedium these tales must have engendered: there were 303 instances of mishearing/deafness alone.[15]) The search for the first time invariably revealed a failed moment with her father: she failed to see him, or hear him, or understand him. Having introjected him, she could not recognize the moment when he "joined in the conversation." Discovering that her father was both an integral aspect of her internal landscape *and* a person who walked in and out of rooms without consulting her, threw her. She both craved and dreaded the idea that he was independent of her. The pain of this "separateness" foreshadowed the separateness that would occur when he died. In reliving each of these moments with Breuer, who emphatically had not died, Anna O. performed the successful talking cure. Every time Breuer had to interrupt their scheduled visits, the "cure" suffered a setback.

By reliving the previous year in such excruciating detail Anna O. made plain that we refuse such repetition as a way of securing psychic health. This is a psychic adaptation – there is nothing endemic to time itself that makes it impossible for the body to relive it.[16] And there is nothing in the body itself that makes such reliving impossible. The body, in short, does not share consciousness' faith in narrative order. The uneven join between the body and a conscious relation to time is filtered through the expansive and expressive force of the unconscious.

This psychic adaptation to the convention of linear, progressive time is one of the founding principles of the social contract, a contract which in turn establishes the classificatory system by which doctors define mental health. The body is always a disciplined entity; one part of its disciplinary training is temporal–linguistic; another part is temporal–physical. Psychoanalysis pursued developing the temporal–linguistic route to the cure in part by attempting to create the talking cure as a performative speech act whose utterances transformed the body. From a system of disarticulated limbs, contractions, and paresthetic seizures, psychoanalysis sought to reproduce a free-moving, coherent, vital body.

The psychic stage on which Anna O. and Breuer danced was a stage attended by other corpses. Breaking open her "private theatre" for Breuer required opening other tombs. Six years before she was born, Anna O.'s older sister, Flora, had died. When Anna was 8, her sister Henriette died. Thus Anna O. was literally her father's "one and only" surviving daughter: she inhabited a private theatre in part because her sisters had left it. Anna O.'s real name, Bertha, was the name of Breuer's mother and of his eldest daughter. (Bertha's father's name was Seigmund.) Breuer's mother had died when he was 3; at the time of her death she was about the same age as Anna O. when she began her conversations with Breuer.[17] These deaths are the historical frames through which the death of her father was experienced, interpreted, and transcribed.

In their somatic and verbal conversations, Breuer and Anna O. learned something about the relationship between language and the body. Anna O.'s conversations with Breuer were not so much a performance in which her body found words, but rather they were performances in which her body found time, and more particularly, found its past. Passing into language, the somatic symptom passes into the past. To put it in a slightly different way: if we think of psychoanalysis as a mode of psychic choreography, we can see the symptom as the body's psychic movement. Psychoanalysis and choreography are two different modes of performing the body's movement. Each seeks to give the body a system of time.

The reproduction and realignment of the symptom suggest a different way to map the body's relation to time and to death. Her father's death terrified Anna O. because she was at once remembering it and anticipating it. Her eye symptoms – periodic blindness and what she calls "clouds" – like her conscious renunciation to dance signaled by the cough – both confirmed and disavowed her image of death. Taking care of her father was traumatic for Anna in part because it reminded her that she had *already survived death.* This is the genius of her symptom. The analysis with Breuer allowed her to transfer her image of death within a narrative structure that assigned images to referents, people to places, events to time.

To say that trauma must be relived or re-enacted in order to be "surmounted," assumes that trauma is or was a lived event. But trauma is an event of unliving. The unlived event becomes traumatic precisely because it is empty; trauma reveals the intangible center of breath itself. As an event of unliving, trauma is a performance in and above the real:

> On one occasion our whole progress was obstructed for some time because a recollection refused to emerge. It was a question of a particularly terrifying hallucination. While she was nursing her father she had seen him with a death's head. She and the people with her remembered that once, while she still appeared to be in good health, she had paid a visit to one of her relatives. She had opened the door and all at once fallen down unconscious. In order to get over the obstruction to our progress she visited the same place again and, on entering the room, again fell to the ground unconscious. During her subsequent evening hypnosis the obstacle was surmounted. As she came into the room, she had seen her pale face reflected in a mirror hanging opposite the door; but it was not herself she saw but her father with a death's head.
>
> (Freud and Breuer 1895: 37)

The repetition of the event, the second visit to the relative, reproduced the symptom. She again saw the face, and like Saul upon seeing the face of God, she fell.[18] With this fall, she stopped moving physically and her psychic progress became "obstructed." Re-enacting the scene and again losing consciousness, she fell into her body. In the act of fainting she became "pure body." She was the body who fell. To re-join her body to consciousness nothing less than the image of death had to be *re-moved*. This is the transfer that the analysis enacted.

Transfer. Transit. Transference. At the heart of psychoanalysis is an ideology of movement, of the curative potential of moving. Under hypnosis after the re-enactment, Anna O. was able to "surmount" the psychic impasse which made it impossible for her to move forward. The trauma that arrested her body's movement also "obstructed" her psychic progress. While narrating her experience for Breuer, a *transfer/ence* took place. "But this transfer into the past did not take place in a general or indefinite manner ..." (ibid.: 33). The act of narrating allows her to interpret the trauma of the unlived event for the first time – and the interpretation created the cure.

On the rehearsal of the original trauma, "she had seen her pale face reflected in a mirror hanging opposite the door; but it was not herself that she saw but her father with a death's head." The analytic cure is enacted in the transfer, the psychic movement necessary for integrating the image of death into her history. Ascribing the image of death to her father, Anna O. positioned herself as the survivor, as the one who, despite falling faint, would witness the death of her father and her own death as the apple of his eye, but would again move, again live. From a killing glance in the mirror that made her fall, to the safe rehearsal of the hallucination with Breuer, she was able to make her trauma history by giving it to her father who was already "safely" dead. The phrase "but it was not herself she saw" interprets the trauma. The analysis generated the curative interpretation by moving the image of the death's head to her father's corpse and taking it away from her own face.

It is important to notice that the interpretation also betrays another level of the unconscious relations among Anna O.'s symptoms. The interpretation suggests that the image of her father's skull was super-imposed on her image of her own face. Her body reproduced an image of his (hollow) body that the mirror reflected. Such a substitution might be said to involve a kind of psychic blurring, a confusion, about the boundaries between her body and his. This blurring occurred across verbal languages as well: during the analysis she translated languages unconsciously and often made sentences out of several different languages. Insofar as language reproduces the body (at least in the talking cure), Anna O.'s case suggests that bleeding between languages might also portend bleeding across bodies. To this idea we will return.[19]

Anna O.'s hallucination of the death's head stands behind the second, remarkably similar hallucination that Breuer believed was the "root of her illness." While nursing her father, "[s]he fell into a waking dream and saw a black snake coming towards the sick man. . . . She tried to keep the snake off, but it was as though she was paralyzed. Her right arm, over the back of the chair, had gone to sleep and had become anesthetic and paretic; and when she looked at it the fingers turned into little snakes with death's heads (the nails)"(ibid.: 38). Having already experienced the image of the death's head in the mirror, Anna O. may well have believed that the image was *in* her body, oozing out of her eyes and her finger nails. She was determined not to let the death's heads alight on her father's body. The analytic rehearsal allowed her to let the image of death escape her body. The willful re-summoning of the traumatic image of the death's head made possible a different interpretation of its meaning.

The final hallucination which was itself a repetition of the previous one was also re-enacted and, as in Aristotelian poetics, catharsis was achieved. "On the last day – by the help of re-arranging the room so as to resemble her father's sickroom – she reproduced the terrifying hallucination which constituted the root of her illness" (ibid.: 40). This transference signaled the passage in which the memory of death's presence became a memory of *his* death: this time, the death's heads are located at the edge of her body, on her fingernails, in her body rather than in the mirror reflecting that body. Lodged inside her body, this image is "the root" that Breuer wants to pull. But in order to do so, he must, as it were, stand-in for the father. Taking Breuer's hands into her own – "But she would never begin to talk until she had satisfied herself of my identity by carefully feeling my hands" (ibid.: 30) – she transferred her image of death to Breuer who, in turn, helped her interpret the image of the death's head as her father's. In this sense, her father's death was almost reassuring. The certainty of his death gave her the psychic freedom to return to the trauma of the death's heads oozing out of her body. "The one thing that nevertheless seemed to remain conscious most of the time was the fact that her father died" (ibid.: 33). The firm fact of his death allowed her to put her symptom in the past. Anna O.'s own body was thus liberated from the psychic death spaces to which she had assigned it during her "absences." Her analysis enacts a movement, a passage, a physical and psychic *transference* from her body to the body of her father. Breuer bridges that transference.

No longer her secret repressed vision, the trauma dissolved as Anna O. gave her image of death away. Once the trauma had been placed in the past her body no longer reproduced the vision and her symptomatic blindness was, in Breuer's phrase, "removed."[20] Finding an event in the past, the death of her father, from which to divide the present from the past, also allowed Anna O. to find a map for her body's movement.[21] Surmounting her fainting fall, she, like psychoanalysis itself, took "a great step forward." The contracture in her right leg disappeared and she moved again, psychically, back into 1882, and physically, out of the sickroom (her father's and her own).

IV

Hysteria, at least in the original and defining case of Anna O., involves the use of the patient's body as a stage for the body of the other. (This is why hysteria has so often been associated with women – and historically with their wombs.) In Anna O.'s case, at her entry into hysteria, she attempted to lend her body to her father. But he had somehow already inhabited her; and her introjection (Freud's later term) of him made it impossible for her to separate her body far enough from his to lend it to him as he fought death. Thus she may have felt herself to be responsible for his death.[22] Traumatized by her images of the death's head reflected in the mirror, and snakes oozing from her finger nails, Anna O. was unsure if she herself had somehow died when her father did.

Insisting that her memories of events of unliving were communicable (across the supple syntax of English, German, French, Italian, and Yiddish) and therefore survivable, Breuer helped Anna O. discover a newly animated body. As this body translated its history into stories for Breuer, Breuer translated their mutually embodied history into stories for Freud.

In such translations, different bodies are reproduced. We shall discuss only one. A crucial aspect of the cure involved the re-enactment of the trauma. The cumulative weight of these performances may have encouraged Anna O. to mark her body itself as auto-reproductive. Her body had been "reconstructed" by her well-timed conversations with Breuer. The body they made was a profoundly new body, one outside the usual order of human reproduction.

This is the frame through which the tricky matter of Anna O.'s hysterical pregnancy must be seen. In an account full of errors,[23] Jones, whom Jean Laplanche calls "the historian of Freud's thought" (Laplanche 1976: 67), claims:

> It would seem that Breuer had developed what we should nowadays call a strong counter-transference to his interesting patient. At all events he was so engrossed that his wife became bored at listening to no other topic, and before long, jealous. She did not display this openly, but became unhappy and morose. It was long before Breuer, with his thoughts elsewhere, divined the meaning of her state of

mind. It provoked a violent reaction in him perhaps compounded of love and guilt, and he decided to bring the treatment to an end. He announced this to Anna O., who was by now much better, and bade her good-bye. But that evening he was fetched back, to find her in a greatly excited state, apparently as ill as ever. The patient ... was now in the throes of an hysterical childbirth (pseudocyesis) the logical termination of a phantom pregnancy that had been invisibly developing in response to Breuer's ministrations. Though profoundly shocked, he managed to calm her down by hypnotizing her, and then fled the house in a cold sweat. The next day he and his wife left for Venice to spend a second honeymoon, which resulted in the conception of a daughter.

(Jones 1954: 246–7)

Jones' contention that Breuer broke off the analysis because of his wife's jealousy is not born out by the published case history, Breuer's notes about the treatment, or the correspondence he maintained with Bertha's mother.[24] Anna O. herself decided upon the day that would end her analysis (7 June 1882) and had accelerated her "chimney sweeping" in order to complete her cure (ibid.: 40). Nor is Jones' implicit suggestion that Breuer displaced his "phantom" paternity by "really" impregnating his wife in Venice credible. Mathilde had delivered their youngest daughter, Dora (!), on 11 March 1882, three months before Anna O.'s treatment ended.[25]

Nonetheless Jones' story, however phantasmal, is worth pausing over. A certain satisfaction emerges in this resolution of the history, a satisfaction that is hard for some readers to ignore. For if Anna O.'s performance of a phantom pregnancy has a certain allure, it comes from thinking of Anna O.'s body as something that cannot be contained by the case history. Independently of Breuer, she went on to mark the effect of their collaborative re-enactments by performing her new self as an auto-reproductive body. Moreover, the pregnancy signifies the supplement that cannot be contained or interpreted by the talking cure, no matter how exhaustive, no matter how loving. For many feminists, this excess is femininity itself – that part of Anna O.'s body that remains outside the discursive frame of the always already "masculine" discursive case history.[26] This excess marks the place of the trauma at the heart of Freud's theory of sexual difference. As Freud developed psychoanalysis, he constructed a theory of anxiety about sexual difference in which penis envy and the castration complex are said to be psychic responses to the fear of somatic absence. But as Anna O. experienced the end of her analysis, an analysis about her response to her father's death, she created a bodily act that was *both* curative and traumatic.

It is necessary to emphasize that the entire report of Anna O.'s phantom pregnancy comes from Freud and his historian – and not from Breuer or Anna O.[27] In his own version of *The History of Psychoanalysis*, Freud admits that Breuer "never said this [that Anna had fallen in love with Breuer] to me in so many words, but he told me enough at different times to justify this reconstruction of what happened."[28] Freud, of course, had his own reasons for wanting to believe in Anna O.'s love for Breuer: it was the most convincing proof of his theory of the "universal nature" of the transference.[29] Since so much of Freud's history has passed for "the truth" of the history of psychoanalysis, and because the story of Anna O.'s pregnancy is continually repeated in critical commentary about this history, and finally because psychoanalysis itself insists that the phantasmatic event and the real event can be equally traumatic, we offer this reading of Anna O.'s phantom pregnancy.

Significantly, Anna O.'s pregnancy returned her to *her* body, in much the way that her fainting spell returned her to her body when she saw the image of the death's head in the mirror. The pregnancy marks her body as sexed, that is to say, as a body other than her male father's or her male doctor's. Anna O.'s body sought a way to carry the hollow, the phantasmatical presence of the dead breath of the other, her father, in her own living body. Her pregnancy was an attempt to make room in her body for the loss she felt at the double death of both her father and herself as his daughter when he died. What is remarkable about the story of her phantom pregnancy is that it registers the attempt to render the fullness of loss somatic.

The somatic reproduction of the trauma of absence is, and can only be, a phantom. The trauma is traumatic because it unveils the material and affective force of the phantom. Anna O.'s reproduction of her father's hollow skull in the analysis is matched by the hollow swelling of her hysterical womb after the analysis. Anna O.'s pregnancy is the reproduction of an event of unliving, a spectacular performance, that makes her body into a living crypt. Accepting her father's death allowed Anna O. her own "re-birth." She sought to mark the entwining of these two events by carrying the breath of his death in her (swelling) body. His death changed her body and she wanted her body to display that change by filling it with the life of his death.

The reasons Anna O. might settle on pregnancy as a way to mark and to make her body into this expansive utterance are overdetermined. Anna O. must have heard in her name "Bertha," "a birth" in English, the language of her initial conversations with Breuer. At the end of her conversations with him, perhaps she wanted to signify the (re)genera-tion of that language in and on her body.

Ten years after her treatment with Breuer, Bertha Pappenheim emerged as a "new woman." She was one of the founders of the Jewish

Feminist Movement in Germany. She became a writer and politician. She devoted herself to caring for unmarried women with children (mothering those she had not conceived – perhaps then another return of the repressed). She lent her body and her life to the making of history, particularly to the making of Jewish feminist history.[30]

Anna O.'s case history, with or without her phantom pregnancy, represents the birth of psychoanalysis. Like all origins, it is also a termination point. It marks the end of historical narratives which assume that pasts are past. "For after the uncomfortable birth of psychoanalysis, time was no longer what it had been, 'before' and 'after' entering into new and hitherto unexamined relations of complicity and interference. . . . Psychoanalysis is . . . time and counter-time at once" (Bowlby 1991: 13). These intricate relations of complicity and interference are the performances which structure the history-of-the-present. These interfering complicities mark the beat of our bodies' dance through the swelling and expiring choreography of time. It is therefore appropriate that the last lines of the case of Elisabeth von R., which concludes *Studies on Hysteria,* should end on the dance floor:

> In the spring of 1894 I heard that she [Elisabeth von R.] was going to a private ball for which I was able to get an invitation, and I did not allow the opportunity to escape me of seeing my former patient whirl past in a lively dance. Since then, by her own inclination, she has married someone unknown to me.[31]
>
> (Freud and Breuer 1895: 114)

Having seen Elisabeth von R.'s legs joining in the conversation of a different lively dance, Freud joins her dancing to marrying. Always partnered by "unknown" bodies (including our own) we attempt to turn time[32] into a bed still enough to lie on. In the still of the night we believe we will be held – until then we hold our own bodies stiff. The legacy of psychoanalysis allows us to see that bodies can be endlessly remade, re-choreographed, outside the traditional architectonics of human reproduction. Psychic health is in part contingent upon the body finding its rhythm in words and time. Choreography and psychoanalysis would do well to join in a conversation about the body's time.

THE RETURN OF THE CORPS

The "logical termination" of the first feminine body reconstructed by the talking cure experiences a phantom pregnancy – or at least Jones introduces the phantom of a phantom pregnancy at the origin of the talking cure. At the "origin" of psychoanalysis we find an hysterical woman, and at the end of her cure she experiences (or is said to experience) an hysterical pregnancy, a somatic event that frames a false or unfulfilled origin, a physical and psychic event with no source in the biological real. Therefore, as Jane Malmo argues, the question becomes "are all origins hysterical?"[33] Perhaps the answer is yes, to the degree to which origins are associated with births and therefore with women. Femininity is that part of bodies that logic can treat only as a question: the feminine body, the psychoanalytic body, can take only an inter-rogatory form. Is she or isn't she? Is she or isn't she making it up? Hysterical pregnancy stages the drama of the question of "the body" – the traumatized body, the seductive body, the pregnant body – on the body of women.

As a phantom, hysterical pregnancy is the somatic form that raises the question of the woman's desire in relation to masculine logic and culture. What does she want? with him? with herself? for herself? Part of what is captivating about the hysterical pregnancy is that the baby never appears; the pregnancy is overwhelmingly powerful because it makes visible the possibility of a body clinging to a permanent present. (One is pregnant as long as one is hysterical. Nine months has nothing to do with it.)

It is here that the phantom pregnancy rejoins the question of dance. Anna O.'s phantom pregnancy points to the limit of the talking cure. Insisting that her performative symptom always exceeds narration and the will to mastery enacted by "masculine" discourse, Anna O.'s phan-tom pregnancy *is* her body's long deferred, long desired, and long renounced dance. At the end of the cure, she partners herself and touches, perhaps for the first time, her feminine body. And it swells. Her hollow hollers. (And he "fled the house in a cold sweat" (Jones 1954: 247).)

One of the biggest problems with reading dance as psychic symptom is that it suggests that dance refers to something other than itself, some-thing behind or beyond the movement itself. Within psychoanalysis, somatic utterances usually refer to something that needs to be unearthed. Dance demonstrates that somatic utterances do not necessarily refer to anything other than movement itself. Ballet, for example, makes mani-fest technique, discipline, and study, but what it "expresses" is bodily movement. (Admittedly this movement is patterned; strictly speaking, spasms might be closer to "pure" movement than dance is.)

Additionally, the emphasis that psychoanalysis gives to the past can seem irrelevant to an art form that can exist only in the present tense. Arlene Croce, writing about the problem of reconstructing Balanchine's ballets, especially his *Agon*, notes: "Like all ballets, it has no past; it happens in the moment" (Croce 1993: 84). But if the ballet is to have a future, like Anna O., it must face the question of history and the attendant challenge of its reproduction/reconstruction. As Balanchine's ballets enter pedagogical institutions, conscious interpretation of tech-nique is turned into science. The success of this interpretation is dependent upon the femininity of *the* Balanchine ballerina. The success or failure of Balanchine's ballet will be measured by her performance of his movement phrases. She will be required to have a technique that leaves "nothing to be desired" and she will be measured according to her skill at reproducing his vision of her moving. And the performance of this transfer/ence is the true *agon* of both the history of ballet and the history of hysteria.

The irreducible kernel of femininity, as a symptom forever in need of interpretation, also returns us to the challenge of reproduction and reconstruction. For if the psychoanalytic symptom is feminine, once it is "re-moved," how is femininity re-enacted? The conjunction of Anna O. and Balanchine's ballerina suggest that femininity is re-enacted through the reproductive body – through a staging of the body as reproductive in the case of Anna O., and through a staging of the body as a "reconstruction" in Balanchine's ballet. That such manifestations can only be reconstructions and therefore to some degree phatasmatical underlines the power of transit, of the force of transferences and transformations, to which both bodies and time continually cling. Moreover, these reconstructions are peculiarly feminine suggesting that the mimicry and masquerade we have so long associated with femininity are themselves attempts to reproduce what is not there. Anna O.'s phantom pregnancy carries the intangible center of her father's last breath; her pregnancy gives an image to femininity's desire to find a way to carry that which is lost.

Patriarchal culture's violent renunciation of femininity has helped to create a feminine body capable of renouncing that renunciation. The feminine body is, profoundly, an auto-reproductive body, one that continues to reproduce symptoms and movement phrases that dance across the slippery stage of the paternal order.

SOLO STEPS AGAIN

> *Whatever else my broken hip was attempting to express, it had something to do with the bafflement I felt not knowing where to put my feet after the music of my own marriage had faded. Lost in a time that seemed to have no order (once the past becomes present it is hard to know where to step), I lost the rhythm of my own limbs' utterance. Computing was an attempt to put that loss in my hands and head, to transfer the grief in my feet that formed the root of my own illness. While I cannot say I am now cured, I can say that observing this psychoanalytic dance*

*has taught me a different way to reconstruct the
loss that numbs me even while I number myself
one of the very fortunate witnesses of a past I
might be able to bear in the near future.*

*The dance that language cannot capture, the
beckoning music that animates our flesh, keeps
us moving beyond the limits of our limbs. While
the corps keeps time, the dance moves beyond
the physical bodies on which it is staged. My
attempt to choreograph Balanchine's ballets for
the computer screen was based on the belief that
his work exists independently of his dancers. I
am not sure I quite believe this now. For the
dance in its very discipline and formal measure
reminds us of a beckoning formlessness to which
we are at once attracted and repelled. Dance and
psychoanalysis capture two different ways of
framing bodies that gesture toward and away
from the formlessness of their own flesh.*

NOTES

1 Insofar as psychoanalysis can be said to be a theory of desire, Breuer's description of its technique as that which "left nothing to be desired" is overdetermined.
2 For more on the instances and justifications for massaging patients see Freud and Breuer (1895: 51–6). Also see Swales (1986) for full discussion of Freud and Breuer's relationship.
3 More precisely, her right thigh (Freud and Breuer 1895: 168).
4 This passage, and the sexual connotations of its language, "arouse," "climax" and so on, is thoughtfully analyzed by Joline Blais (Blais 1995).
5 These "critical" words rejoin their conversation – but we can only press on the textual body that the doctors have created, and, of course, on our own.
6 This formulation of the body as "joining in" is a common one in Freud's case histories. In the wolf-man's history, for example, Freud notes: "his bowel began, like a hysterically affected organ, to 'join in the conversation'" (Freud 1918: 76).
7 This reading of hysteria is ubiquitous: see Showalter (1993), Marcus (1984) and White (1989), for representative examples. Showalter's essay also provides an excellent survey of the literature.
8 Sometimes it may impose an "excess" of order. Breuer's narrative case history ends with Anna O.'s cure, but as Albrecht Hirschmuller has demonstrated, Breuer knew that Anna was not "well" when the analysis concluded. (She was, however, "well" when Breuer wrote his case study.) See Hirschmuller (1989). Breuer's "act" in writing the case study is a willful re-imagination of the past of their sessions no less than Anna O.'s conversations with Breuer were a re-imagination of her own past. And our narrative re-construction here

repeats the act of re-imagining the past that they re-imagined together. In joining their conversation, we experience, again, the physical and psychic imperatives to discipline the textual body, and learn again, how much an "act" of imposition that ordering was – for Breuer, for Anna O., for us.

9 See Chapter 8 for a discussion of one way to edit that order.

10 For Lacan the symptom is never "gone." But the analysis can achieve the cure by realigning the analysand's relation to the symptom, to the inevitability of castration. For Freud, the symptom does "disappear," but because of "somatic compliance" the same body part might become symptomatic again as the patient faces other traumas.

11 In the "Preliminary Communication" of *Studies*, Freud and Breuer report Anna O.'s paralysis: "A girl, watching beside a sick-bed in a torment of anxiety, fell into a twilight state and had a terrifying hallucination, while her right arm, which was hanging over the back of her chair, went to sleep; from this there developed a paresis of the same arm accompanied by contracture and anesthesia. She tried to pray but could find no words; at length she succeeded in repeating a children's prayer in English" (1895: 4–5). In Breuer's case history, the "prayer" is a nursery rhyme. The case history, like psychoanalysis more generally, partakes of the nursery rhyme, the fairy tale, and the prayer. In Anna O.'s case the allegorical implications are especially hard to ignore: a young unmarried woman cares for her father; she exhausts herself and falls ill; he dies; when he does, she becomes even sicker. The mother calls in the good doctor who loves her like a father and cures her. And they all live happily ever after. In embryo then here are the same seeds that develop into narratives of Revolution (the ailing father and the death of the State); of Romance (the reintegration of the household); of scientific progress (from chaos to clarity); and of Redemption (from suffering to salvation via faith in the cure).

12 From Breuer's original notes (the notes he used to compose his case history) in Hirschmuller (1989: 279). Anna O.'s talking cure is doubly marked as translation from one sign system (the body) to another (speech) by virtue of the fact that she unconsciously translates everything into English (see Freud and Breuer 1895: 26). The echo of her father's call in English ("Na, how are you, Miss Bertha?") is most likely reproduced as Breuer hypnotizes her and asks her, in English, how she is. She eventually "joins in the conversation" by (re)producing nursery stories. This interpretation lends credence to Freud's (early) view of the transference – here, from the father to the doctor.

13 It seemed very likely to me, incidentally, that each of these repetitious citations was an attempt to partner – for my lecturer and I are both also very fond of dancing – to partner Anna O.'s stutter step with prose.

14 For Anna O.'s mother, one of her daughter's most alarming symptoms was the loss of her ability to speak her "mother tongue" (German); it is therefore fitting that it is her mother's words, her private diary, that maps Breuer's reading of the temporal "truth" of Anna O.'s symptoms.

15 But perhaps the process of uncovering held its own allure. Breuer notes that during these recitations, Anna O.'s deafness would increase and he had to write down his questions in order to be "heard" (Freud and Breuer (1895: 37)).

16 The repetition of course marks the time as "different" – that is to say, as a "second" time. In physics, classical thermodynamics proved that the same events can occur forward or backward in time. Much of Freud's theory of the drives is predicated on classical thermodynamics. For a discussion of contemporary physics' notion of a "second time" see Phelan (1993: 126–9).

17 For an exhaustive tracing of these and other correspondences, see Hirschmuller (1989: 129–30).
18 For a fine reading of "fall," "fallen" and "falling" in Freud's case histories of women, see Fuss (1993).
19 For now though let me just note that in the bleeding from Breuer's German to the English of the *Standard Edition* this question of translation is re-enacted. I am satisfied that what I say here about the English text applies as well to the German.
20 When blindness, the absence of sight, vanishes, the eye/I decides it is safe to return. Note that the symptom which negates must itself be negated before it can disappear. Thus the double narrative transcribed by Breuer also corresponds to the double narrative (the two negations) which enable the symptom's "removal."
21 Michel de Certeau argues that the "making of history" always requires the production of a division between the past and the present. Insofar as psychoanalysis is the search for the history of the symptom, the "historical cure" reproduces the interpretation of this division. See de Certeau (1988: 1–15, *passim*).
22 Lacan's famous dictum, "woman is the symptom of man," is reversed by Anna O. Her father is her symptom. One wonders what transpired between the two of them. I know the "truth" is not recoverable, but when I read this in Breuer's notes I wonder: "One evening she told me a true story of long ago, how at night times she would creep in to eavesdrop on her father (at that time, night nurses could no longer put up with her), how she slept in her stockings for this reason, then on one occasion she was caught by her brother, and so on. As soon as she was finished she began to cry out softly, demanding why she was in bed with her stockings on" (from Breuer's case notes, in Hirschmuller (1989: 288)). And what was she eavesdropping on? What conversation was she seeking to join with her "creep"ing, dancing feet covered in stockings? And what is in that "and so on" after her brother "catches" her? In the published case history, Breuer notes that one cause of Anna O.'s symptomatic deafness had its origin in the trauma of being "shaken angrily by her young brother when he caught her one night listening at the sickroom door" (Freud and Breuer 1895: 36).
23 For a discussion of the many errors in Jones' account, see Bowlby (1991: 10–19) and Hirschmuller (1989: 126–32).
24 The correspondence and case notes are reproduced in Hirschmuller (1989).
25 It is possible that there was a miscarriage or a still birth but I have not found evidence to support this. It is unlikely, however, that Jones would specify the gender if he were referring to a miscarriage or still birth.
26 The best analysis of femininity and Freudian psychoanalysis I know is Brennan's (1992).
27 I am not trying to suggest that the transference and counter-transference played no part in Anna O.'s case history. I am trying to question, however, Freud's version of it. Breuer, writing in 1907, did say that Anna O.'s case history taught him a lot: "I learned a very great deal: much that was of scientific value, but something of practical importance as well – namely that it was impossible for a 'general practitioner' to treat a case of that kind without bringing his activities and mode of life completely to an end. I vowed at that time I would *not* go through such an ordeal again" (Cranefield 1958: 319–22). It certainly seems clear that Breuer's counter-transference was not worked through with Anna O., anymore than her transference with him was successfully analyzed.

28 *History of Psychoanalysis*, quoted in Bowlby (1991: 11).
29 For a fuller treatment of this motivation see Bowlby (1991).
30 See Marion A. Kaplan (1979); Dora Edinger (1968); Lucy Freeman (1972); and Hirschmuller (1989) for full accounts of Bertha Pappenheim's life and work.
31 Part of the reason that Anna O.'s hysterical pregnancy is so difficult to decipher is because all of the case histories end so "novelistically."
32 Time and its attendant copyists – narrative and history.
33 Jane Malmo, personal communication, December 1995.

4

Uncovered rectums: disinterring the Rose Theatre[1]

In 1989 one of the most dramatic plots in Renaissance theatre unfolded in London. In a six month dig in Southwark, archaeologists unearthed the startlingly well preserved remains of the Rose Theatre, the first home of Christopher Marlowe's dramatic plays. That the Rose, whose span as a "living" building had lasted but eighteen years (1587–1605), could be unearthed some 400 years later was extraordinary. The disposition of the remains of the Rose incited a controversy whose consequences are still being felt in Southwark, "the third poorest local authority in England."[2] In addition to the Rose's structural remains, coins, jewelry, shoes, and hazelnut shells ("Elizabethan popcorn") were found.[3] Over the course of the dig, it became clear that this was a very valuable site for historians, archaeologists, architectural historians, geologists, and other scholars. Notoriously difficult references in Renaissance plays to the theatre space were tantalizingly close to being deciphered. (Or at least new conjectures could be based on "real" and "better" evidence.) As Andrew Gurr and John Orrell put it early on:

> In the last three months theatre historians have been given more fresh and utterly reliable information about the design of the Shakespearean stage than they have managed to scrape together from written sources in the past three centuries. To lose it would be a new kind of Shakespearean tragedy.
>
> (Orrell and Gurr 1989: 429)

The idea that archaeology provides "utterly reliable information" is a curious one. For as Christopher Tilley points out, "All archaeology is an interpretive activity. This hermeneutic dimension to archaeological research is absolutely fundamental. . . . We can regard archaeology itself as the largely unconscious but nevertheless rule-governed production of statements about the past" (Tilley 1989: 277). These "largely unconscious" ideas controlled the reception of the Rose remains as much as they informed the archaeological framework of the excavation itself. Before we examine the cultural unconscious at play in the hole in

Southwark's streets, it is worth pausing over Gurr and Orrell's characterization of what the Rose's excavation has "given" theatre historians. "Utterly reliable information" is rare and especially so when it is derived from rotting wood and old artifacts. The baldness of the claim, the lack of hedging or apology, can perhaps be attributed to the authors' awareness that the fate of the Rose excavation would be determined by politics and economics. To hedge on the scholarly value of the site would perhaps make continued excavations more difficult to justify. But more than the *realpolitick* at work in Gurr and Orrell's characterization is a belief, a statement of faith, that by recovering the architectural design of the physical theatre, one can recover the truth of Renaissance theatre. For Gurr and Orrell, the physical object has an enormous truth-value. "To lose it would be a new kind of Shakespearean tragedy."

Shakespeare's own tragedies were themselves far less sanguine about the truth-value of physical objects. In *Othello*, for example, Desdemona's handkerchief is used by Iago to convince Othello of her infidelity. Enclosed within Iago's interpretative framework, the handkerchief, "the ocular proof," is profoundly deceiving. Orrell and Gurr are indeed correct to suggest that the prospect of losing the disinterred Rose signals a new kind of Shakespearean tragedy, although not for the reasons they imply.

The 1989 discovery of the Rose was surrounded by the prospect of loss. In an effort to preserve the site, the Shakespeare connection was heightened and the Marlowe connection played down, in part because Shakespeare has a cultural capital that Marlowe lacks. But only two of Shakespeare's plays, *Titus Andronicus* and *I Henry VI*, were performed at the Rose, and some evidence indicates that they had originally opened at The Theatre.[4] Nonetheless, the Rose in 1989 became, if not quite "Shakespeare's stage," certainly a "Shakespearean stage." The reasons for this emphasis cannot be completely explained by noting the economic and intellectual dominance of Shakespeare over Marlowe – although these two factors played a decisive role in the debate about saving the Rose. For modern archaeology, like modern theatre, is a hazard of politics, of money, and of ideology.[5] It participates in and is a product of cultural attitudes toward history. These attitudes, like the unconscious, are informed by selective memory, anxiety, and desire.

Surprisingly thus far almost all of the scholarly work on the Rose excavation has concentrated on the "products" of the archaeological findings, and/or has analyzed the political conflicts of interests that were exposed by the public protests that arose when the Rose was feared to be lost.[6] What I am interested in here is something closer to a psychoanalysis of excavation: I am interested in what it means to disinter a theatre, what anxieties it creates and what fantasies it fosters. Our attitudes toward the return of buried bodies, including architectural ones, like our attitudes toward the return of the repressed, have much to tell us about our ideas and fantasies about living bodies.

The Rose is assuredly a special case – not any theatre remains would incite the intense feelings created by the return of the Rose. The polygonal structure was built in 1587, only the third solid theatre built in London. Philip Henslowe owned it and in 1592 he recruited Edward Alleyn and Strange's Men to act there. Shortly thereafter, the Rose mounted Christopher Marlowe's great plays – *Tamburlaine* I and II, *Doctor Faustus*, and *The Jew of Malta*, with Alleyn in the lead roles.[7] In 1594, the Lord Chamberlain set a new Privy Council policy permitting only two companies to play in London in designated playhouses. Alleyn became the lead actor in the newly formed acting company, the Admiral's Men, and the Rose became their permanent theatre. (The other licensed theatre was The Theatre, owned by James Burbage. When it was dismantled in 1598, the Globe was erected from The Theatre's old scaffolding. The Globe was of course the home of Shakespeare's company, the King's Men. Shortly after the 1989 excavation of the Rose, excavation began on the Globe, but the poor condition of the remains made that excavation less compelling.)[8]

To put the complicated story of the Rose excavation very briefly:

In the 1950 *Survey of London* an 1875 Ordinance Survey Map was reprinted which clearly displayed the location of the Rose on Maiden Lane in Southwark (now called Park Street, it abuts Southwark Bridge Road). In 1971, Richard Hughes, an archaeologist hired by developers interested in building on the site, advised them not to. He wrote, "Since the water table is relatively near the ground surface and since the area before the initial occupation was marshy, structural timbers are likely to be preserved, as are leather, wood, and fabric artefacts. ... [T]his should be considered one of those areas where public action could make excavation and preservation a national issue" (in Eccles 1990: 160).[9] In November 1987 the site was purchased by the Heron Group, which applied to Southwark Council for planning permission to construct a nine story office building. After consulting with the Museum of London, Southwark Council granted permission contingent upon the developers' funding excavation of the site before building. After the agreement was brokered, the Heron Group sold the site to Imry Merchant, another developing firm. Imry Merchant agreed to fund ten weeks of archaeological research before building would begin. As the value of the excavations became clear, the ten weeks turned into six months (although during that time Imry Merchant did begin to build in the opposite corner of the lot), all of which was funded by the developers. The delay cost them over £1 million (Wainwright 1989: 430).

Having concluded six months of excavation, the developers were legally scheduled to proceed with building on Monday morning 15 May

1989. All archaeological research and the chance to preserve the Rose would end as soon as the developers' tractors moved in. During the weekend of 13–14 May, a series of protests led by the actors Dame Peggy Ashcroft and Ian McKellen alerted Nicholas Ridley, then the Secretary of State for the Environment, that he would have a serious problem on his hands if the developers were allowed to build. On that morning, Ridley and Virginia Bottomley, the Under Secretary of State for the Environment, met with representatives of Imry Merchant, English Heritage, and Simon Hughes, the MP for Southwark, in an effort to resolve the crisis. And a crisis it had become: Peggy Ashcroft had threatened to throw herself in front of a tractor and the protesters had suggested she be handcuffed to the fence surrounding the construction site in the manner of a hostage (Eccles 1990: 178). The protesters had also quickly organized themselves into an official group called The Rose Theatre Trust.

The Trust organized a petition to have the site scheduled as a national treasure so that its preservation would be funded by the government. Ridley, often described as "the architect" of Margaret Thatcher's economic policy whose cornerstone was "privatization," eventually rejected the petition.[10] Had the site been scheduled the government would have been obligated to compensate Imry Merchant because, by law, once permission to build has been granted it cannot be revoked without compensation. Compensation, which always exceeds simple reimbursement, was estimated to be about £60 million.[11]

At the meeting on the morning of 15 May, Ridley was able to persuade Imry Merchant to delay building for a month by committing the government to pay the developers £1 million to compensate them for the new delay. During the thirty days, Ridley hoped that a new architectural design that would preserve the remains, give the public access to them, and give the developers their office building, would materialize.

Later that afternoon, Ridley announced the thirty day reprieve to the House of Commons. He took pains to state that the government would not underwrite the cost of preserving and displaying the remains of the Rose, as many people not of his party had urged. He told the House, "The Government's financial commitment finishes with this statement."[12] To which, Mr John Fraser, the Labour MP for Norwood replied, "I hope the Right Honorable Gentleman [Ridley] is not like Oscar Wilde, who believed where architecture starts, art ends." And Ridley retorted, "I claim dissimilarity with Oscar Wilde in more than one respect." The transcript of the meeting published in *The Times* the next day notes that "(laughter)" punctuates the close of Ridley's statement. It's difficult to know exactly who is laughing or why but it is not irrelevant to point out that Ridley was a vocal supporter of the infamous censorship law in the United Kingdom, Clause 28 of the Local Authorities bill, that banned the "promotion of homosexuality." The bill was passed in March 1988. We will return to the consequences of this bill later.

In an effort to return Ridley to the question of government funding for the Rose, Eric Heffer (Liverpool, Labour) then took up the standard banner that English culture's claim to greatness rests with Renaissance theatre. Heffer urged Ridley that "the Government must now consider what financial help it could give to preserve the theatre, which was vital to the cultural development of the nation." Ridley deflected the comment by assuring Heffer that he would be give him an opportunity to donate to any public fund drives undertaken to preserve the Rose. Whereupon Mr Anthony Beaumont-Dark (Birmingham, Conservative), growing impatient with the whole drift of the debate, yelled, "This is *not* a building!" He went on to say that the Rose was not even a ruin; it was merely "footings." If the government tried to preserve "the footings every time some experts said that they were the remains of a theatre or a brothel, London would still be composed of the ruins of Rome."[13] Drawing on one of the most historically sustained links between the similar "ruins" produced by theatres and brothels, Beaumont-Dark thereby suggests that there is no real difference between a theatre and a brothel. Philip Henslowe, the original owner of the Rose Theatre, might agree. For in addition to owning the theatre, he owned several properties that housed brothels.[14] Beaumont-Dark concluded that if the government had £10 to £20 million to spend, it should be spent on "living theatre" and not on something that looks like "a disused mine." In response to this outburst, Ridley returned to Wilde's distinction between art and architecture and contended that the excavation of the Rose was neither. He preferred the term "archaeology," to which Beaumont-Dark retorted, "It's rubbish!"

Beaumont-Dark's point, for all its bluster, is actually very important. The remains of the Rose do not reveal "a building." They are literally the building's remains, the foundation's footings, the structure upon which the building stood. To preserve such footings, Beaumont-Dark suggests, is to degrade architecture and, by implication, culture itself. It is to elevate old brothels or disused mines to the status of art objects. On an unconscious level also, associations among empty cavities, hollow caves, and open holes are consolidated as so much "rubbish" in need of psychic repression. Given the Tory government's attitude toward coal mining, disused mines were particularly potent symbols in England throughout the mid- and late 1980s.[15]

Beaumont-Dark's argument rests on a distinction between the living and the dead: within his logic, "living theatre" lies at the opposite end of the death space of brothels and "disused mines." Government funding, in this argument, must be devoted to the reproduction of a living theatre and a living architecture: it must not support the mere remains of myth and memory.[16] (Thatcher's government had consistently cut funding for the "living" arts. Perhaps Beaumont-Dark is just covering the government's bases: no money for theatre, living or dead.)

For Beaumont-Dark, it was unclear if the Rose could be a productive player in the construction and reconstruction of a national myth and memory. The heritage industry, as Christine Eccles points out, is huge. In Stratford-upon-Avon alone, £50 million a year is spent by 2.5 million tourists (Eccles 1990: 243). This kind of money has made it very tempting to play fast and loose with historical accuracy. As Eccles puts it, "If history could not confirm the fact that William Shakespeare was born in a thatched cottage in the market town of Stratford-upon-Avon, right in the geographical heart of England, then history would have to invent it" (ibid.). But it is not some neutral, albeit economically driven history that invents birthplaces for cultural patron saints. The invention of history springs from a dense nexus of competing and often contradictory moral, nationalistic, economic, and unconscious factors. These factors themselves change over time, thus making the production of the nation's past contingent upon the material, moral, political, and psychic needs of the present – as they are understood by those in power.[17] In the case of late-1980s England, the heritage business was securely in the oh-so-sure hands of the Right:

> [T]he culture of the New Right has actively fostered [the growth of the heritage industry]. The heritage is everywhere, all around "us," nothing less than a kind of collective memory of an entire people or nation. Such a notion of heritage does not involve a recognition of the *difference* of the past (thus enabling it to put the present into a comparative perspective) but an assertion of sameness and identity, the creation of the fictional unity of a national consciousness.
>
> (Tilley 1989: 279)

In the creation of such a consciousness, the cultural unconscious works double time. The invention of cultural history is generally not the product of a progressive, liberatory enterprise, in part because those powerful enough to impose that "invention" tend to be entrenched within the conserving and conservative apparatus of the state. Furthermore, what Tilley refers to as the "largely unconscious but nevertheless rule-governed production of statements about the past" is, like all productions of the unconscious, subject to repressive disavowing. Such strict limits and rigid control over "historical invention" emerged in the political discussion of the Rose remains.

These remains represent the "excess" that will not stay repressed, no matter how carefully mainstream culture works to solidify the normative. Oscar Wilde's name resounded in the House of Commons on 15 May 1989 because he is the symptom which signals the (failed) repression of that other body, the "non-normative" homosexual.[18] As Ridley demonstrated, Wilde functions as a foil for heterosexuals; in declaring themselves "dissimilar" to Wilde, they claim a non-excessive or flamboyant theatrical life. Politicians such as Ridley use Wilde as a way to legitimate their own public performances as anti-theatrical. In contradistinction to Wilde, they are "straight shooters."

Moreover, an unconscious link between Wilde and Marlowe may be at play in these debates as well. The Rose was Marlowe's stage, not Shakespeare's. Marlowe wrote plays about a man who consorted with devils, about a homosexual King, about the persecution of a Jew; he also allegedly wrote "all they that love not tobacco and boys were fools."[19] Marlowe was murdered by a man in the courtyard of an inn. He was 29 years old. Legend has it that he and his killer, Ingram Frazier, were fighting over the inn's reckoning; then as now disagreements about *footing* the bill can be fatal. Thinking of the deaths of artistic young men at the hands of other men who spend nights together in hotels touches another contemporary cultural narrative: the deadly reckoning exacted by AIDS. Thus, Marlowe is a much more ambiguous cultural patron saint than the Bard of Avon. The ambiguity about Marlowe may well inform the attitude about the remains of the Rose as well.

In 1592, Henslowe expanded and renovated the Rose – enlarging audience capacity by about four hundred. The Rose remains discovered in 1989 then turn out to be the remains of two theatres. One can discern how and where the second, larger theatre enveloped the first. What we have then is a mutating architectural body in which the boundaries of the previous body determine the growth and development of the new body. Discovering the remains of the Rose actually meant discovering the remains of a double architectural body. The question posed to the architects who were hired to revise the plan for the original office building was: "How can we make this new building allow us to see multiple distinct architectural bodies?"

I am using the word "body" here quite deliberately; I'd like to suggest that the Rose Theatre is and was a mutating, "theatrical" body. As the demands upon Henslowe's theatre increased in 1592, he transformed and added to the building; as the archaeologists and politicians debated the remains of the Rose in 1989, new plans were drawn up to re-animate the footings that remained. In these mutations, the Rose of 1989 changed from an archaeological site into an architectural one. In this transformation, the Rose became less an "object" full of rocks, coins, and artifacts, and more a "subject," an unruly, even contradictory form that refused to stay dead. In short, reversing Beaumont-Dark's prediction, the "rubbish" of the Rose became a *building* – a structure and an activity.

The architectural question about the Rose can best be understood as a theatrical challenge: how can the single body of the actor display two (or more) distinct but coherent "selves"? And how is the articulation of that doubleness always already dependent upon a notion of a "proper" (singular) body? How do buildings themselves, in their solidity and singularity, contribute to the notion of "a proper body"?

These questions take on particular force in relation to the excavation of the Rose. As only the third solid theatre built in London, the Rose re-presents the historical moment when theatres became buildings. In *The Illusion of Power*, Stephen Orgel indicates the importance of this architectural consolidation:

> Before this moment, the concept of theatre had included no sense of *place*. A theatre was not a building, it was a group of actors and an audience; the theatre was any place they chose to perform. . . . [Once] embodied in architecture . . . theatre was an institution, a property, a corporation. For the first time in more than a thousand years it had the sort of reality that meant most to Renaissance society; it was *real* in the way that real estate is real; it was a location, a building, a possession – an established and visible part of society.
>
> (Orgel 1975: 2; emphasis in original)

But disinterring the Rose rendered theatre itself spatially and temporally fluid, a focus of passionate debate: it put into question "location, building, possession." If Renaissance theatre architecture inaugurated an assured and certain place for "legitimate" theatrical activity (in the benign reading of theatre history), or if it provided a spatial confinement and rigid border for illicit theatrical activity (in the "hegemonic" reading of theatre history), the return of the Rose made that theatrical place radically insecure. Who owned the Rose remains? How could the new building relate to the old building? Where was the theatre actually located? The question of ownership raised ancillary questions about the relation between "public property" and commercial development, and about the relation between historical preservation and contemporary revitalization. Similarly, the question about "location" led to the complicated negotiations about where to place the pilings for Imry Merchant's new building. The developers wanted to maximize the size of their building, and the historians wanted to maximize protection of the Rose. What I am trying to suggest is that the excavation of the Rose literally unearthed the epistemological claims about "the place of theatre," claims that had been made possible by the construction of Renaissance theatres themselves. And these claims became particularly traumatic in relation to the male body.

The moment in which theatres became consolidated in and as buildings, the moment which returns in the re-discovery of the Rose, is the moment when the male body joins an ongoing epistemological history of display. When theatres re-established a place for the male body to play, they made possible an enormous array of interpretive frames by which that body could be apprehended. These frames include acting books, books of gesture, handbooks on expressing emotion, and all the other discursive "arts and sciences" that begin to emerge in the Renaissance. In short, architecture informs and defines the epistemological possibilities of the male body once theatre itself "takes (a) place."

Architecture has of course long been considered theatrical. Buildings are said to "stage" ideas about space and time, to dramatize arguments about form. Architecture also establishes a specific relation with and among its inhabitants (think of Foucault's Benthamite prisons), and often insists on a mimetic relation to the human body. In this insistence, architecture is performative as well as theatrical, for it actively shapes and forms the bodies that inhabit it. Denis Hollier's brilliant reading of Bataille allows us to see the intensity of the anthropomorphism often embedded in architecture and Bataille's radical resistance to it: "[E]ven though he seems to denounce the repression exercised over man by architecture, Bataille is really intervening against the catachresis requiring that man only take form with architecture, that the human form as such, the formation of man, be embedded in architecture. If the prison is the generic form of architecture, this is primarily because man's own form is his first prison" (Hollier 1989: xi–xii). Housed in flesh, we build houses; human form forms the buildings which keep us in them. The mimetic relation between buildings and bodies is difficult to destabilize. Theatre architecture is often doubly mimetic: it is constructed around an image of the bodies to be staged in its building; and these theatrical bodies display themselves in relation to architectural rules that govern their staging.

In the odd and complex dialogue between representational forms and "real" behavior, the possibilities of the body opened up by theatre architecture extend and sometimes even invent bodily practices, while also creating a distinction between the "theatrical" body and the "normative" body. The body is routinely *made "normative"* – consistent and whole, the property of one person who has one gender, one proper name, one self – by virtue of *becoming anti-theatrical*. This schooling in making the body requires both a positive and a negative other.

Within the normative Symbolic of contemporary heterosexuality, the positive other is the singular self of the other gender with whom one will join in a monogamous union until "death do us part." The negative other is cast as the promiscuous homosexual who, in addition to seeking an other of the same gender, also eschews monogamy and long-term relations. Within this Symbolic, the heterosexual's quest for the "true" singular body it longs to (re)join is set against the homosexual's wandering and false "body in disguise." Wandering actors, like wandering homosexuals, are dangerous because they threaten to expose the fictional stability of homes. These are emphatically not ontological claims: I am merely plotting how the Symbolic opposition between homosexuality and heterosexuality that so rankles the Right and Left today, for very different reasons, employs ideas about the body derived from theatre to carry out its oppositional thinking. Such thinking is not confined to the genre of theatre as such: the homosexual "body in disguise" fuels the Right's paranoia about the gay male body far beyond the solid architectural confines of theatre. From the phantasmal image of the homosexual predator about to be "unleashed" in the United States military, to the terror-filled narratives of infected and infecting "AIDS-carrying homosexuals," the figure of the male homosexual as "the [dangerous] body in disguise" stalks the cultural imaginary and is fed by the paranoid fervor of the Right.

This imaginary framed the discussion about the Rose remains in London. To put it perhaps too crudely and far too swiftly, I am suggesting that just as Renaissance theatre helped focus the discursive and pragmatic possibilities of the arts and sciences and led to a "new conception of man," so too does the contemporary theatre of AIDS help focus discursive and psychoanalytic tensions around repression and death, leading to a new conception of the male body. This body is marked by the aggressiveness that accompanies disavowal and is rendered as a form full of holes. The 1989 Rose, a hole, "a disused mine," so much "rubbish," is the emblem of a body that carries death in its newly-exposed holes and hollows.

I realize this is largely speculation based on retrospective revision. My own conscious allegiance to the conventions of the academic subject force me to abandon these associations in favor of "empirical" facts. So entering from another angle, let us return to the narrative of the Rose debates.

Instead of contracting to develop an office building in Southwark as Imry Merchant had proposed to do, the developers were suddenly in the business of designing a building which could stage the remains of a theatre. In short, the building could no longer correspond to a normative body – singular and whole – but had to become a theatricalized, double body. Staging the remains of the Rose required a new architectural model. And, in the strange form of reproduction that prevails between buildings and bodies, several different proposals were conceived.

These plans are at once architectural and anatomical. For just as an anatomy makes visible the interior structure of a body, so too must the new Rose display, architecturally, the ground, the skeletal set, upon which the building takes its current form. Within the history of human anatomy, a history enacted through public dissections which were frequently held in medical theatres, the accuracy of the anatomical drawing depended upon securing a corpse. Only the dead could be legally dissected: a dead body was required for anatomical representation to be born. In the case of the Rose, the dead architectural body was, if anything, all too present: before it could be erected as a "new" building, it had to make its own corpse visible. The foundation of the new building would be the disinterred skeleton of the old.

Hollier points out that the invention of architecture was motivated by a desire to forestall and forget death. This desire functions according to the rule of psychoanalytic desire, which is to say the desire is focused on an object which perpetuates, rather than satisfies, that desire. In order to forestall or forget death, architecture invents the tomb which both distracts us from the specificity of the dead body and underlines the stone cold fact of death itself.[20] As Hollier puts it:

> The monument and the pyramid are where they are to cover up a place, to fill in a void: the one left by death. Death must not appear: it must not take place: let tombs cover it up and take its place. . . . One plays dead so that death will not come. So nothing will happen and time will not take place.
>
> (Hollier 1989: 36)

The tomb is appealing precisely because it is static and still, unlike the decomposing body it covers.[21] If death were guaranteed stillness perhaps it would be less dreadful. Architecture offers us this monumental stillness and helps transform dying into death.[22] When Hollier claims, "One plays dead so that death will not come," he implicitly links architecture to theatre.[23] Theatre itself is the space in which death is made to play, to be a play. (Marlowe's *Faustus* is still perhaps the best example of the dramatic conjunction between plotting a death and plotting a play.) And the drama of the Rose excavation, complete with actors jumping in and climbing out of the grave-like pit (and in their zealousness almost ruining the ruins they wanted to preserve), threatened to make death in the contemporary city too visible.

The disinterment of the Rose Theatre raised a question about the place of play that contemporary culture accords to death itself. The architectural challenge inaugurated by the Rose necessitated a shift in the notion of architecture itself, a shift whose causes and implications are much larger than the local challenge of the Rose. The story of the Rose's remains is a significant one because it dramatizes an art form – architecture – inverting its ontological paradigms in response to a past that continually irrupts into the present. The Rose forced architecture to abandon its customary notion of itself as a spatial art, and to reinvent itself as a temporal one.[24] This reinvention parallels the re-imagining of the erotic male body as it confronts the grave of AIDS.

D.A. Miller has argued that we now live in what he calls "morbidity culture," in which social life, public discourse, and art are preoccupied with questions of health, and of death and dying (Miller 1990: 70–4).[25] While many things account for our new consciousness of morbidity, from the structure of health care to the increase in cancer, AIDS is surely the most explosive catalyst for the formation of this new culture.

As I have argued elsewhere, AIDS is and will remain indelibly linked to "promiscuous gay men" in the cultural unconscious, despite statistics which reveal that the level of HIV infection in that group has been decreasing (Phelan 1991). As Leo Bersani has astutely demonstrated, the cultural anxiety generated in relation to gay men's sexual practices, especially "passive" anal sex, is tied to particular psychic anxieties about male submission itself (Bersani 1987). This leads him to the central question of his essay, "Is the Rectum A Grave?," a question he was prompted to ask after reading Simon Watney's study, *Policing Desire*. Watney contends that AIDS "offers a new sign for the symbolic machinery of repression, making the rectum a grave" (Watney 1989: 126). Bersani returns to Watney's thesis that the mainstream media is displaying a kind of paranoid reading of gay male sexuality and suggests that male submission, and male masochism itself, is deeply subversive in a culture which insists on male dominance. While Watney bemoans the logic which renders the rectum a grave, Bersani hopes that it may portend the welcome death of the belief that male sexuality is completely expressed in acts of penetration. This belief, Bersani insists, is undone by a consideration of male submissiveness in "passive" anal sex.

Let's compare an anatomical diagram of the male rectum and an aerial photograph of the Rose remains (see Figures 4 and 5). I am aware that on one level this comparison is comical, and I hope to recall the laughter in the Commons when Ridley claimed his dissimilarity from Wilde. When Ridley suggested that the Rose excavation was neither art nor architecture, but rather was archaeology, he evoked Freud's favorite analogy for psychoanalysis: "The analyst's 'work of construction' or, if it is preferred, of reconstruction, resembles to a great extent an archaeologist's excavation of some ancient edifice that has been destroyed and buried" (Freud 1937: 259). For the psychoanalyst, like the theatre historian, the project of ex-cav-ation always involves mapping the hollow which is not there and the hollow that is.

In the ground of the Rose there is plenty present to help recall what is missing, and plenty to create an uncanny new presence. I cannot be alone in thinking that there is something *in* this archaeology. The Rose remains retained the theatre's drain: the single best preserved feature of the dig was the original timber drain pipe made of Baltic pine and measuring 18 feet. For Renaissance theatre scholars, the excavation's deepest revelation is the size of the Rose. It is much smaller than any one figured. The stage seems to have been only about five to six meters from front to back. The pit also appears to have been raked, not flat as previously assumed, thus giving a whole new conception of the experience of being a "groundling." The capacity of the 1587 theatre was about 1,400–1,800 people depending on how packed one assumes people were willing or were forced to be, and roughly 1,800–2,200 after the 1592 expansion (Orrell and Gurr 1989). All of these calculations are based on the assumption that the average Elizabethan was 5 feet 5¾ inches tall. This number is in turn based on one firm fact: the size of the contemporary burial plots for plague victims (Eccles 1990: 133).

The deadly reckoning of measurement also led to the contestation over the placement of the pilings for the Imry Merchant office building. The developers wanted to place them directly beneath their building so that the structural support would be in smooth verticals. They wanted to have the legs of the building (the pilings), as it were, placed directly beneath the building itself. English Heritage wanted to spread the legs of the building, place the pilings far apart, and have them lead to a central beam which would support the office building well above the remains. This plan was dubbed "the office on stilts." Since the whole site had not been excavated, architects had to guess the actual dimension of the remains. Pilings placed too close to the site risked damaging the Rose. Drawings rendering the piling positions were done in the same way crude drawings render the rectum – as a circular bold line covering a hole.

Ian McKellen, Dame Peggy Ashcroft, and Lord Laurence Olivier were the three most prominent members of the Rose Theatre Trust. When Olivier died in July 1989, the members of the Trust wanted to mark his death by placing a wreath at the Rose construction site. Imry Merchant viewed this gesture as "deeply provocative and [in] extraordinarily bad taste" (Souster 1989). Eccles notes that this was the first time during the long campaign that Imry Merchant "got into a direct confrontation" with those who sought to preserve the Rose (Eccles 1990: 221). She attributes the developers' "tetchiness" to the impending takeover of the company by Marketchief, a large conglomerate. Perhaps Eccles is correct, but I think the developers' heated rhetoric may well have sprung from the implication that by placing a wreath, an encircled hole, at the site, the campaigners would have directly converted Imry Merchant's building into a grave site. Exploiting the idea that the developers were going to erect a building against the wishes and "over the dead bodies" of actors, the protesters apparently wanted to place a wreath on the construction site as a calculated gesture that would portray Imry Merchant as uncaring capitalists. The developers' aggressive response implied that the protesters were using Olivier's death to make a political point, an unseemly use of a dead man.

But the desire to place a wreath commemorating the death of an accomplished actor on the site of a "dead theatre" is also a desire to

Figure 4 Rose Theatre, aerial view. Copyright Andrew Fulgoni Photography. Reproduced with permission.

create a tradition, to establish a connection between Renaissance actors and contemporary ones. More profoundly though, the gesture expresses a desire to transform the economic, architectural, future-directed aspiration implied by a "construction site" into a place of retrospection, memory, and history. "Nothing defines the specific rootedness of a

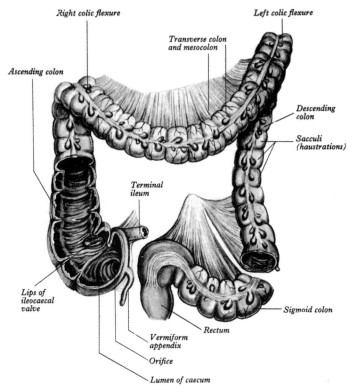

Figure 5 Anatomical drawing of the male rectum. From Frank Netter's *Atlas of Human Anatomy*, 1989, Ciba-Geigy Corporation: Schmit, NJ. Reproduced with permission.

location – the transformation of a place into a site – more than its being founded on a grave" (Pellizzi 1990: 84). The failure to secure the boundaries of the Rose site led to a desire to insist on mapping the past by turning the location into a grave site – a tomb, a place meriting deeper, "grave-r" contemplation.

For those in the homosexual community who have had to replot the "usefulness" of death, finding new ways to memorialize the dying has become a common preoccupation. McKellen had, in the course of campaigning against Clause 28 in 1988, at the age of 50 come out as a gay man. As we think about the male homosocial environment of the Rose Theatre, all the men playing all the parts under the protection of Queen Elizabeth I and then under a reputedly homosexual King James I, in relation to the male homosocial environment of the 1989 Parliament, the invocation of Oscar Wilde begins to make more sense. These sites harbor more than a passing interest in the politics of the display of the male body. Just as the architectural solidity of the Renaissance theatre served as an epistemological consolidation of the "art and science" of the actor's body, the prohibitions and possibilities of displaying contemporary bodies were given new anatomies after Clause 28 was added to the Local Authorities Bill and approved by the House of Commons on 28 March 1988, a few months before the first digging for the Rose began. Clause 28 reads:

A local authority shall not:

a) intentionally promote homosexuality or publish material with the intention of promoting homosexuality;
b) promote the teaching in any maintained school of the acceptability of homosexuality as a pretended family relationship.
   Addendum: Nothing in subsection one shall be taken to prohibit the doing of anything for the purpose of treating or preventing the spread of disease.

(*Index on Censorship*, September 1988: 39)

In short, representations of homosexuality are acceptable if yoked with disease: all "positive" representations are prohibited. At the Olivier Awards in 1988 McKellen came out again and outlined the danger Clause 28 would do to theatre in particular.[26] Under the rules of Clause 28, Marlowe's *Edward II*, an uncannily frequently cited example in the press coverage of the bill's passage, could not be taught or performed in schools.[27] By the time McKellen began campaigning to save the Rose he was a well-known political fighter for gay rights. And by the time Ridley publicly claimed his dissimilarity from Oscar Wilde he was a well-known opponent of such rights. In short, the opposition between McKellen and Ridley had a history before the Rose was unearthed.

At the end of 1990 McKellen was awarded a knighthood, which he accepted. On 4 January 1991 Derek Jarman, a self-identified "queer artist with HIV" whose film of Marlowe's *Edward II* makes the parallels between contemporary gay society and Marlowe's world very clear, wrote a letter to the *Guardian* criticizing McKellen for accepting a knighthood from a government "which has stigmatised homosexuality through [Clause 28] . . . and is poised . . . to take important steps toward recriminalizing homosexuality." Jarman continues, "I think it's a co-option and allows anyone to say: 'The Tory party isn't so bad: it's not really anti-gay. After all, it gave Ian McKellen a knighthood.'" Jarman's letter set off a round of defenses, in which more theatre professionals came out as lesbians or gays.[28] Many of the letters noted McKellen's public attacks on the homophobia of the Tory Party. He was also roundly praised for his efforts to raise funds for AIDS research with his one-man Shakespeare performances.

At the heart of the debate about the Rose is another debate about access to vital and fatal male bodies, a debate which is informed at every turn by the AIDS crisis. That this debate would touch a political discussion about the remains of a theatre, Marlowe's theatre, is not a coincidence. Acting has long been associated with male homosexuality in part because mainstream modern Western acting is about the creation of a *double* body. The actor is trained to reproduce the gestures, bearing, and "being" of some other body, the "character." In this culture, the visible display of a double body is naturalized by the body of the pregnant woman – which is not to say that this image creates no psychic anxiety.[29] Adrian Spigelius' *De formato foetu*, a plate prepared by Casserius, but first published in Padua in Spigelius' 1626 text, shows the fetus growing out of a woman's body in the manner of a flower. She stands in a field of dying trees, with her left hand out as if a character speaking on a stage ("suit the word to the gesture") and her eyes downcast. The fetus is marked with letters and is framed by lettered leaves that look remarkably like petals (see Figure 6).[30] Spigelius imagines the pregnant woman as a fecund human flower, a doubly flowering Rose.

The architectural challenge raised by the excavation of the Rose asked that an office building become a double body. In the proposed plans, there is an implicit femininization of the building, and a marked theatricality to the designs. The architectural proposal of John Burrell imagines the building as a tall column abutted by a swollen base (see Figure 7). This double body was rejected because at twenty-six storeys it was seen as "too tall" (Eccles 1990: 227). The so-called "office on stilts" was the preferred plan. The office on stilts, in name, if not in design, may remind us of the "intolerable image of a man, legs high in the air, unable to refuse the suicidal ecstasy of being a woman" (Bersani 1987: 212). But in the course of building the office on stilts, the plan was modified allegedly because the cost of displaying and preserving the Rose remains was prohibitive. Legs akimbo, the office building squats on the Southwark bridge. Beneath it, the Rose remains remain covered in sand.

It comes as only a dull surprise to observe that the magical office on stilts which would preserve *and* display the remains "intact for all to see" (the phrase is Ridley's) *and* allow "office business" to be performed, has not yet materialized. Imry Merchant was purchased by Marketchief in July 1989. A year later, Ridley resigned his post after an interview, in which he spoke skeptically about Germany's role in the new European Community, caused outrage. Displaying his "private" opinion "intact for all to see," Ridley exposed his own vulnerability. Drawing on the Tory version of national myth and memory, Ridley said it was up to

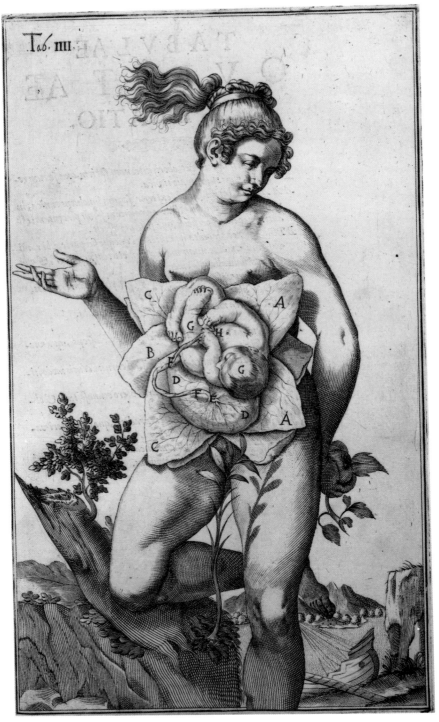

Figure 6 De Formatu Foetu, Adrian Spigelius, 1626. Copyright The British Library. Reproduced with permission.

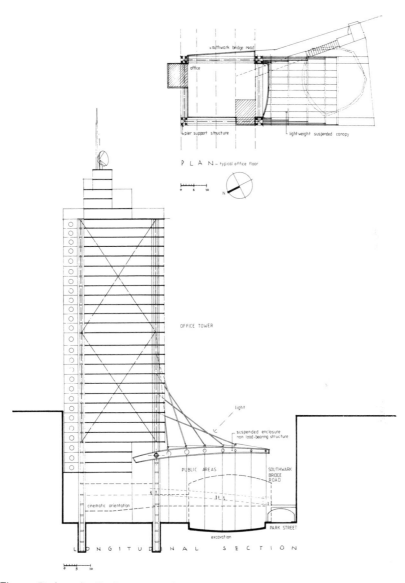

Figure 7 Longitudinal section of the Burrell Foley design viewed from Rose Alley. Reproduced with permission of John Burrell.

England to hold the balance in the new Europe against the "uppity" Germans (Ridley 1990). While this was an attitude that Thatcher was acting on without announcing, Ridley's public exposure of this belief let out a dark secret, and thus Ridley himself was le(f)t out of Thatcher's cabinet.

After the new building was complete, the government did schedule the Rose, thus avoiding the cost of compensating the developers and leaving the problem of finding the funds to display the Rose in the hands of John Major. The minimum estimate for display is £1.65 million (see Tait 1991).

As of this writing (August 1996), the remains of the Rose are in a deep hole, covered in sand and invisible to the public. Above them, the new office building, aptly called Rose Court, has struggled to find tenants. Thus, what has been produced is the *preservation* of the remains of the Rose; there is no public display and no office business. An ironic monument to monuments, the new building's tombstone-grey facade faces the austere black and gold of The Financial Times building directly across the street.

During the 14 May 1989 protests at the Rose, when it seemed likely that the Rose would be lost, a statement by Lord Olivier was read to the crowd. Olivier may have expressed a deeper sense of "terrible" oppression and "shame" than he had intended: "It seems terrible to me that one's heritage can be swept under the concrete, as though it never existed. It is a vitally important part of our theatrical history, a very great shame" (in Eccles 1990: 175). Left hanging on that last comma, a dramatic and too long interred history of the theatrical "body in disguise" awaits its mourners.

NOTES

1 This paper has benefited from the opportunity I had to read it in various forums: The American Society for Theatre Research meetings in November 1992; the University of Exeter, Department of Theatre, March 1993; and the University of Bristol, Department of Theatre, Film, and Television, March 1993; Cornell University, February 1994. Remarks made in the ensuing conversations have influenced the current version and I would like to thank my interlocutors. I am also grateful to Christina Duffy, Carolyn Shapiro, Robert Sember, Lynda Hart, Timothy Murray, and Elin Diamond for helpful suggestions on previous drafts.
2 See Drakakis (1988) for full historical and economic account.
3 The popular press took up the idea that the nutshells found in the site were vestiges of Elizabethan audiences' food. But see Orrell (1992) for a full explanation of how the shells came to be there. The shells comprised part of the soap yard used to make the mortar for the theatre. (They were also found at the Globe site.)
4 See Gurr (1991) for a full discussion of the production history of these plays.

5 For an extremely interesting analysis of the relationship between theatre and archaeology see Tilley (1989).
6 See Eccles (1990), Biddle (1989), Orrell and Gurr (1989), Wainwright (1989), Foakes (1991), Kohler (1989), and Tait (1989, 1991).
7 One of the most famous stories about Marlowe's *Faustus* is relevant here. Apparently during Act V when Faustus is carried off to Hell, the curtain at the Rose cracked and spectators became convinced that they saw a real ghostly devil and rushed out of the theatre screaming. The remains of the Rose that appeared in the cracked ground of contemporary Southwark can be said to have promoted a similar panic about ghostly bodies.
8 For a comparison of the two excavations and their value for theatre historians see Gurr (1991).
9 One section of this quote is taken from Tait (1989).
10 It is only fair to note that both Thatcher and Ridley were in favor of preserving the Rose; they simply were trying to avoid paying for it. Ridley's decision not to schedule the Rose was made after the thirty day "breathing space" had been granted. He said that he believed the site would be preserved "voluntarily" and that it was not necessary for the government to prohibit the developers from having their building. He did say that it might be necessary to schedule the Rose at a later date. See Chippendale (1989). On 11 May 1989 Thatcher said, "everything must be done to preserve those remains so that one day they may be on public display" (in Eccles 1990: 170). This statement probably inspired Ridley's million pound thirty day "breathing space" four days later.
11 The legal obligations are summarized straightforwardly in Chippendale (1989).
12 See "Transcript from House of Commons," *The Times* (1989). All quotes from the politicians are taken from this piece and supplemented by Parris (1989).
13 Beaumont-Dark's impatience with urban archaeology may have been due to the fact that the Rose was the third archaeological crisis to reach Parliament that year. The Huggin Hill site in London and the Queen's Hotel site in York had also prompted public outcries. See Chippendale (1989).
14 For a more detailed discussion of the historical links between theatres and illicit sex see Sinfield (1991).
15 Regarding the 1985 miners' strikes see, for example, Getler (1985); and for the 1992 legacy see Robinson (1992).
16 As we shall see, it is my contention that the Rose itself could not be smoothly reproduced within the heterosexual reproductive economy upon which the construction of national myth and memory depend.
17 For a fascinating post-Foucauldian discussion of the "invention" of history see Davis and Starn (1989).
18 Lynda Hart has argued that much of the "drama" around homosexuality involves a challenge about seeing homosexuals at all. For an extended argument about this in relation to lesbians see Hart (1994); for a briefer treatment see Hart (1993). For a discussion of visibility, theatre, and gay men see Sinfield (1991).
19 This is what is stated in the Thomas Baines note, the note supplied to the authorities after Marlowe's death.
20 These remarks are confined to modern Western burial practices. In no way are these remarks intended as an "anthropology" of burial practices.
21 One of the most intriguing motivating aspects of the political uncertainty and about-facing done by the Tory government in relation to the Rose derived from the fact that the theatrical "body" of the Rose had not fully

decomposed, disappeared, died, as most people would expect a building built in 1587 to have done. The very fact that it could be recovered and seen at all was an enormous shock – despite the fact that Hughes (and others) had predicted that it would be well preserved. Not above exploiting the psychic consequences of this shock, George Dennis, from the Museum of London, "brandished the bone, now known to have come from a European Brown Bear, as evidence that the spoil produced by piling was not being recorded by English Heritage" (Eccles 1990: 230). The bear bone, found at the Rose site, functioned as the indexical image of the always shocking and uncanny force of the dead body that never permanently vanishes.

22 I am adapting Leo Bersani's argument about literature, especially Proust, in the opening chapter of his *The Culture of Redemption* (1990).

23 For different contemporary meditations on the ontological relationship between theatre and architecture see *Perspecta* (1990).

24 Rachel Moore argues: "we look across boundaries of space at the living rather than across time at the dead" (Moore 1992: 23). It may well be that spatial art forms are fundamentally philosophies of vital bodies and temporal art forms are philosophies of dying bodies. It may be that the work of mourning requires movement and motion – the transformation of space into time.

25 For a discussion of contemporary art as the art of dying see Phelan (1993a).

26 For a very inspiring and helpful conversation about McKellen's coming out I am grateful to John McGrath.

27 For a representative article see Billen (1988). Note the word "even": "Since most regional theatres are in part funded by local authorities, the Bill, if it becomes law, could preclude [teaching/presenting] such plays as *The Normal Heart*, *Bent* and even Christopher Marlowe's *Edward II*."

28 In a group letter from "gay and lesbian artists" defending McKellen, twelve men and two women sign. In debates such as these women usually take up about one/seventh of the visual field.

29 For a fuller discussion of the psychic anxieties raised by pregnancy for men see Phelan (1993b).

30 I am grateful to Jane Malmo, Department of English, New York University, for calling this image to my attention. Her own fascinating work, *The Melancholy of Anatomy: Violence, Law and Subjectivity in the Renaissance Theatres of the Body*, is forthcoming.

5

Bloody nose, loose noose: hearing Anita Hill and Clarence Thomas

Sexual injury illuminates a broad problem in the performance of legal justice. Some of the most culturally troubling legal cases of the past decade in the United States have involved sexual injury, a concept recently re-defined by feminist legal scholars and activists. I am interested here in how a psychoanalytic concept of sexual injury, usually called sexual trauma (which encompasses incest, child abuse, eroticized beatings) informs and distorts the legal notion of sexual injury (which encompasses rape, sexual assault, incest, and sometimes sexual harassment). The Anita Hill–Clarence Thomas hearings provide an interesting case through which to consider legal and psychoanalytic understandings of sexual injuries because the hearings were conducted between these two discursive systems. Precisely because they were not conducted in a court of law nor on a psychoanalytic couch, the hearings can illuminate how each system of understanding has both perils and possibilities for redressing sexual injury.

The logic of law and the logic of sexual injury have an uneasy, often hostile, relationship. The logic of law seeks to draw a line between the truth of the empirical and the fiction of the lie; the force of sexual injury often makes it impossible to make this distinction. Insisting that it is possible and necessary to separate "objective" evidence from subjective testimony when assessing damages, the law prefers firm test results as against medical speculation or claimants' descriptions of pain. The law, in other words, believes that while people may lie, the body generally tells the truth, providing the test and diagnosis are clear enough. Medicine, for law, functions to guarantee body-truth. But when the injury is sexual, it is virtually impossible to separate the empirically verifiable from the phantasm of the trauma. Sexual trauma tears the fabric of knowledge itself: it is a wound in the system of meaning through which the subject knows the world, knows him or herself. Sexual trauma can perhaps never be fully interpreted, but the tear it creates may be mended as it is rehearsed, rewritten, revised (see Caruth 1994).

Part of the social function of law is to assure the populace that the law can redress injury. If the claimant suffers an unfair or avoidable harm at the hands of a defendant, the law promises the claimant an opportunity to receive moral solace and/or financial compensation. In terms of injuries to property or names, claims are evaluated according to a rigid notion of "proof" – in which the claimant is asked to produce visible and/or material evidence that the injury occurred and that the defendant had an obligation to avoid causing injury to the claimant. In cases related to sexual injuries, however, the law is asked to interpret and adjudicate "evidence" that is informed by the complexity of the unconscious. It is with a great deal of uneasiness that law "submits" to the rules of the unconscious, rules most fully articulated by psycho-analysis. This uneasiness surfaced in the long battle over criminal procedure statutes that required corroboration of sexual injury – for example, physical evidence of penetration in addition to a claimant's account of rape or sodomy. At the heart of such a battle lies the question of whether or not any sexual injury ever happened. ("She asked for it." "She consented." "She is hallucinating.")

Law attempts to make clear rulings, to establish guilt (innocence is assumed, not established), and to name winners and losers.[1] Legal hearings often involve two competing versions of narrative sequences that proceed according to the logic of cause and effect. The unconscious eschews the logic of cause and effect and achieves coherent mental associations and sequences through the logic of repression.

The Anita Hill–Clarence Thomas hearings occurred at the threshold between the opposing discursive practices of psychoanalysis and the law. What was deeply unsettling about the hearings was the exposure of their acute inadequacy to interpret satisfactorily what had and had not occurred between Hill and Thomas. Moreover, the hearings raised several profoundly important questions for those interested in rethinking the contemporary purpose of the "talking cure." Can law redress sexual injury? How must the terms of sexual injury be translated into a language that law can decipher? How can law find a logic supple enough to follow the repressions and distortions that psycho-analysis tells us always accompany sexual trauma? And how can these distortions be separated from legal definitions of "temporary insanity"?[2] I cannot answer all of these questions here but I hope that this chapter will map the chasm between the logic of law and the logic of sexual trauma that was so dramatically revealed in the Hill–Thomas hearings.

The Senate Judiciary Committee hearings in October 1991 investigated Professor Anita Hill's allegations of sexual harassment against President George Bush's nominee for the Supreme Court, Judge Clarence Thomas. But the hearings uncovered and concealed much more than anyone had intended. Part of the fascination of the hearings derived from their form, their mutating genre. National and international "from gavel to gavel" television and radio coverage, unprecedented numbers of viewers, and the nature of the accusations themselves, quickly transformed the hearings into a riveting public display of the nation's sexual and racial wounds. The hearings seemed, at times, to turn into a criminal trial – although everyone, except for Thomas, denied that that was happening. Hill continually emphasized that she was not making a criminal charge of sexual harassment and Joseph Biden, chair of the confirmation process, repeatedly said the hearings were not "a court of law." At other times the hearings turned into a kind of public psychotherapy session in which terms like "erotomaniac," "proclivities" and "fantasy world" were bandied about as "explanations" for Hill's motives.[3] Poised midway between criminal trial and public psychotherapy, the televised hearings generated a furious momentum that displayed the searing limitations of both criminal trials and public psychotherapy as truth-finders. These limitations were in turn amplified by the disjuncture between the media's boasts of complete coverage and the content of the hearings which made repeated references to secret conversations, badly summarized FBI reports, inaccurately dated phone logs and secret "leaks" to the press. All of these gaps underlined the fact that the televised mediated hearings were a mere surgical cut, a small incision, in the larger political struggle for control of the Supreme Court, that supreme judicial body whose main political function is now often understood as legislating sexual reproduction and abortion.[4]

The chasm between the formal claim to see-all and to show-all and the constant references to a past that could not be agreed upon drove the search for the truth of the authentic body – a body – any body that could not, would not, lie. Thus the racist fascination with the size of Thomas' penis, quickly gave way to a fascination with the interior spaces of Hill's body – particularly, her stomach.[5] Psychoanalysis elaborates the impossibility of ever mastering the truth of the body; law insists that the truth can be uncovered. In the liminal zone between law and psychoanalysis where the Hill-Thomas hearings occurred, disturbances in the corporeal were interpreted as truth-meters. While Hill argued that her stomach pain was the result of stress on the job, and Thomas argued that his weight loss was attributable to the stress he felt from the hearings, his somatic response was read as normal and hers was seen as pathological. Thomas' character witnesses argued that it was more than Hill's "stomach" that was upset; Hill herself was unstable and motivated by unrequited love, they argued. Eventually many senators concluded that her claims "came out of nowhere," and that they had "no substance."

Confirming Thomas, however, required that the senators adopt the structural logic of the criminal trial where guilt must be established beyond a reasonable doubt. Many senators said they voted to confirm Thomas because they believed that they owed him, as they would an alleged criminal, the presumption of innocence, even though Thomas was not charged with a crime. The question of whether or not Thomas was qualified to be a Supreme Court Justice was repressed in the frantic attempt to establish Thomas' "innocence." Thomas understood that this was impossible; I suspect his explicit reminder of that impossibility led some senators to vote to confirm him as a form of compensation.

It is useful to tell the story of the hearings again, and again differently, for repetition contains within it the possibility of reversal.

President Bush's decision to nominate Thomas to replace Thurgood Marshall was immediately seen by many as a desire to fill the "black man's seat" with a conservative, "white man's Negro."[6] Attempting to dispel this interpretation, the Republican administration insisted that Thomas' race had no relevance in his nomination. Bush put it with typical inelegance at the initial press conference announcing Thomas' nomination: "[W]hat I did is look for the best man. The fact that he is black and a minority had nothing to do with this in the sense that he is the best qualified at this time. . . . I don't feel he's a quota" (in Phelps and Winternitz 1992: 15). The very terms of Bush's "defense" are themselves offensive, and Thomas, perhaps cynically, perhaps naively, decided to take Bush at his word. In the first round of the confirmation hearings, Thomas simply performed the part of a man with a worrisome amnesia but who was nonetheless the "best qualified." Wagering that the Senate did not have to like him, or agree with him, Thomas was content to be confirmed. But in declaring himself a victim of a high-tech lynching in the second round of the hearings, Thomas accented his identity as a black man. This move helped set up the curious parallel he drew between himself and Martin Luther King. Thomas' lynching comparison, coupled with his "you don't have to like me" stance, echoed Martin Luther King's famous statement during his trial in Alabama, "The law may not be able to make a man love me, but at least it can keep him from lynching me" (quoted in K. Thomas 1992: 1431).

By invoking lynching, Thomas insisted he was a black man who was being unfairly judged by white America. For the white senators, Thomas' masculinity was never an issue; but his relation to race was. As a successful conservative married to a white woman, a man who said that "the civil rights groups had done 'nothing right' and that all civil rights leaders do is 'bitch, bitch, bitch, moan, and whine,'" Thomas posed several dilemmas for the white male senators even before round two (quoted in Chrisman and Allen 1992: 241).[7] Throughout round one of the confirmation process, (what Thomas called "my real confirmation hearings" as against the "Kafkaesque" drama of the second round),

Thomas simply said that he could not recall discussing any controversial legal cases. His strategy was that if he did not admit to having any controversial opinions he would be confirmed, if only because many white senators feared being labeled "racist" for voting against a black man. But by employing the lynching analogy in round two, Thomas fundamentally recast the form and the substance of the hearings. He placed himself firmly in a historical plot in which he was the victim. In this script, if Thomas cast himself as the falsely accused black man hanged in the town square, he cast Hill as the white woman who lusted after a black man and who, when he spurned her or when she found herself caught out, falsely denounced him as a rapist. In his drama, Hill perforce played the part of the white woman and, as Kimberle Crenshaw put it, was thereby "de-raced" (Crenshaw 1992: 420–39). Once positioned as a white woman, Anita Hill became susceptible to the historical strategy that emerged in the nineteenth century and continues to greet white women who protest men's sexual appetites: she became pathologized.

Thomas' lynching strategy was clever because it allowed him to play the part of the dead man; he had already "died a thousand deaths" before he appeared before the cameras. The blood was dry in him, but it was still flowing in Anita Hill. As a dead man, his relation to sex was arrested and buried in the past. His sexual behavior was merely a matter of his imperfect recollection; moreover, it was trenched in on all sides by a newly awakened fidelity to privacy. Ironically, Thomas' new language echoed the language of Justice William Brennan when, in *Eisenstadt v. Baird* he laid the groundwork for *Roe v. Wade* which was decided one year later: "If the right of privacy means anything it is the right of the individual, married or single, to be free from unwarranted government intrusion into matters so fundamentally affecting a person as the decision whether or not to bear or beget a child" (*Eisenstadt v. Baird*, 405 U.S. 438, 453 (1972)). This is precisely the logic that Thomas took up to defend himself from "unwarranted government intrusion" when he told the senators: "I am not going to engage in discussions nor will I submit to roving questions of what goes on in the most intimate parts of my private life, or the sanctity of my bedroom. These are the most intimate parts of my privacy, and they remain just that: private." This is a statement that can go unchallenged when uttered by a heterosexual man of a certain class. We still live in a culture where economically secure heterosexual men can either brag about sexual conquests or claim "privacy," while gay men, women of all sexual preferences, and those who seek financial assistance from the state, must endlessly "confess" their sexual histories.

During the Hill–Thomas hearings, a strange link between gay men and women was evoked. While the language of "privacy" has been most resonant in legal decisions involving women's reproductive choices, it has also played a decisive part in case law involving gay male sexuality.[8] In 1986, in a very controversial opinion, the Supreme Court held (five to four) that the right to sexual privacy does not extend to male homosexuals. In *Bowers v. Hardwick*, the court ruled that "the presumed belief of a majority of the electorate in Georgia that homosexual sodomy is immoral and unacceptable" is sufficient to justify the prohibition of sodomy between homosexuals.[9] Given that this presumed belief is also presumed rational, the statute only needs to pass the requirements of "minimum scrutiny" for the statute to be upheld. Under the requirements of minimum scrutiny, the state need only demonstrate some "rational basis" for the discriminatory law, rather than demonstrate that the law serves the state's "compelling interest." Thomas' claim that he was going to protect the "sanctity of [his] bedroom" was a right he enjoyed because of his heterosexuality: a similar claim could not be legally made by a homosexual man in Georgia.

In addition then to staging a conflict about race and gender, the Hill–Thomas hearings, I am suggesting, also staged a conflict over heterosexuality and homosexuality. This is a crucial, if often unmarked, aspect of the hearings. The hearings created a crisis about *diagnosing* the nature of the accusations themselves. This doubt led to troubling questions about the nature of Hill's sexuality.

In contrast to Thomas' "private" (hetero)sexuality, the story of Hill's sexuality, in Alan Simpson's insidious description, was coming in "over the transom. . . . I've got letters hanging out my pocket, I've got faxes . . . saying 'Watch out for this woman.' . . . And I'm talking about the stuff I'm getting from women in America . . . and especially women in Oklahoma." After bemoaning the fact that the Senate could not spend 104 days investigating Hill's "proclivities," Simpson neatly found a different reason to elicit the word "faggot" from Thomas. He asked Thomas why he had fired Angela Wright, another African-American woman who had told the FBI that Thomas had made inappropriate advances toward her while she was working at the Equal Employment Opportunity Commission (EEOC).

> Simpson: Did you fire her, and if you did, what for?
> Thomas: I indicated, Senator, I summarily dismissed her. . . . I felt her performance was ineffective. . . . And the straw that broke the camel's back was a report to me from one of my staff that she referred to another male member of my staff as a faggot.
> Simpson: As a faggot.
> Thomas: And that's inappropriate conduct and that's a slur, and I was not going to have it.

Simpson: That was enough for you?
Thomas: That was more than enough for me.

Simpson wanted to demonstrate that Thomas would not tolerate homo-
phobic and offensive remarks in his office. Framing the discussion of
"homophobia" within an interrogation that begins with the assertion
that Hill is a woman of unknown, or unnamable, proclivities, Simpson
continues to weave the theme of "a love that dare not speak its name"
into the public hearing. Furthermore, this exchange has the effect of
dismissing Angela Wright's accusations against Thomas. Had Wright
been asked to testify and could corroborate Hill's story, it may well have
been considerably more difficult, if not impossible, for the senators to
have confirmed Thomas' appointment to the Supreme Court.

If Thomas had made "inappropriate remarks" to Wright as she stated
in her sworn testimony to the FBI, and she had rebuffed him, he may
well have wanted to "summarily dismiss" her – both at the EEOC and
from the hearings. But if the account of Timothy Phelps and Helen
Winternitz in *Capitol Games* is accurate, Thomas' and Simpson's version
of Wright's dismissal is almost impossible to believe; she claimed that
Thomas left a note on her chair saying she was fired (1992: 280–5).
When she asked him why, he said she had not fired enough people in
the agency during a time of budgetary cutbacks. But even if we grant
that the story Thomas tells in the hearings is absolutely true, it raises a
different, but equally difficult, problem. Thomas is boasting of
dismissing an employee because of an unnamed staff member's report
of Wright's inappropriate and sexually offensive remark. Hill started
out as an unnamed staff member who was accusing Thomas himself of
inappropriate and offensive sexual remarks. While it is enough for him
to fire a member of his staff based on such a report, he is outraged at
the possibility that his confirmation might be in jeopardy because of
Hill's allegation of his own sexually offensive language. Thomas objects
that Hill's "unsubstantiated rumors" are being used to "lynch" him even
while he boasts of acting on less cause when he fired Wright. I will
return to the role of rumors in these hearings later, but for now I want
to point out that the hearings circulated rumors that led to dismissals
of women and the confirmation of men.

Quite apart from the rumors, however, some of the language of
the hearings took on a rather surreal tone. In his opening statement, for
example, Thomas made this strange boast: "As a boss, as a friend, and
as a human being I was proud that I never had [a sexual harassment]
allegation leveled against me." To me, this is a peculiar thing to be
proud of. A little later on, Thomas, after "categorical[ly] deny[ing]
Hill's allegations," remarked, "if there is anything I have said that
has been misconstrued by Anita Hill or anyone else to be sexual

harassment, then I can say that I am so very sorry and I wish I had known. If I did know, I would have stopped immediately." In other words, if his comments were taken to be sexually harassing he wished he had known they were being interpreted that way. But after Hill's seven hour testimony in which she endeavored to make plain what she took to be Thomas' sexually harassing remarks and behavior, he returned to the Senate hearing. The first question was from Senator Howell Heflin (D-Alabama) who said he "supposed" Thomas had heard Hill's testimony. "No, I haven't," said Thomas. Heflin, incredulous, "You didn't listen to her testimony?" Thomas again, more flatly, "No I didn't." Heflin, still stunned, groping now, "On television?" Thomas, for the third time, like Peter with those other crowing cocks, denied it. "No I didn't." After claiming he "wished" he had known what he might have been doing to make Hill think he was sexually harassing her, his refusal to listen to her seems – in the most generous word I can summon – overdetermined. If he expressed power over her by forcing her to listen to things he knew she found offensive, he underlines his power over her again by refusing to listen to her testimony. Hill could not choose not to listen to him, but Thomas could, and did, choose not to listen to her.

Not confident about what anyone had heard, when the senators read back parts of previous transcripts, they continually asked to be corrected if they had in any way mistaken the actual words of the witness. An extraordinary amount of energy and time was spent trying to reproduce and re-cite the actual words of the testimony. The senators wanted to appear as if they were benign recorders rather than active instigators of the hearings. Moreover, presiding over something that was harder and harder to contain or explain away, the senators wanted to prevent any more "foreign bodies" from infecting the true and "healthy" political-legal body. Containing the words, stopping the multiplying signifiers, seemed to promise a way to control the content and impact of the hearings. This verbatim quoting of the witness's recitation is a symptomatic consequence of law's belief in the true past as reflected in the speech act.[10] But such purity cannot be had. Despite the senators' attempts to keep the facts straight, they consistently misnamed Hill and Thomas. "Judge Hill" and "Professor Thomas" were frequent slips. This confusion extends to critical commentary as well, often with hilarious implications. In her brilliant reading of the hearings, "Whose Story Is It, Anyway? Feminist and Antiracist Appropriations of Anita Hill," Kimberle Crenshaw refers to Virginia Lamp Thomas, Clarence Thomas' wife, as Virginia Hill (in Morrison 1992: 439 n.16). Proper names often bump and bleed into one another, upsetting the security of appellation, memory, interpretation. In reciting the past, it becomes transformed. The hearings demonstrated how difficult it is to legislate these transformations.

The political-legal body is rife with "foreign bodies" whose phantasmatic force must be contained, even incarcerated. The black male body is the "representative" criminal body in the contemporary United States, and the criminal justice system is charged by the political-legal body with managing the "dirt" that that criminally-black body carries. As Thomas himself put it, "This is a case in which . . . dirt was searched for by staffers, . . . and was then leaked to the media, and this . . . body validated it and displayed it at prime time over our entire nation." So traumatized by the "filth and dirt" generated by the hearings, Thomas' own body wasted away. He complained that he had lost 15 pounds in two weeks. The hearings were "eating his insides out."

While Thomas said he spent two weeks "eating his insides out," Hill's "insides" had been eaten out, she testified, by the alleged events which gave rise to the hearings. Hill told the senators that she had been hospitalized for "five days on an emergency basis for acute stomach pain, which [she] attributed to stress on the job." The psychic trauma she believed she had to endure from her boss manifested itself in physical symptoms. But these symptoms were interpreted in the hearings according to the distorted logic of sexual difference.

The psychological interpretation of the structure of the socio-political relation between Hill and Thomas went unexamined. During the time of the alleged harassment, Thomas was Hill's boss. Thus they had an asymmetrical social relationship: he was her superior. Psychoanalysis helps us see that such structural asymmetries can produce psychological violence – before a word is spoken. These consequences can be heightened by the particular performative (speech) acts of those in power; these acts can also be made "more" violent by the ways in which individual subjects interpret these acts. (These interpretive processes are established by earlier schooling in asymmetrical social relations; classical psychoanalysis examined the pedagogy of asymmetry undertaken in and by the family.) Parents and children, teachers and students, and employers and employees, are engaged in social relations which, because they are also always already asymmetrical relations of power, produce psychic violence.

The energy of this repressed violence enables the return of the repressed. The Hill–Thomas hearings staged the return of the repressed in relation to two different narratives of the past. The "truth" of the past is located in both unconscious and conscious memories. Thomas and Hill have a past social relation that can never be re-presented entirely accurately. Each of their narratives about it will be partially phantasmatic, partially real. Hill's testimony indicates that she truly believes herself to be the victim of Thomas' sexually harassing speech. In this sense her testimony is at once a performative and transformative speech act in which her public account of that private sexual *victimization* attempts to repudiate – in the very public and politicized form of its telling – her position as "victim." (It is precisely the transformation accomplished by the voiced speech act that makes the psychoanalytic talking cure possible.) But if Hill's speech act is taken to be "the truth" (if her accusation is believed), then that very success makes possible the truth of the other, the other truth articulated by Thomas. Thomas' testimony is organized around his belief that Hill's public speech act victimizes him; her accusation transforms him into a victim. His protest against this positioning was evident in his counter-charge that he is a *victim* of "a high-tech lynching." In order for the narrative truth of the asymmetrical social relation to be maintained, which is one of the functions of "confirmation" hearings – a performance of gathering evidence to *confirm* the legal order, the order of (white juridical) discrimination – the hierarchy of the criminal/victim relation must itself be confirmed. Thomas' lynching analogy underlines what exactly is in need of confirmation even while he fights to hang the noose around Hill's neck rather than his own: the discriminating order of justice. This order of justice is itself more sympathetic to men-as-victims than to women. Hill's performative speech act makes it possible for her to evacuate the position of victim, but it also leaves the position of victim open. Thomas claimed that vacated position. In his performative speech act, Thomas confirmed the power given to men by the asymmetry of the social relation we call sexual difference.

In failing to address the structural asymmetry of the political-social relation between Hill and Thomas (both when she worked for him and when she appeared in Congress), the hearings reproduced the violence of that asymmetry. But perhaps they also made it more difficult to keep such violence repressed. It may well be that the most salutary result of the Hill–Thomas hearings is the conscious attention they called to the unspoken violence of the routine performance of discriminating justice. The return of this repressed may help to transform the narratives through which individuals (and cultures) interpret asymmetrical social relations, especially those we attribute to sexual difference.

One could go on in this way for a very long time and there have been many excellent analyses of the subtexts of the hearings.[11] But I firmly believe the "truth" of the relations between Hill–Thomas is not recoverable. What matters now is the way in which the public exposure of the uncertainty of their relations makes a wedge into political history itself. The question that is still open, I believe, is how retrospective critical interpretations of the hearings will analyze the psychical trauma they inflicted on the contemporary cultural unconscious. Anita Hill's allegations helped expose the fact that official political history is the smooth story of solid non-leaking bodies, bodies who learn not to bleed in order to assure their political immortality. The dramaturgy of the hearings made clear that real political power lies in the interpretation of the always bleeding line between public and private bodies. Moreover, these interpretations must be seen to repeat historical patterns – what law calls precedents and psychoanalysis calls reminiscences – whose symbolic force is great and whose details are vague. Thomas' invocation of the lynching script provided an interpretative model that the befuddled senators were all too happy to seize upon. Given a choice between being immortalized in history books as racist or sexist, the majority of the senators decided they would rather have the blood of a "de-raced" black woman on their hands than the blood of a black man who denounced them as a lynch mob. Hill accused Thomas, but Thomas accused them. Thus, in order to defend themselves and prove him wrong, given the perverse logic of psychic trauma, they had to confirm him. The crudity of the perception that that was the choice makes it likely that the injury will be repeated until we see it differently and change the usual outcome.

The Hill–Thomas hearings dramatized a crisis about law's inability to heal a sexual wound. Traumas that involve the sexualized body and the "neutral" corpus of law contain within them reminiscences of events – imagined or real – that repeat other traumas. Our best hope is that the exposure of these repetitions may bring about a critical reversal of the trauma. By trauma I mean a hole in the symbolic network that cries out to be mended, rehearsed, revised. Perhaps a performative psycho-analysis of this public trauma might begin to inscribe a different political history, a history written with and through the bodies of women as they appear and disappear in the discursive narratives of both law and psychoanalysis. By performative psychoanalysis, I mean a calculated public rehearsal of the psychoanalytic "reminiscence" undertaken within the contemporary event. I am not suggesting that the reminiscence consciously informs that event; but I am suggesting that, by using the psychoanalytic reminiscence as a way to interpret the contemporary event, a way to temper (if not quite reverse) its effects may emerge. One of the central assertions of theatrical performance is that the affective experience of the body can be authentically conveyed regardless of whether or not such experience is the consequence of a "real" event or a well-rehearsed repetition of an imagined one. Thus psychoanalysis and performance are congenial enterprises and, when strategically marshaled, can help us to reassess what bodily truths signify.

Hill testified that while she was working for Thomas she was hospital-ized for "five days on an emergency basis for acute stomach pain, which [she] attributed to stress on the job." No further testimony about this injury was heard. Few emergency rooms would allow a patient to stay for five days. Or perhaps she meant that she went to the emergency room five different times during her tenure under Thomas. Hill probably meant that she was admitted to an emergency room and then transferred to a regular hospital room for four additional days. If this is what she meant, it is likely that she was treated for a bleeding ulcer, the most common cause of acute stomach pain due to stress. I am interested in what such a bleeding inner cavity in the body of a woman might set off in the unconscious of the male senators. For the hearings staged an accusation against more than Thomas. The senators well knew that they themselves were on trial, and like medical doctors (and lawyers), the men were terrified of being accused of malpractice. Their terror of course only guaranteed their inept performance. The whole bizarre scene recalls the strange and sad case of one of Freud's patients.

Emma Eckstein "came from a prominent socialist family and seems to have been active in the women's movement in Vienna" (Masson 1992: 57). When she was 27, Eckstein was analyzed by Freud. The "exact nature of [Eckstein's] complaints is unknown, but it appears she suffered from stomach ailments and menstrual problems" (ibid.). After some discussion of her early experiences with masturbation and her continuing interest in it, Freud suggested that Eckstein submit to nose surgery. Very much under the influence of Wilhelm Fliess, who believed that: "[W]omen who masturbate are generally dysmenorrheal. They can only be finally cured through an operation on the nose if they truly give up this bad practice" (quoted in Masson 1992: 57), Freud seems to have believed that nose surgery would regularize Eckstein's menstrual bleeding.

While much of Freud's support for the idea that a nose operation could cure menstrual irregularity has been attributed to his intense and blinding love for Fliess, it is worth noting that in *The Interpretation of Dreams* Freud argues that the unconscious engages in a general system of psychic displacements from the lower region of the body (the genitals) to the upper region (the face). Within the unconscious, Freud argued, the nose can easily become a stand-in for the penis. (Since Freud believed that the clitoris was a deformed penis, this view had implications for Eckstein, as we shall see.) As is so characteristic of Freud in his work at this time, he was unable to make a firm distinction between a "psychic" link between the nose and the penis and a biological link. Fliess' proposal to manipulate Eckstein's nose surgically in order to realign the nature of genital excitement was a literalization of Freud's theory of the psychic link between the two bodily zones.

Fliess came from Berlin to Vienna in early 1895 and operated on Eckstein's nose. Several days after her surgery – Fliess had already returned to Berlin – Eckstein was still bleeding and a "fetid odor" was emanating from her nose (Freud 1985: 116). She was also in considerable pain. After waiting another week, Freud called in a second doctor, Ignaz Rosanes. In his letter to Fliess, Freud describes the scene:

> Rosanes cleaned the area surrounding the opening, removed some sticky blood clots, and suddenly pulled at something like a thread, kept on pulling. Before either of us had time to think, at least half a meter of gauze had been removed from the cavity. The next moment came a flood of blood. The patient turned white, her eyes bulged, and she had no pulse. Immediately thereafter, however, he again packed the cavity with fresh . . . gauze and the hemorrhage stopped. It lasted about half a minute, but this was enough to make the poor creature . . . unrecognizable . . . At the moment the foreign body came out . . . everything became clear to me – . . . we had done her an injustice; she was not at all abnormal, rather a piece of . . . gauze had gotten torn off as you were removing it and stayed in for fourteen days, preventing healing; . . . That this mishap should have happened to you; how you will react to it when you hear about it; what others could make of it.
>
> (Freud 1985: 116–117)

The scene of Emma Eckstein's physical trauma was overtaken by Freud's fear of Fliess' interpretation of it. "That this mishap could have happened to you," that is, to Fliess and not to Eckstein. The one who had to be protected and cared for was Fliess, whose reputation and name would surely be injured because he inflicted unnecessary trauma on Eckstein's body. Faced with the oozing fluid of a woman's body, Freud's unconscious seemed to work double time (the scene echoes his dream of Irma's injection where the oozing pus of her throat cavity undoes him). In narrating the story to Fliess, Freud moves quickly from the scene of his own fainting to an assessment of what the two doctors must do to prevent injury to Fliess' name. This same fear of an injured reputation also predominated the Hill–Thomas hearings. Thomas' worry over his name elicited excessive sympathy from the senators who were themselves constantly calculating how to protect their names. Thomas put it with typical bluntness: "I find myself here today defending my name, my integrity, because somehow select portions of confidential documents . . . were leaked to the public. . . . My name has been harmed. My integrity has been harmed. My character has been harmed. . . ." Thomas was there because of a leak, not because of an injury that Hill attributed to him. The leak in Eckstein's case came from her nose; in Thomas' case it came from nosy women reporters, as we shall see.

When Freud told Fliess "we had done her an injustice" he does mean "we." While Fliess had performed the surgery and left the gauze in her nasal cavity, Freud had been using Eckstein to develop his embryonic theory of transference. Freud had told Eckstein that she was bleeding excessively and resisting the surgical cure because she longed to have Freud's attention. By continuing to bleed, she was assured of Freud's continuing care. The logic of this interpretation, with its attendant unconscious arrogance so characteristic of the powerful, was also in circulation, without irony or horror, during the Hill–Thomas hearings. Phyllis Berry bluntly declared that Hill "had a crush on the chairman" [Thomas] and the hearings were merely a way for her to regain Thomas' attention. John Doggett went further and suggested that Hill often longed for the attention of men who had no interest in her and that he himself had been the object of Hill's "romantic fantasies."

After Emma Eckstein's nose stopped bleeding and she had recovered from Fliess' operation, she continued her psychoanalysis with Freud. Shortly after it concluded, she wrote an essay about the law entitled "Servant as Mother." The essay systematically demonstrates the failure of Austrian law to protect servant girls and women from sexual abuse at the hands of their employers. Eckstein writes: "So we see: according to Austrian law, a woman serving in a household can well be punished as a seducer, but cannot, by the same law, be herself protected from seduction" (quoted in Masson 1992: 249). The servant, like women slaves in the United States, could be tried as perpetuators of sexual crimes, but they could not be victims of sexual assault by more powerful men. It is not for nothing that Eckstein looks to the law as a way of redressing the trauma of sexual abuse just after she believed she had recovered from her own surgical/psychoanalytic trauma. Law promises recoveries from unjustly inflicted wounds; it functions as a civil forum for redressing injury. Knowing herself to have been wounded, and that the wound was somehow related to her sexuality, Eckstein turns to law's treatment of sexual wrongs.

Like Eckstein after her trauma, Anita Hill found herself drawn after the hearings to the laws concerning seduction and rape. Whereas Eckstein, writing in Vienna in 1905 as an economically privileged white woman, turns to the inequities faced by servants, Hill, writing in the United States in 1992 as an African–American woman law professor, turns to the history of slavery. Racism and economic inequality are pronounced aspects of both women's commentaries: Eckstein and Hill connect sexism with the history of systematic racial and economic injustice.

Hill returned to the 1855 case of "The State of Missouri against Celia."[12] Hill's decision to read this case was shrewd for several reasons. It can be seen as a brilliant rejoinder to Thomas' use of the lynching analogy. Male slaves were sometimes lynched in the South in part because white women were thought to be completely sexually innocent and therefore incapable of voluntary sexual intimacy with a black man.

Female slaves, however, were routinely raped by their white masters.[13] Their reproductive capacity and sexuality were part of the "property" slave owners purchased when they acquired female slaves. Rewriting the script in which Thomas placed himself in the historical narrative in which he, as a black man, was subject to unjust lynching, Hill force-fully counters that her historical analog is Celia, a woman who was repeatedly raped by her boss and owner. Celia's lack of recourse, during the five-year period in which she was subject to rape, and during her brief trial in front of an all-white male judicial body, might be seen as parallel to Hill's sojourn with Thomas and her treatment during the hearings.

Celia murdered her slave owner because he had repeatedly raped her. At the time of the trial, Robert Newsom, the slave owner, was 65 and Celia was 19. She had borne him two children, and at the time of the murder, she was pregnant again. Celia was tried for first degree murder. The only female slave on Newsom's property, he had made her a small cabin about fifty feet away from his house. He had come to her cabin after she had told him not to bother her anymore. When he arrived, she hit him with a stick. He fell to the ground, and his hands reached up for her. She hit him again, on the head, and he died instantly. Apparently she then put his body in her fire. In the morning, she asked Newsom's grandson to clean the ashes out of her fireplace. The next day she was questioned and she eventually confessed.

During the trial, the defense argued that Celia was not guilty of first degree murder since she was acting in self-defense. The Missouri statutes of 1845, in effect at the time of Celia's trial, made it a crime "to take any woman unlawfully against her will and by force, menace or duress, compel her to be defiled" (quoted in McLaurin 1991: 91). The defense argued that since she was a woman and rape was illegal, Celia, who explicitly stated she did not want to have intercourse with Newsom, could not be guilty of murder in the first degree, since she acted in self-defense. In essence, the defense argued that just as the law allowed one to kill in self-defense against another person's attempt to kill, it must also allow one to kill in self-defense against another person's attempt to rape. The defense argued that the fear of being raped was equal to the fear of being killed.

As a slave, Celia could not testify against a white person. Her confession was legally admissible as evidence, but not her testimony as a victim. In short, as a slave, Celia was vulnerable to the power of the law, but she could not seek redress from it. The state argued that Celia's "consent" to Newsom's advances was immaterial since she was a slave, and therefore by definition, Newsom's property. It is worth noting that white married women at this time also had no legal right to protest their husband's rape of them. Even now some states have been reluctant to criminalize the act of a husband raping his wife (see Buckborough 1989). The judge, over the defense's objections, let stand the prosecutor's instruction to the jury that "If Newsom was in the habit of having intercourse with the defendant ... and [she] struck him ... and killed him ... it is murder in the first degree" (in Higginbotham 1989: 683). In other words, if the repetition of rape has become a law between them, Celia had no legal right to begin to defend herself. Not surprisingly, the all-white male jury found Celia guilty of murder and she was scheduled to be hanged. The defense appealed the decision and petitioned the state supreme court to stay her execution (a request the trial judge had denied).

Celia could not legally be hung in the state of Missouri while pregnant. For slaves this apparent benevolence had its own sinister logic. As Leon Higginbotham points out, the "baby would have been an asset of Celia's master's [that is, Newsom's] estate" (ibid.: 684). While incarcerated, Celia delivered a stillborn child. Three days before she was scheduled to be hanged, and with no action from the Missouri Supreme Court regarding a stay, Celia escaped, probably aided by her lawyers. Sometime after the execution date had passed, Celia was returned to jail. The Missouri Supreme Court reviewed her file and on 18 December 1855, they decided that they would not hear her appeal. Three days later she was hanged.

Hill, remarkably enough, read the case optimistically. She argued that the outcry over the case, which was covered extensively in the press, and the escape, which probably involved powerful white men coming to her aid, helped expose the unfairness of the law. Celia's case, Hill argued, led to a public awareness of the inequities of slavery and eventually to its abolition. While not explicitly stated, the parallel that Hill seemed to want to draw was between the sexual domination of slave women on plantations and the sexual domination of women in the contemporary workplace. Hill also left the impression that the public outcry over Celia's treatment, like the public outcry over her own, was a good thing because it forced people to confront things (routine rape of slaves then and sexual harassment now) that they would have preferred to ignore.

A few years after Emma Eckstein published her essay on the failure of the law to protect servants from sexual abuse, she suffered another breakdown and returned to Freud.[14] After investigating the law and finding it unfair and inadequate, Eckstein was still looking for a cure. Freud agreed to see her again as a patient but he was unable to schedule her immediately, and there was some conflict over fees. In the meantime, Eckstein, who was having difficulty walking, and may have been feeling ambivalent about returning to Freud, saw another doctor, Dora Teleky. Teleky found an abscess near Eckstein's navel and drained it.

She told Eckstein that she had found the cause of the trouble and she was now cured. Apparently Eckstein's nephew told Freud what had happened with Teleky. Furious, Freud withdrew from Eckstein's case and said, again according to the nephew, "This is Emma's end. Now she will never get well" (in Masson 1992: 258). Shortly thereafter Eckstein had another breakdown and stopped writing. She spent the last ten years of her life confined to her room.

Of course it is difficult to know what really transpired, if anything, beyond the discussion of fees and scheduling, between Freud and Eckstein. It is tempting to fill in the gaps in this story with rumors, hearsay, speculation. One constructs other stories to interpret confusing and dense narratives, and especially when these stories involve sexual injuries. Just as law relies on precedents and psychoanalysis relies on "reminiscences," rumors rely on the mediated structures we associate with melodrama, soap operas, and tabloid journalism.

Acutely conscious that the Hill–Thomas hearings were not revealing "the whole story," auditors began to invest belief in other systems of explanation. Rumors about the hearings were almost as riveting, in some ways perhaps more riveting, than the formal hearings. One of the most persistent rumors was that a deal had been made before the hearings. One version of the rumor goes like this: Thomas' side agreed not to mention that Hill once had a lesbian affair, if Hill's side agreed not to produce receipts from Thomas' x-rated video rentals (including the *Long Dong Silver* flick).[15] In the second version of the rumor, Thomas' side agreed not to mention that Hill was a lesbian if Hill's side agreed not to mention that one of the grounds for divorce from his first wife had been that he beat her.[16] These rumors help explain detailed and otherwise inexplicable references in the hearings – Thomas' allusion to news reporters' trying to get hold of his divorce papers by searching his garage and his suddenly razor-sharp memory of Hill's basketball playing roommate and her sweat pants. Asked if he had ever met Hill's roommate, Thomas replied, "Yes. . . . She was, as I remember, a basket-ball player. I think she was in a basketball league. And occasionally she would walk by in her sweats, or be there in her sweats." In testimony filled with large overdetermined gaps in memory about significant legal cases, Thomas' detailed memory about Hill's roommate's sartorial habits seems strategically rehearsed.

Rumors function to sustain the belief that the "real truth" is, ulti-mately, recoverable. But even as they declare themselves "rumors," they disable the recovery of truth. By virtue of their status as rumor they displace what they seek to restore. Multiplying and mutating as they go – from one lesbian relationship to the ontic status "lesbian" – from porn-flick watcher to wife-beater – rumors underline the incoher-ence of the story they seek to verify and explain. In the face of the painful gap between the structure of legal inquiry and the psychic trauma and doubt the story unleashed, rumors worked to link what many experienced as a chasm between the empirically verifiable and the phantasmatic.

The legal category of sexual offense, which includes crimes of rape, sexual assault, sexual harassment, incest, and sodomy, continues to bedevil the law because it lends itself so promiscuously to the phantasmatic. The law currently provides a sorry forum for the redress of sexual injury. At best, it can make transfers of injury between the victim and the criminal, but it can do little to heal the psychic injury of sexual trauma. Psychoanalysis must re-theorize the distinction between genuine sexual abuse and seduction fantasies before it can effectively instruct law on rules of evidence. Until this happens, we will continue to live with what resembles a gossip network between the two modes of thought: the crudity of the law's understanding of sexual injury, for example, is itself arrived at from an analysis that is, essentially, psychological (as against psychoanalytic) gossip.[17] The inadequacy of the join between law and psychoanalysis makes it almost impossible, under current arrangements, for the law to redress sexual trauma. This near impossibility fuels the circulation of rumors which restage the desire for a cure, for a full explanation, for a way to know. In that restaging the phantasmatic is "explained"; but that explanation can satisfy only at the level of rumor. Once the phantasmatic is interrogated according to the strictures of legal "proof" it becomes incoherent.

Recognizing the bias and flaws in the discursive framework of the law, feminist scholars and lawyers have worked hard to introduce a new legal standard for sexual injury cases. Instead of having to prove that remarks or behavior would be offensive to "a reasonable man," the traditional legal measure for over 150 years, judges in several federal courts have begun to acknowledge that men and women might, reasonably, interpret the same event quite differently. In a sexual harassment case in Jacksonville, Florida, the judge allowed testimony that reported a poll in which 75 percent of the men said they would be "flattered" by sexual advances in the work place and 75 percent of the women said they would be "offended" by such advances (in Hayes 1991: B1). The judge then went on to rule in favor of a woman who alleged that pornographic pinups in the work place and "a boys' club atmosphere" violated Title VII of the 1964 Civil Rights Act. Some feminist legal scholars are betting that the "reasonable woman" standard will make it easier for law to redress sexual injury. While it is still too early to know if this bet is sound, it is significant that the law is beginning to recognize the ways in which the so-called "neutral" language of rationality may be gendered male. As the Ninth U.S. Circuit Court of Appeals in San Francisco argued, "we adopt the perspective of a reasonable woman primarily because we believe that a sex-blind reasonable person stan-dard tends to be male biased and tends to systematically ignore the experiences of women."[18]

But these apparently progressive movements forward must be tempered by the brute facts of the Hill–Thomas hearings.[19] During the hearings, the majority (approximately 58 percent) of people polled said they believed Clarence Thomas, while only 24 percent said they believed Hill. There was "little difference in response between men and women, or between blacks and whites. But Republicans were more inclined to believe Judge Thomas than were Democrats" (in Kolbert 1991: A1). Several months after the hearing, when the legal apparatus had disap-peared and people evaluated what had happened, the majority of people said they now believed Hill. It is hard to "explain" the shift since no new evidence emerged,[20] but it may have something to do with the fact that political and legal hearings – in their physical and psychic settings – underline the associations between power, rationality, truth and masculinity – before a word is said. Women, on the other hand, and perhaps especially black women, may seem simply not to belong in such a setting and therefore are judged to be wrong.

The story of Anita Hill's allegations was first reported by Timothy Phelps in *Newsday* on Sunday 6 October 1991. At 9 a.m. the same day, Anita Hill was interviewed on National Public Radio by Nina Totenberg. Both stories, the senators believed, were the result of a "leak." But as the hearings grew in complexity, Phelps' coverage of the Hill story was downplayed and Nina Totenberg came to be associated with breaking the story. The political leak, like gossip and rumor, is non-verifiable. Despite a subpoena, Totenberg never told "the law" who gave her a copy of Hill's affidavit.[21] The leak has a close association with the enig-matic nature of women's sexuality. It is the mystery around which law, psychoanalysis, and perhaps even the beleaguered "nice guys at the office water cooler" circulate.

Totenberg came in for some hard hits herself as a result of her "leaking" the story (see Hunt 1991). Totenberg had claimed that her own experience of sexual harassment had led her to take Hill's charges against Thomas seriously from the start. This claim left her vulnerable to the charge that her reporting was not objective. Senator Alan Simpson made that charge and more on *Nightline*; he accused her of "bias" and, with stupefying logic, claimed Totenberg had "destroyed this woman [Hill]" (quoted in Kurtz 1991: D6). But the accusations against Totenberg did not stop with charges of "bias." At the time Totenberg herself was allegedly sexually harassed (in 1972), she was working for the now defunct *National Observer*. Admitting that she plagiarized an article ("I made a mistake"), Totenberg "claim[ed] the harassment was the reason she quit."[22] In a piece in *The Washington*

Post, Howard Kurtz reported: "Totenberg was dismissed by the *National Observer*, where she says the harassment took place over a period of months, over an allegation that she had plagiarized part of a story. Totenberg would not identify the man she says harassed her or say whether or not it was connected to her dismissal. 'It happened and I left,' she says, 'that's all I'm going to say.'" Responding to this claim in *The Wall Street Journal*, Albert Hunt (1991) argued that Totenberg's comment "left the impression that the harassment was behind her firing over charges of plagiarism." Then documenting Totenberg's plagiarism from twenty years ago, Hunt concludes: "Purposeful plagiarism is one of the cardinal sins of journalism from which reporters can never recover their credibility: There is no statute of limitations on that judgment."

In light of Totenberg's dismissal, it is interesting to reconsider Thomas' firing of Angela Wright. Asked if she thought Thomas had fired her because she did not respond to his sexual overtures, Wright told staff members of the Senate Judiciary Committee: "'[H]e did tell me at one point during that conversation when I asked him why he was firing me that he was real bothered by the fact that I did not wait for him outside his office after work.' [Wright was then asked:] 'Well, did that comment make you think that perhaps the firing had to do with your failure to respond to his comments?' 'It did not make me think that at that moment. What I was thinking at that moment was he was grasping for all kinds of reasons. In retrospect that was a possibility'" (quoted in Phelps and Winternitz 1992: 283). For Totenberg, it may well be that "in retrospect" the harassment was the reason she quit. In short, much turns on the "in retrospect," which is a psychic rewriting of an event in the past. In Totenberg's case this rewriting is particularly dense because the "cardinal sin" she has committed is plagiarism, a rewriting of someone else's version of a story. Who knows? Perhaps the only way she thought she could escape the harassment was to get herself fired – to literally re-write the present story. And then, "in retrospect" to rewrite that rewriting. My point here is not to discover "the truth" of Totenberg's dismissal, or Wright's, but rather to underline the point that doubly traumatic events (being harassed and getting fired) produce many rewritings "in retrospect." For such a rewriting was part of what motivated the testimonies of both Hill and Thomas. For if Thomas was not traumatized at the time of the alleged harassment, he certainly was traumatized when he heard of "the leak" that led to the hearings.

During the hearings Juan Williams wrote a piece in *The Washington Post* entitled, "Open Season on Clarence Thomas," defending Thomas and accusing "liberals" of becoming "abusive monsters" in their attempt to discredit him (Williams 1991: A23). The piece was praised by Orrin

Hatch (who is quoted in it) during the hearings. But at the time the piece appeared Williams himself was facing charges of verbal sexual harassment filed by female employees of the *Post* (see Elson 1991: 30).[23] Unlike plagiarism, sexual harassment is apparently not one of the "cardinal sins" of journalism.

The intertexts of the hearings – innuendoes about homosexuality, circulating rumors, and the "cardinal sins" of reporting – all serve to illustrate the ways in which the hearings failed to provide the truth of what or may not have happened between Hill and Thomas. But they did offer insights into the different ways in which law and psycho-analysis treat sexual injuries and traumas. Asymmetrical social relationships (in the classroom, the church, the office, the family, the state) produce and reflect sexual violence. If we are ever to imagine a way to redress sexual injury and trauma, the law must learn to address the psychic consequences of the asymmetries that constitute the law of the sexual relation itself.

NOTES

1 For interesting new approaches to legal theory see: Young (1990), Minow (1990), and Patricia Williams (1991). For new critical approaches to law and culture see *Representations 30*. Unfortunately, the valuable insights of these texts and critical legal studies more generally were nowhere in evidence at the Hill–Thomas hearings.
2 For a fascinating analysis of the law and delirium see Lane (1993).
3 No licensed psychologists were called as witnesses; legal experts in sexual harassment law were also prohibited witnesses. Unless otherwise stated all quotations come from *The New York Times'* transcripts of the trial published between 12–15 October 1991. For important analyses of the hearings see Morrison (1992), Phelps and Winternitz (1992), Brock (1993), and Chrisman and Allen (1992).
4 Abortion is "the most volatile legal issue in the country" (in Phelps and Winternitz 1992: 18). Therefore, controlling the judicial body is central to controlling women's bodies.
5 Hill claimed that she was hospitalized for five days "on an emergency basis" with stomach pains which she attributed to stress from Thomas' sexual pursuit of her.
6 William Schneider, a fellow at the conservative American Enterprise Institute, remarked early on: "The cynicism of this choice – the white man's Negro – may be transparent. It could backfire. Liberals will once again argue that the President is using race for political advantage and that he is not really committed to a civil rights agenda" (in Phelps and Winternitz 1992: 16). For a different analysis of the Marshall-Thomas connection see Brock (1993: 27–9). Brock argues that Thomas had been Bush's choice to succeed William Brennan who retired in 1990, but his advisors insisted that Thomas did not have enough experience on the federal courts.
7 For further illumination of Thomas' political beliefs see "In Opposition to Clarence Thomas: Where We Must Stand and Why," Congressional Black Caucus Foundation September 1991 (please note this report was written

before the Anita Hill charges were made public) in Chrisman and Allen (1992: 231–54).

8 In "The Miscegenation Analogy" Andrew Koppleman (1988) begins his argument by noting: "While enforcement of [sodomy] laws is sporadic at best, this is as poor a measure of the injury they inflict as the relative infrequency of lynching in the post-Civil War South." Koppleman's essay appeared in *The Yale Law Journal*, and as alumnae, Thomas and Hill may have kept up with the *Journal*. Thomas told the Senate he had read a lot about the history of lynching and he may have had a personal interest in miscegenation analogies since he himself was married to a white woman. But my point is not so much that Thomas read Koppleman; but rather that the languages of lynching and privacy used so effectively by Thomas had been analyzed by Koppleman in relation to the sodomy statutes. Both lynching and the sodomy laws do great symbolic injury, and Thomas wanted the historical weight of the injury of lynching to be on the white senators' minds.

9 It is important to point out that the Georgia Criminal Code does not make a distinction between homosexual and heterosexual sodomy, although the Supreme Court did. In Georgia, the statute simply reads: "A person commits the offense of sodomy when he performs or submits to any sexual act involving the sex organs of one person and the mouth or anus of another." In the lower courts, Michael Hardwick was joined in challenging the constitutionality of this statute by John and Mary Doe, a heterosexual married couple. But the district court and the court of appeals agreed that the Does had no standing (they had not been arrested; Hardwick had). The Supreme Court opinion asserted that its decision only applied to homosexual sodomy and "express[ed] no opinion on the constitutionality of the Georgia statute as applied to other acts of sodomy" (478 U.S. at 188n.1). For a brief polemic against the reasoning applied in *Bowers*, see Stoddard (1987). For a thorough and brilliant deconstruction of the language and logic of the opinion see K. Thomas (1992) (and citations therein).

10 For an excellent treatment of racism and sexual harassment as performative speech acts see Lacour (1992).

11 See especially Morrison (1992), and Chrisman and Allen (1992). When I say that we will never get to the "truth" of what happened between Hill and Thomas, I do not mean anything remotely like Senator Alan Simpson who complained that the "truth" was not recoverable in the Senate hearings but surely would be in a court of law: "I'll tell you how to find the truth. You get into an adversarial courtroom, and everybody raises their hands once more, and you go at it with the rules of evidence, and you really punch around in it, and we can't do that. It's impossible to do that in this place" (quoted in Ross 1992: 50).

12 For excellent discussions of this case see Higginbotham (1989) and McLaurin (1991). My summary of the case comes from these two sources; in some cases the two disagree, and I have followed McLaurin because his study is a comprehensive look at all the relevant documents and newspapers from the case. As far as I can ascertain Hill has not yet published her talk.

13 Under the law, a black woman slave could not be the victim of rape; so even black male slaves were not charged with the rape of black female slaves. Saidya Hartman's forthcoming work on this topic discusses the ideology and consequences of this inequity in the law.

14 Between the time of her recuperation from the nose surgery and her second breakdown, Eckstein offered psychoanalytic treatment to patients of her own.

See Masson (1992: 114–15 and 242–3). Freud seems to have asked her to report on her progress with her patients and in this sense can be seen as her supervisor.

15 No evidence supports the idea that watching pornography would make one a sexual harasser. But the perception of Thomas as a "porn watcher" would not have helped his case. Nor for that matter would a public discussion of Hill's "proclivities" have helped hers.

16 Even the obvious objection that Kathy Grace Thomas could easily say if he had beat her is disposed of neatly in this rumor. One of the conditions of her alimony, this story goes, is that she never accuse him of it. If she says he beat her, she would lose the money. (In fact, however, the legal documents only revealed a no-fault divorce. Clarence Thomas was granted custody of their son Jamal.) As Phelps and Winternitz point out, the rumor about the divorce began long before Anita Hill arrived in Washington: "There was a rumor that something nasty had happened between the judge and his ex-wife, though there was absolutely nothing to substantiate it. The rumor had been unwittingly fueled by *The Wall Street Journal*, which had championed Thomas on its editorial pages. In its initial story about the nomination, the newspaper had mentioned, but not explained, the existence of some concern in Republican circles about the divorce affecting the nomination. *The Journal* had said too much and too little, thus setting off the sort of manic speculation that happens all the time behind the often pretentious facade of the media" (1992: 68–9).

17 The lack of understanding about the distinction between genuine sexual abuse and seduction fantasies has made it possible, on occasion, for frivolous, but nonetheless extremely damaging, claims of sexual abuse to be too easily granted legal grounds for criminal accusation. (This seems to be especially true in cases involving child care workers and the testimony of large groups of children.) For further discussion see Wright (1993).

18 Quoted in Hayes (1991: B1). While the new standard has been developed in relation to sexual harassment, it can be applied to negligence and self-defense cases as well.

19 It is useful to be cautious in claiming victories over these kinds of "concessions." They work to perpetuate essential gender differences, a reasonable man and a reasonable woman, that may not, in the long run, make law an ally in progressive struggle. Moreover as the lawyer for the plaintiff in the Jacksonville case pointed out, "We have a male judge who thought the conduct was genuinely trivial. How is he going to think like a reasonable woman?" (in Hayes 1991: B5).

20 The shift may be due to the manner in which the poll was taken. Anthropologists in Detroit found the majority of women believed Hill. Of 101 interviews conducted three weeks after the hearings, 53 percent were strong Hill supporters and 16 percent supported Hill with some reservations. See Rauch (1992: A3). For another interpretation of the polls and their bias, see Fraser (1992).

21 A special independent counsel subpoenaed both Phelps and Totenberg. Neither would cooperate – that is, divulge their sources. Citing the First Amendment, both Phelps and Totenberg insisted that the inquiry was unfair and possibly illegal. Eventually, the Senate Rules Committee, headed by Wendell Ford, a Kentucky Democrat, called off the inquiry. See Phelps and Winternitz (1992: 430–3).

22 In Reed and McElwaine (1991: 56). This piece, just to give this whole episode another dizzying turn, is itself a re-run of Kurtz's article (beginning with

the title and lifting many of the quotations from Totenberg). Technically I suppose it's not plagiarism as the *People* authors do mention "a recent article in *The Washington Post*."

23 Apparently Williams was not notified of the charges at the time his piece defending Thomas appeared.

6

Shattered skulls:
Rodney King and Holbein's
The Ambassadors

We were just about to paint the green living room white when the phone rang. Dolores and her husband, Tom, our next door neighbors, were arguing again. We had heard them earlier; but I was intent on keeping us both working the paint across the walls, so I kept my mouth shut. I don't know what kept you silent. But now it was Dolores on the phone asking for you, asking for your help. "Please come over and be our good will ambassador." Everyone knew your rule: if someone has the intelligence to ask for help, anyone intelligent enough to hear it is obligated to respond. You smiled at me eavesdropping and observed my slow rage starting. Into the receiver you said firmly, "I'll be right there." Laughing at my jealousy, you held my body against the green wall and painted my outline really fast across it. My green jealous body traced in thick white. When we stood back to admire your handiwork, I grabbed you. Holding you tight (my left shoulder against your chest) I placed the paint brush between your legs, traced your thighs, your hips. You bolted forward and hit my hand: I got paint all over the right thigh of your tight blue jeans. You kissed me – hard – and left. I stared at the wall, a mess of our bodies' shadows.

Later that night Dolores in tears explained, brokenly, that Tom held the camera up to you and said he wanted a picture of her favorite ambassador. You were mugging for them, mugging for peace. When the shutter clicked, instead of the lens dilating, a bullet shot out of it and shattered your skull.

I took three years to finish painting the living room.

If I called you by all your names, would you appear here beside me? If I went from green to white, from white to green with my brush, my hand, my words, my eye, would you return to me? Do I have to live forever with your shadow – a fast white outline on a green wall? I'm calling you. Looking for my peaceful ambassador. Trying to repair the broken line. Is history a cable? a telephone? a faded memory? a painting we keep copying?

Figure 8 Holbein, *The Ambassadors*. Copyright The National Gallery. Reproduced with permission.

That painting, Holbein's famous one, they say is a study in surface (see Figure 8). Under the surface of this book will you read me again? Can these words map a way for you to find your way back to me? Reverse photography. No bullet. Just light. A negative in the pan. No light. No camera. Holbein worked his charm before all that. Just paint. Why couldn't I have held you to the walls of my skin? I have looked so long at my fast copy of half your body I sometimes have lost the feeling in mine.

Pliny says the first painting was done by a young man about to go away on a long sea voyage. The night before he left he went to see his weeping girlfriend. To comfort her, he traced his profile on the wall above her bed and told her that his image would console her, make her feel less lonely. (Painting his profile probably helped him believe she wouldn't forget him either – but Pliny doesn't go into that.) Pliny's painter was some kind of sea explorer: an ambassador of the waves. You were an ambassador for Dolores, traveling across the waving lawn. I painted you on your pants and on our green wall.

In Holbein's painting, *The Ambassadors*, he pictures two men, friends from France. Both had been visiting England briefly: one for nine months, the length of a pregnancy; the other for six weeks, long enough to pose for a portrait. In the painting everything is elegant, orderly, shiny. Except the skull. In my mind I saw yours shattering endlessly, as if you were caught on a home movie projector stuck on automatic rewind. I went to see a psychiatrist, told her about my non-stop movie. She said I was obsessed with the skull because I hadn't seen you die. She suggested that I study Holbein's painting. She thought that it would intervene in my memory-machine and provide a "real" object for what she called my "obsessive neurosis." She said that I was stalled in "the grieving process." I believed her.

To feed my obsession with the painting (she called it an "enabling displacement") I bought a magnifying glass to look at all the details I could see. I kept buying stronger and stronger glasses.

In the painting two books are open. One is for people who count, the other for people who pray. The German hymnal is open to Luther's translation of the "Veni Creator Spiritus" on one face and on the other his "Shortened Version of the Ten Commandments." I imagine Martin Luther nailing up his proclamations on the wooden doors of German cathedrals. Martin Luther King singing at the March on Washington. The copyist. Why did Luther want to shorten those commandments? Why did King want to dream out loud? Was King your peaceful Ambassador? King, Martin Luther. Martin Luther King, Junior. Hans Holbein the Younger. I hunger for you still.

Martin Luther King was assassinated for trying to live his dream. Maybe I wanted too much with you: maybe you were shot because you would not stay in "your place." A black man moving faster than they liked. Rodney King was beaten for moving too fast – speeding too fast from drugs, from a heavy accelerator, from the thud of a police stick. Martin Luther King. Rodney King. King Henry VIII executed Anne Boleyn because she could not reproduce sons and the Pope told him no divorce. Henry wanted a copy, a way to reproduce himself to maintain succession as King. That was his dream.

Holbein painted *The Ambassadors* in 1533. It seems I've been staring at it ever since. I know too much about the painting. Kafka said that he wrote to forget. Am I forgetting you? Painting you over. 1533 was a thick year at the English Court. Henry married Anne Boleyn in secret in February. Her public coronation was held in May. Her image was copied majestically by Holbein in the weeks before the ceremony. He portrayed her as official queen before she was one. He rehearsed her for it. Showed herself to herself. She saw herself as Queen through his painting. He coronated her on his canvas before she walked through London. The image was complete before "the people" saw their Queen. When Anne told Henry she thought Holbein was a genius for the way he painted her, Henry hired him. Holbein was for a while the royal painter, the court's official artist.

While Holbein was waiting to paint Anne he rehearsed. In April he was practicing on *The Ambassadors*. The "s" of the title is an extra, a redundancy, the sign of the copy. The painting depicts only one ambassador, Jean de Dinteville. He worked for King Francis I of France. While Jean was in England observing the strategic unveiling of Anne, his brother was at the Vatican negotiating a marriage between Francis I's second son, the Duke of Orleans, and the Pope's niece. Henry wanted to talk to Jean about persuading the Pope that divorce was allowable. Wives should be required to produce sons.

Maybe nothing really changes. I don't know anymore. Oliver North and friends offered arms for hostages. Are arms for hostages different from divorces for Kings? North and Henry probably believed they were helping to save the lives of hostages, of wives. You made me believe there might actually be a difference between the two. Now I've lost you; I don't know anymore. Wives, hostages, arms, divorces, deaths. Executions for dreamers and mothers who produce only daughters. Pardons for those with state credentials. Diplomatic immunity from criminal contagion. Oliver North had us pay for a fence for his house while he fenced arms: North to South.

In Holbein's painting, the means of measuring the axis goes from globe to quadrant to star. Holbein added the six-pointed star to the pattern of the floor in his painting. He was copying the floor mosaic from Westminster Abbey – the section designed by Abbot Ware to memorialize Edward the Confessor. State secrets. The ambassador enjoys a privileged confidence.

Jean de Dinteville is standing next to his friend Georges de Selve. Georges had been appointed Bishop of Latour in 1526 and counseled any one who would listen that religious tolerance was a good idea. He put off his official consecration until 1534. By then Anne Boleyn had been executed. In the painting, he wears the robes of a scholar, not the regalia of Bishop. Next to Jean, he looks a little dour and aesthetic. Holbein, a German living in England, loved to criss-cross things. Everyone sees the painting as a *momento mori*, a reminder of death's moment. I don't know. I think it really is a painting about you. No stillness in the thing at all. You posing for a photograph and in an instant you were exploded by a bullet. The United States government officially considered assassinating Fidel Castro with an exploding cigar. Jump back fast when the lighters light and the shutters click. Don't move when the police sticks beat your body like a rolling drum. This still life moves. Still moves me. Your life stilled by his camera shot. These words recalling you, whispering to you in the sheets of this book.

Anne Hollander wrote a different book about how paintings have motion in them. She calls it *Moving Pictures*. Still lives fecund and rotting. Little deaths. Holbein's skull, the scholars (the skull-ares?) say is a *momento mori* because it shows the vanity of knowing. I don't think so. Death is what we cannot know: the end point that we can never see. We make up "knowledge" because we cannot see that skull, cannot see what we know we must absorb without our eyes, our I/s. Holbein's models are standing the way I imagine you stood when Tom said he wanted your photograph: attentive, but slightly preoccupied. They are so busy posing that they never notice the skull. I wonder when Holbein showed them it was there.

To look at the men, we must overlook the skull. To look at the skull, we must lose the men. The skull is a blur when the painting is seen straight on. It is anamorphic: death is its own distortion. Waiting for mine, trying to recover from yours: I cannot get to it, to you. Not even after all this time.

The painting is six feet square. Inside his square canvas, another square – this one for mathematical computations. It props open the book for counters. It is a German book of tables for merchants who wanted to add the price of commodities quickly and accurately. Holbein knew that buying and selling, like state negotiations, are often a matter of timing. No time to add while the customer reconsiders. Better to have the sums ready before the reckoning. Numbers in tables, read in criss cross. Our wedding rings, six weeks old, were white gold braids. Criss cross. Tom was tried and let off. Temporary insanity. Dolores divorced him right after the trial. I heard he took to drink.

With the magnifying glass cupped to my eye like a shot glass, I noticed that one of the strings on Holbein's lute is broken. Discordia: life's sweet music stopped by death. You loved jazz and scotch and could not play a note. Lutes were suppose to convey harmony, concordia. What was Holbein mourning? Maybe he was homesick? Or maybe it is dour Georges who mourns, in love with someone other than the one he has to bishop? Jean? Envious of his brother's job at the Vatican? Jean knowing he is playing Henry fast and loose, worried he is about to snap?

On the top shelf of the book case behind the men, Holbein included two different instruments that tell the time: a Shepherd's dial and a polyhedral sundial. He had painted the same instruments in a portrait he did in 1528. Holbein was always practicing, rehearsing, painting the same strokes over and over again, making the same objects. I was getting sick of all the copies. I wanted to see something real, not these endless mediations between me and that skull.

I was fed up with reproductions and magnifying glasses. I had missed your death, only heard Dolores' descriptions and Tom's trial testimony. I wanted to see the real event. I flew to London and went to the National Gallery. I walked all around the room waiting for the skull to rise up and walk off the painting with me. It didn't. I used to stare at the wall of the living room, willing your shadow to fill up. I had only gotten the lower part of your body. Is your torso roaming around looking for a cast? Is Holbein's skull casting about looking for a body?

When I was in London I met a young man. He was a socialist, a member of the Labour Party. I met him in an Indian restaurant. He was angry for reasons I could not always follow. He was a lecturer at a London polytechnic. He wanted to create collectives of subversive action: he kept telling his students that they had to become cultural ambassadors for the new state. I don't know why I liked him so much. He was kind of mad, really. He yelled a lot. Smoked cigarettes. Drank pints of Guinness for hours and the only consequence seemed to be that he talked more.

We had an affair. He was the first since you. Since him there have been others. He helped me rehearse, fed me my lines. I liked learning them again. It all came back quickly actually. I was relieved.

I was getting over you. I could tell. I finished things, started others. I hardly ever thought of Holbein's painting. It had become a "hollow bone" in my memory. But recently, since the police in Los Angeles were found not guilty for beating Rodney King, I started thinking about Martin Luther King and Martin Luther and the painting. I started dreaming of you and of my professor friend in London. I wanted to be an ambassador for the new state.

I went to the mall. There was a demonstration scheduled to protest the Rodney King verdict. Across the country ambassadors for the New State were rising up knighting themselves in King's name. I listened to the radio as I drove to the mall. Woodbridge Center in New Jersey. Action everywhere. New York's Wall Street closing down. Atlanta rioting. Miami marauding. A New World Order, and I was going to be part of it. I got to the mall. There were a few dull speeches. A kind of stunned crowd. Someone suggested we loot the mall. Someone else counseled tolerance and slow action. Someone invoked Martin Luther King. Someone else countered that Martin could not help his brother Rodney King. Malcolm X, he said, could handle this. I thought about Holbein's *The Ambassadors* again. The painting was a series of feints: the ambassador that mattered to Henry VIII was not the one Holbein pictured, but his brother, who was off negotiating a different marriage with the Pope's niece. Holbein wanted painting to be able to convey the force of what it could not show. The anamorphic skull sits in the foreground of the painting, begging us to change our position, to find another perspective through which to read the painting. Holbein reminds us that what grips us in the field of the visual is hardly ever the thing we need to see. In the mall's parking lot, we were all staring forward, straining to hear the speakers who seemed not to want the attention. They were not the ones who needed to see us. Surely there must be some other way to negotiate justice, to see self defense, to gain a more profound perspective on the killing force of that verdict.

I had read the accounts. I knew the police, especially Stacey Koon, believed that what they did to King that night was an excellent use of force. Hours of testimony were given to discussions of how and where the police delivered blows to King's head. His skull was not shattered but it was bruised and wounded: his face repeatedly hit the concrete. Koon argued that King kept moving when they tried to arrest him for speeding: the police wanted him to stop and he would not and so they hit him until he could not move and then they arrested him. They kept him in handcuffs in the emergency room. When King would not stop moving and lie on the ground when Koon told him to, Koon concluded King was on PCP and therefore had super-human strength and a huge tolerance for pain. So they shot him with the stun gun, they knocked him down, they tied his arms behind his back, put him in handcuffs, and took him away.[1]

Standing in a parking lot a year later on the opposite coast, I thought that Holbein's 1533 painting would help us. I wanted to conjure the action of that painting, that dynamic double perspective toward and away from the objects at hand, there in the parking lot of the mall. I was trying to imagine how to tell my fellow demonstrators about the painting. How could I tell them about it without the whole place shouting me down? I did not even have a slide.

Knowing it was futile, I shouted out, "We need *The Ambassadors.*" Someone pushed me forward. I kept shouting. Other people started to chant with me but like a game of telephone the words kept shifting. First they were yelling, "We need ambassadors." Then they were shouting, "Storm the doors." Everyone was shoving and pushing. I thought I'd be killed: my skull crushed by a crowd at a mall. I remembered again that Holbein's paintings had a killing force. Anne Boleyn dead, you dead, and now maybe me.

But eventually we did all tumble into the mall. The doors opened and the mall seemed to be a big enough home for us to hang our hope. I was elated, thrilled. I rushed to the center to hear the speeches. On the way, I noticed the crowd was thinning. People were stopping at the little shops. "Just to pick up some batteries." "My daughter needs some socks. Be right back." When I got to the center, only about twenty people were there. The crowd had decided to go shopping.

I gradually drifted away from the center and found myself in Abraham & Strauss's appliance section. There, twenty television sets were turned on, all tuned to Oprah Winfrey. She was interviewing some Los Angeles looters. She was really working. Calling her black guests "Brother" or "Sister," she wanted to know why the people had looted the stores in Los Angeles. They told their stories. One woman, about 25 (the age of Georges in Holbein's painting), said she looted because she knew it would take her years to have enough money to buy the color television set she stole. She reasoned that since the whole city was burning down even if she could get the money she'd have to drive too far to get it. And she didn't have a car anyway. Oprah, in exasperation and perplexity, asked, "But what's your life gotta do with a color t.v.?" The question exploded across my body the way Tom's shooting camera took yours: click and the whole picture changes. The appliance department started shimmering all around me. Oprah, in her coiffured hair and belted jacket, rich and smart and unable to understand one bit of what her guest was saying. Class wars. Oprah, I wanted to ask, "What's *your* life gotta do with a color t.v.?"

Oprah's moral shackles raised by poor people looting. I wonder if she did a show on the rich looters who pillaged the banks. I wonder if she tried to book George Bush's son, Neil. Who can nail Neil? (No more brother-to-brother plots between the Vatican and the English court. Those other brothers, William and Henry, argued over the structure of Henry James' novel version of *The Ambassadors*. The King James version of the Bible came out after Luther founded his church, after Holbein finished painting. Henry and William had a sister, Alice. She fell down a hole. I saw her once in an imaginary bed: it was made of paper and she was writing all over the sheets. I have talented siblings too. But now it takes at least two generations to nail down the plot: George to Neil. Kneeling before the magic of the state still. Keening for its lost aura. It is the grief, it is the grief, endures.)

While the twenty televisions all switched to the commercials, like the horns in a great orchestra each finding the intermezzo, I thought about Oprah's own melodrama. A melodramatic life story so well suited to the malls. A piece of us all at the mall, a piece of us all on her television studio chairs. They were not made of paper I was sure. My skull was banging. Migraine coming. I turned on my heel as the Oprah music started to play. It was a lute. All my strings broken.

When I had my last child, my water broke in the elevator. She was my third lovely daughter. No sons and still no execution. We moved out of the house with the green white walled living room. I am going back to school at night. Art history. The girls are beautiful. Mixed blood.

They travel all the time. Sometimes I look at their passports: official stamps from all over the world. Cambodia, El Salvador, Johannesburg, Athens, Tel Aviv, Nigeria, Hong Kong.

Holbein included a terrestrial globe in his painting. Inscribed on the surface depicting France, is POLISY, the name of the small town in which Jean de Dinteville was born. Can all the facts assembled here, like so many stores in the mall, give me what I want? A way to you – through your eye, or ear, through the fragments of your body invoked in these ruins and ruminations? I'm trying every voice I know. Now I am the professor, the subject supposed to know:

Holbein is doing more than invoking a patron's favor by including the name POLISY in his painting. What is the origin of our ambassador's policies? Who are we copying when we dissolve our political rallies to go shopping? Who were the Los Angeles looters copying? What is police policy?

> POLISY. POESY. PROPHESY.
> MONEY. MELODRAMA. MYSTICISM.

Modern ambassadors perform the urban prophesy of Kings in malls. Mauled too often these ambassadors have abandoned the speech of diplomacy. They speak with computer images, rap samples, archaic and cutting edge technologies. Virtual reality and the hyper-real. Mickey Mouse and Philip Glass. Nostalgia and the avant garde. Modern ambassadors wear many odd hats. The keys to the kingdom are hanging around their necks. Execution is their only goal.

Melodramas. Fairy Tales. Children's rhymes. Biblical allegories. Take the keys and throw them here. My fair lady.

No, tell me true. What have I learned from you?

1 There is no one.
2 When you died I lost my sight.
3 When I was blind my fingers learned to count.
4 When I counted too closely I broke my hip.
4 When my hip was broken, I got pregnant.
5 After I delivered, my nose bled.
6 I could not decide if I could bury you and so I practiced putting wreaths on construction sites when famous actors died.
7 I went into analysis. The talking cure made me mute.
8 I drew buildings that were never built.
9 I went to the movies and sat still.
10 I lied when I told you I lied.
11 (morning sex so moving yes I am still mourning sex)
12 Freud himself wanted the cure by love and so he invented the counter-transference: psychic health is the ability to love and to work.

13 Your skull is in the cupping of my hands when I wash my face.
14 I see your shadow on every green wall.
15 I love you here and there body to body word to word.
16 Time can be made: let's do it again.
17 We always miss the ending.
18 You are painted on the inside of my skin; the hard paint is cracked now, a hollow skull.
19 I left the house, the buildings I could not build, the vows we made.
20 I am dead. I have not survived our death.
21 In this after death, I stare for hours at crows, pluck black feathers from their heads, feel the curl of your hair where the bullet sliced through your head.
22 Darling I would hold you if I could.[2]

NOTE

1 See Koon (1992) for a full account.
2 This text began as part of a multi-media installation I made entitled "Knowledge Bazaar" as part of a group show held at the New Museum in New York called "The Art Mall: A Social Space." The installation, and the collaborations it launched, will be on the worldwide web after August 1997. It can be found at: http://www.nyu/projects/phelan/.

7

Failed live(r)s: whatever happened to her public grief? In memory of Rena Grant (1959–1992)

I

PREFACE: THE SET UP

In my high school English class we read Gerard Manley Hopkins' poem "Spring and Fall." The first line – "Margaret, are you grieving?" – and the last line – "it is Margaret you mourn for" – had one of my names in it and as I read I waited for that slow burn of pride and embarrassment that I had come to expect any time a famous person noticed me or said my name. But the burn never came: a new kind of sorrow suffused me. The nun who was teaching us explained that Hopkins' poem was about grief. She said that each person's soul is uniquely summoned by another soul and when the summoner dies, that part of our soul which had been summoned by the dead dies too. That was one of the most coherent things I had ever heard about partial souls. I wondered if the soul of the one addressed by the dead person died instantly or malingered and had to be actively killed off after the beloved died. Maybe grief was another version of a partial death which, from other experiences, I believed could not be worse than sudden deaths.

Years later when I read Freud's essay "Mourning and Melancholia," I thought again of Hopkins' poem even while I realized Freud was thinking of his own earlier essay, "On Narcissism," his prose version of Hopkins' poem. Freud conceives of narcissism as a form of grief: not a quiet whimpering grief, but an aggressive, keening howl. Lacan's reading of Freud's essay underlines the connection between grief and narcissism: "There is something originally, inaugurally, profoundly wounded in the human relation to the world ... that is what comes out of the theory of narcissism Freud gave us" (Lacan 1988: 167).[1] For Freud, narcissism emerges as a response to the loss of the ego-ideal of childhood, a loss that haunts all subsequent love. Narcissism is laced through with grief because we have lost the ego-ideal, *and* with aggressivity because the ego is not an adequate substitute for the ego-ideal.

Lately, I've been wondering about the relationship between private and public grief and trying to figure out if there is any political agency in public grief for women. In his 1989 essay, "Mourning and Militancy," Douglas Crimp argues that for gay men responding to the AIDS crisis, mourning has been efficiently converted into political action – what Crimp calls militancy. He thinks, on the whole, that this is a good thing, but he does not want to forget mourning altogether. For Crimp, mourning can itself be a form of militancy – an expression of the ego's defense against its own death. Within Freud's scheme, the ego conquers the death drive through narcissism. Perhaps narcissism and militancy share more than a similar goal; if so, how would such a goal be enacted within a psyche that is continually marked by racial and sexual differ- ence? For white women, the problem of linking mourning with militancy is especially difficult because the structure of identification between women proceeds through physical mimicry and resemblance,[2] and because racial stratification in the contemporary U.S. positions white women in a psychically ambivalent position in relation to their own identifications with other women – white and "non-white."

Crimp's essay is an homage to and revision of Freud's "Mourning and Melancholia" essay of 1917. Freud argues that grief always effects and is the result of a prior internalized relation we have with ourselves. These internalized relations, however, are deeply coded by external values – the ones I would like to discuss here have to do with race and gender. These internalized relations are (substitute) identifications which provoke both the memory of the ego-ideal and the aggression prompted by the realization that subsequent love objects must struggle to replace that lost idealized relationship. In short, the on-going reinterpretation of the loss of the ego-ideal determines all subsequent love. Therefore, grief and aggression are the foundations of narcissism. Narcissism emerges not out of an excess of self-love as is commonly assumed, but rather as a "militant" acknowledgment of loss.[3] It is that loss, and the ego's aggressive response to it, that motivates cultural and psychic reproduction – again Lacan's gloss on this point is wonderfully blunt: "[N]othing fruitful takes place in man save through the intermediary of a loss of an object" (Lacan 1988: 136).

For Freud, the psychic process of mourning can take one of two paths, depending upon the prevailing form of identification between the one who grieves and the lost object. Freud (at this point) believed that iden- tifications were either narcissistic or hysterical.

> The difference between narcissistic identification and hysterical iden- tification may be seen in this: that, whereas in the former the object-cathexis is abandoned, in the latter it persists and manifests its influence. ... In any case, in the transference neuroses, too, identifi-

cation is the expression of there being something in common, which may signify love.

(Freud 1917: 250)

If identifications are expressions of "something in common," the mode of recognizing that commonality differs. If the person who is mourning has had a hysterical identification with the lost object, he or she retains that cathexis and develops what we might call a contiguous relationship to the lost object. Hysterical identifications, as we shall see, operate metonymically. Narcissistic identifications, on the other hand, cause the person who mourns to abandon the cathexis when the object is lost. This abandonment, however, is not accomplished simply. The object-cathexis must be aggressively killed off and discarded. This is part of the work of mourning.

Earlier in "On Narcissism" Freud states that love is a necessary precondition for psychic health: "[W]e must begin to love in order not to fall ill, and we are bound to fall ill if, in consequence of frustration, we are unable to love" (Freud 1914: 85). He goes further too and quotes what he calls Heine's "picture of the psychogenesis of Creation" in which God confesses that illness was "no doubt the final cause of the whole urge to create. By creating, I could recover; by creating, I become healthy" (ibid.). Narcissism is the name of both the wound and the cure: the ego attempts to "become healthy" – to recover from the loss of the ego-ideal by creating out of itself a substitute object for that loss. This view of love and illness exerted a strange pressure on the project of psychoanalysis itself for it forced Freud to recognize that most of his patients sought "the cure by love, rather than a cure by analysis" (ibid.: 101).[4]

The transference/counter-transference structure repeats the structure of the narcissistic/hysterical structure of identification. While the analytic session dramatizes "something in common" between the analysand's identifications outside the session and those within it, this commonality is not exact. The analytic frame assures that the "reproduction" of the identifications within the session are different, if only because they are no longer unconscious. Serving as part of the "content" of the analysis, the identifications activated by the transference are what allows repetition (as activated through the processes of substitution and mimicry) to bring about reversals or, indeed, "a cure." (Although not alas "*the* cure by love.")

While psychoanalysis is often said to be itself a melancholic, even nostalgic pursuit, we do well to remember that for Freud psychic health meant being able to work and to love. Love, despite its loss and grief, was for Freud productive, positive, and "healthy." The project of psychoanalysis is to chart the intellectual, psychic, and affective movement from the structure of love-as-loss to love-as-splitting. This project can be usefully and quickly rehearsed in the history of the movement between Freudian and Lacanian theory. For Lacan the psychic subject is quintessentially a split subject. For Freud, who believed that "We must begin to love in order not to fall ill," the success of psychoanalysis is related to the "creation" of substitute objects which can stand up to the same attachments that the lost object – especially the ego-ideal – provoked. The *creation* of these substitute objects produces a split in the psychic subject – and the *work* of splitting, although alienating and even in Lacan's sense castrating, requires both aggressivity and creativity.

Aggression and creation are themselves encouraged and discouraged by the political field in which this psychic work must, perforce, take place. For example, it may well be that for women, loss would be accompanied by guilt and shame – what did I do to drive the ego-ideal away? How will I explain this loss? While for men it might produce less ambiguous aggression, in which case it would be a relatively short step to militancy. But this is crude and broad speculation; clinical evidence would be necessary for any further pursuit of this proposition.

Nonetheless, it does seem clear that for white women, the mimicry motivated by the loss of the ego-ideal is related to the image of the female body, an image often associated with reproduction itself. If identification expresses "something in common," the visible body, especially skin color and physical resemblance, is often the stage on which identifications are made. For white women, the political imperative of reproduction informs the ability, indeed the often coercive compulsion, to reproduce an/other object. The reproductive imperative at the heart of white feminine mimicry determines whether or not erotic love is melancholic or "happy" and whether or not the analysis is a success or "broken off."

II

A FRAGMENT OF AN ANALYSIS OF A CASE OF REPETITIVE HYSTERIA

In all respects, save one, the patient I'd like to describe here appeared to be well adjusted and psychically robust. She did however display an extraordinary ability to mimic the actions, thoughts, and physical gestures of those with whom she had contact. She was a kind of Zelig-like creature. Her mimicry was responsible for much of her professional success as a critical writer, but it also led to personal unhappiness. In the course of the analysis, she began to mimic me so completely that I was forced to suspend our investigations. In the three years since I have seen her, I have spent considerable time reflecting on her quite remarkable case.[5]

In a nutshell, my patient's identificatory abilities were so strong the rest of her personality was shriveled and underdeveloped. As a professional critic her identificatory eagerness provided her with keen insight into the art work that she wrote about, for she could see almost everything the artist was trying to see and she could hear the art saying almost everything it was trying to say. My patient, whom I will call Echo, ran into trouble, however, when the art documented death. For then she herself felt obligated to die. Because she knew enough to know that this response was not proper, she usually was able, albeit sloppily, to put on the brakes.[6]

This aspect of Echo's symptom was deeply intriguing to me. More than any patient I'd ever seen, Echo's ego operated according to a principle of pure mimesis. Her unconscious was organized around the principle of mimicry: she was trying to train her mimetic faculties so astutely that eventually she would be able to mimic and thereby reproduce her ego-ideal. She was, nonetheless, terrified by the logical temptation of her mimicry; for its termination point, she understood, would be a form of suicide. For if she could indeed reproduce her ego-ideal she knew it would necessitate her own self-annihilation (why would she be necessary if the ego-ideal was there?). Her original reason for seeking my counsel came from her desire to channel her mimicry more effectively. She did not want to "stop" it, she wanted to use it in a way that would allow her to work, to write, and to love. To an extraordinary degree her unconscious controlled her critical writing and thus early in the analysis we decided to use her critical writing as our "text." Under normal situations, I would not use a patient's work in this manner, but I believed it would save us time and would allow us to isolate her relation to mimicry. For it was within this writing that she was able to enact most fully the positive force of her mimetic desire.

When she was commenting on the work of other writers she assumed, incorrectly of course, that they wrote as she did: with a complete introjection of and identification with the subject of their writings. And, ironically enough, it was this problem and not the other ostensibly more dangerous symptom that undid our work together. Her use of quotation, allusion, citation was so pronounced that I began to see her voice as a camouflage: so thoroughly did her own word work "blend in" with the words of others that it was sometimes impossible, at the level of pronouns and syntax, to decipher where her voice began and the other's ended. This blending of voices entered our sessions and her miming of my own voice disrupted the analytic work.

Shortly after the death of her colleague, Professor Rena Grant, my patient wrote an essay about Grant's last work, an analysis of Joan

Riviere's essay, "Womanliness as a Masquerade." Discussing Echo's essay in our sessions gave them a very dizzying aspect. Echo was miming my responses to her remarks about Grant's interpretation of a psychoanalytic essay. The *mise en abyme* we found ourselves in made it impossible for the analysis to go forward and it was at this time that I terminated the treatment. I gave her several referrals and encouraged her to see a male analyst, for I believed that gender difference might slow her mimicry sufficiently for Echo and a male analyst to study it as it formed. As a white woman myself I felt its effects, but I could not see, until later, what exactly provoked it. Unfortunately none of the colleagues whose names I gave her ever heard from her. Echo has weighed on my mind in the intervening years. I would like to reconstruct the final part of our work together for I believe it may shed light on an aspect of psychoanalytic theory that needs further development.

While the following analysis may seem overly textual, I must remind you that we worked with Echo's writing more than her talking. Perhaps this was an error on my part. But at least initially her writing helped us isolate Echo's problem. While composing this essay I have myself gone back and read Riviere's essay, the essay by Rena Grant, and Echo's essay. All three papers mark an explicit identification between the writer and her subject: Riviere identifies with her patient; Grant identifies with Riviere; and Echo identifies with Grant. In their essays both Grant and Echo are also engaged in a process of grief: Grant seems to be grieving over the curtailment of erotic choices for women and Echo's paper is an explicit mourning for Rena Grant. In writing about Echo's writing about Grant's writing about Riviere's writing I am myself identifying with Riviere writing about her patient. The fact that all these voices "emanated" from white women who were seeking to articulate something central about the psychic force of femininity has something important to say about the way in which writing and psychoanalysis are implicated in the peculiar structure of identification that white women experience in relation to one another.

I would like to quote at length from Echo's manuscript because it is through this text that I can best articulate her case history. Particularly large jumps in Echo's manuscript are indicated by ellipses and short summary statements of the excluded material. Smaller cuts are left unmarked.

III

EXCERPTS FROM ECHO'S ESSAY

About two weeks before she died Rena Grant called her editor, Josefina Ayerza, and told her to change the title of her essay from "'Womanliness as a Masquerade,' Reconsidered" to "Let Daddy Do It For You." In Grant's first title, she quotes the title of Joan Riviere's 1929 essay, and adds the final word, "reconsidered," a word which promises a retrospective of the object that constitutes her essay's subject. Ayerza, busily packing for her trip to Buenos Aires, said the new title was fine. She had not yet read the essay. When she had been in Buenos Aires for about ten days, she received a telegram: "Rena Grant is dead." She read Rena Grant's essay on the plane back to New York. When she finished, she could not understand why Grant wanted the title changed. When Ayerza arrived in the city, she was told that the official cause of Rena Grant's death was liver failure. Liver failure at the age of 32.

A few weeks ago, the editor gave me Grant's essay. The last writing, the final word. It's an amazing piece, quite apart from the extraordinary title change . . . .[7]

"Womanliness as a Masquerade," Riviere's 1929 essay, has been subject to several powerful feminist re-readings; it is integral to Mary Ann Doane's formulation of the female cinematic spectator (1987) and to Sue-Ellen Case's "Butch-femme aesthetic"(1989). [. . . a long summary of these arguments.] Rena Grant's piece is a re-reading of all of these re-readings. It circles back and, as her original title put it, reconsiders.

When Rena Grant decided to reconsider Riviere she must have also reconsidered feminist theory's object-cathexis with the essay. Do feminist academics love this essay so much because it concerns a woman who gives public lectures, much like the ones we routinely offer about her case history? Is our identification with Riviere's patient itself narcissistic – a form of reproducing ourselves on both sides of the psychoanalytic couch – and/or hysterical, a form of melancholic brooding? Do we love the essay because Riviere allows for ambivalence around sexual object choice and still allows that such ambivalence may nonetheless make women happy? Do we cathect so deeply and frequently with Riviere's essay because it says women strive mainly to understand that unfathomable thing we can never recognize, that unfathomable thing Lacan called sexual difference? In the face of this unfathomableness do we shore up "womanliness" by repeating its tropes, its conventions, and by endlessly reconsidering its theoretical conundrums, including the conundrum of womanliness itself? We reconsider what is unfathomable because we do not get it: we think if we return one more time this time just maybe we will get it. So Rena, revering not Riviere herself, but the painful project of repetition, returned to Riviere's essay – and this time she returned not through the mother, but through the father. Let Daddy Do It For You.

[Long discussion of the law of the father . . .]

But within the economy of the academy, the return itself already involves a wager. It exists in another currency: in returning to Riviere's essay Rena Grant also reconfirms her womanliness: the academy reads Grant's "reconsideration" of Riviere as a confirmation of Rena's own womanliness and feminism.

What would it take, within the frame of the academy, to invent another form of identification among women? One not read as confirming and conforming to "womanliness" at all? An identification in which resemblance was based not on physical or psychic mirroring but rather on uncertainty, doubt, the unfathomable? How might such a phantasmatically compelling identification be performed?

IV

A FRAGMENT OF AN ANALYSIS OF A CASE OF REPETITIVE HYSTERIA, CONTINUED

Echo's paper goes on at some length describing what such an identificatory performance might be. But I feel compelled here to interrupt her essay in order to contextualize her relation with Rena Grant, as she represented it to me during our sessions, both before and after Grant's death. Professor Grant was Echo's colleague at the University of _____. They were hired the same year and while they were in different departments and schools, they taught similar subjects and read the same kinds of books. Professor Grant was in the English Department and had earned her Ph.D. from Yale. She was originally from Scotland. As I understand it, she specialized in Lacanian and Marxist theory, wrote and taught in a variety of fields, and was deeply interested in psychoanalysis as a mode of interpreting art – especially literature and film. Her death at 32 was a shock, although her heavy drinking was an open secret.

The modes of identification Echo experienced in grieving over Professor Grant's death are relevant to a larger consideration of white women's relation to the difficult psychic process of mourning. What follows is a transcription from an audio tape I made (with Echo's permission) of a brief part of one of our sessions before Professor Grant's death. We taped only Echo's narrations of dreams. She was particularly eager to have this dream recorded. And she always insisted on framing the narrative of each dream by the activity engaging her right before sleep. The first sentences of this excerpt which frame the dream function in much the way her prologue about the editor who goes to Buenos Aires frames her reading of Grant's essay. We spent several sessions analyzing this dream. Please note the prominent role of the university in the dream work:

I had been out with Rena for about six hours, drinking heavily. She was drinking scotch and I was drinking beer. When I came home I was exhausted, anxious, very upset. I took a long shower and had what I can only describe as a terrifying dream. I dreamt that the University of _____ was a hospital. I saw myself lying in the hospital as a newborn infant. I was behind the glass in one of those crowded incubator rooms. I remember noticing the glass window, the glass cribs, the glass covering the fluorescent lights above my infant, half-blind eyes. Next to me was another little baby girl and I knew she was Rena. Somehow we got mixed up. I was supposed to go down one hall and grow up in the English Department and become a writer. She was supposed to go down another hall to the Theatre Department and become an actress – she was supposed to be Professor Bette Davis. But somehow we got switched, and I grew up to be who she should have been and she grew up to be who I was meant to be. Except of course I was neither Professor Bette Davis nor Professor Rena Grant. But I always felt I was acting. And she had tortuous bouts of writer's block and complained brilliantly about being miscast. It was all a terrible mistake but by the time we realized it, it was too late. We decided to keep it a secret. We both were deeply ashamed to have discovered the mistake. We wished we hadn't known.

When Echo recounted this dream I was quite struck for she seemed not to be identifying with anyone other than the dreamer – that is, for once she seemed to be identifying with "herself" rather than with someone else. The dream seemed to indicate a healthy narcissistic identification with Grant. But as we continued to speak, and now that I've read Echo's essay, I see that Echo also was experiencing an hysterical identification with Professor Grant. When I suggested to Echo that she was perhaps abandoning her mimetic desire in the dream, she dismissed my theory and said that no, she was identifying with the university. She said that this part of the dream frightened her for she realized she had come to regard the university as an institution that labeled and named the ill, rather than cured them. When I pointed out that a university is not a hospital, that the students there are not seeking a cure, she looked at me blankly and after a long pause said, "You do not teach." I assured her that I did and that my students wanted information, knowledge. She shrugged her shoulders and said, "Mine want to be loved."

Echo was terrified that her writing could only label and name and beyond that it did nothing. Without work that had some consequence other than nomination, she said, she saw no reason to continue working, and by implication she seemed to suggest, no reason to continue living. She said that she also feared the dream for it seemed to tell her that she was able to see "herself" only as an infant; after that she was always pretending to be someone else. I told her birth dreams usually indicated an important psychic shift but she resisted this line of my thinking. She told me bluntly that I was naive. I was glad that her identification with me had enough room in it to allow her to make this assertion, for it seemed to indicate that her mimetic compulsion was slowly being overcome by our work together. My optimism was short-lived however.

Echo and I spent many hours trying to piece together how she and Professor Grant had discovered that they were switched at birth. Echo insisted she could not recall any information from the dream about it. I wish I had pressed her a little more on this point for it really is too remarkable that she could have repressed so completely such a vital piece of knowledge. It is my contention that in her essay about Grant (written about a year after the dream) she displaced this knowledge into a kind of critical riddle. I return now to Echo's essay:

V

EXCERPTS FROM ECHO'S ESSAY, CONTINUED

The symptom Riviere wants to untangle is her patient's contradictory perform-
ance of femininity. A highly successful professional woman, Riviere's white
patient "reverts" to "typical" feminine behavior after giving successful public
lectures – more particularly, she flirts with the men in her audience, regard-
less of their ability to help her in her career. It's this last that seems to Riviere
troubling – flirting with men who might help one's career makes sense, she
seems to suggest, but flirting when there is no potential payoff seems to Riviere
problematic, a symptom in need of psychoanalytic interpretation. Grant,
however, proposes an alternative "explanation" of Riviere's patient's perfor-
mance: she wonders if this patient is not displaying a "quite high (if cynical)
degree of adaptation to reality. Experience tells us that unremarkable outfits,
straightforward presentation of arguments, and an expressed lack of heteroerotic
interests will do us no good in professional situations" (Grant 1992: 57).

Grant's cynical candor displays her own highly adapted relation to sadism
(aggression's sexual partner) which Riviere suggests is the key to her patient's
remarkable sexual fantasy. Moving then from a reading of "real" flirting, to
an interpretation of a sexual fantasy, Riviere's analysis seeks to explain the
nature of her patient's sexual desire, a desire which negotiates between the
power of white masculinity and the "innocence" of white "womanliness."
Riviere's patient, who had spent her childhood in the southern states of America,
fantasizes that a black man comes to attack or seduce her sexually. She allows

him to touch her because she rationalizes that she might "defend herself by making him kiss her and make love to her (ultimately so that she can then deliver him over to justice)" (Hughes 1991: 93).

In Riviere's analysis of her patient, she interprets her patient's post-lecture flirting as a response to her "theft" or appropriation of her father's phallus (her father was also a public speaker). Her flirting, Riviere argues, is an attempt to disguise her castration of him and to render her innocent of any theft at all. She so fears his retribution for her castration of him she, as it were, disowns the theft. Her flirting returns the phallus to him and the excessiveness of her seductive behavior works to absolve her from any illegal appropriation.

Grant astutely re-reads Riviere's analysis and traces the two different versions of the phallus activated by "real" flirting after her lectures and this sexual fantasy. Grant argues that Riviere's patient can only have the sexual fantasy (can only "have" the black man) because of the Symbolic phallus, the legal and psychic order policed by white men. Grant contends:

> *The distinction between the phallus that the white woman imagines herself to have stolen from her father . . . is shockingly different from the phallus that "justice" will appropriate from the black man; and the status of the woman in this scene becomes less clearly one of innocence, even in the terms that her own fantasy dictates. She begins instead to take on the role of . . . one who justifies the unwritten law whereby castration is seen as socially useful, and whose theft is indictable only at severe cost to her supposed judge. If "the purity of white womanhood" is the stated cause for an unofficially-sanctioned violence, the question of an ultimately pure enjoyment becomes extremely troubling, and we have to add to our analysis of Riviere's patient that she is masquerading not only as a woman, but as white.*
>
> *(Grant 1992: 60)*

The sadistic pleasure as against "ultimately pure enjoyment" in this fantasy then derives from the fact that "Daddy Will Do It For You." Riviere's patient's sexual pleasure is purchased by the tyranny of the lynch mob, who cannot conceive of white women as anything but sexually innocent. Riviere's patient participates in this masquerade. Disguised as innocent, she structures her erotic life, both phantasmal and actual, within the frame of this "justice."

Therefore in the strange calculus of erotic desire – desire that often converts narcissistic aggression into sadism – the performance of white women's false sexual innocence constructs another subject position, another body, in this case the black man's body, upon whom difference (and sexual guilt) is inscribed. This body, in turn, is introjected back onto the white women's psyche as contiguous with her own (in part because she has created it, reproduced it, made it). It is precisely the contiguity of the other's body that motivates hysterical identifications. Discovering then what a white woman wants, Grant suggests, will then be a matter of reconsidering her relation not to the drives as Freud proposed, but rather in relation to the All, the white patriar-chal Symbolic where woman is not-All. And, Grant concludes, "what this relation is, God only knows" (ibid.: 64).

VI

A FRAGMENT OF AN ANALYSIS OF A CASE OF REPETITIVE HYSTERIA, CONTINUED

I have come to think that the hysterical kernel of Echo's identifica-tion with Rena was related to their both being white women working in an institution that used their "womanliness" as a way of forestalling racial equality. Affirmative action quotas could be filled, for example, either by a white woman or a "person of color." In this arithmetic a white woman equals one point, a male person of color equals one point, but a woman of color equals two. As victims of patriarchy, women masquerade as feminine. As among those who contribute to and benefit from racism, they masquerade as non-complicit and indi-vidually benign – purely "white." Recognizing their complicity with this system complicated Echo's and Grant's pleasure in their profes-sional lives; further discovering that they each saw the other's complicity led them to form a kind of hysterical identification with one another. Their shame and guilt gave them an odd bond. This bond may be a key to the embarrassed recognition they experienced in relation to "the switch at birth" recounted in Echo's dream. They both had to recognize and forget (and in Echo's case actively repress) how they learned of their own switch from "benign" infants to complicitous masqueraders. Grant's essay and Echo's essay reveal and conceal their own implication in the critical problem they each address. For if they are masochists in relation to patriarchy they are sadists in relation to racism. And therefore no part of their erotic or professional desire is "innocent." As witnesses to one another's double positioning, Echo's dream constructs a scenario in which each woman is ashamed of the belated knowledge that they discover about a terrible mistake which makes it impossible for either of them to be who they intended to be. And in this discovery the malignancy of the university's labeling practices is exposed. But not before the women are each infected and implicated in the illness they can diagnose but cannot cure.

Echo attempted to transform the grief and melancholia she felt in relation to Rena's death, a death Echo referred to as a slow suicide, by writing her essay. I imitate her writing here by recognizing that my own counter-transference with Echo led me to recognize *and* forget (and no doubt actively repress) my own complicity with the structure of psychoanalytic accounts of female desire, a structure that makes it quite often impossible, as it was for Riviere, to see the way in which racism inscribes psychic desire itself.

But something troubles me about Echo's essay. Her close reading of Grant's close reading of Riviere is undertaken because of Rena Grant's death. Writing, as a public enactment of her own psychic "working through," also allows Echo to repeat particular letters, and find another order of alignment within them – a psychic poetics of rhyme one might say. But not just any rhymes: for whatever else Echo was working through in relation to Grant's death, she was attempting to come to terms with psychic and somatic resemblance.

In her essay Echo notes that the cause of Grant's death was liver failure. In our sessions she always referred to Grant's death as a "slow suicide." Within the logic of the letter, the failure of the liver was itself a symptom of the failure [of her will] to live. Echo seemed to suggest that "livers" signify both somatic organs that flush liquid through the body and, more baldly, those who live, especially those with an aggressive grip on life.

Moreover, in Echo's reading of Grant's reading of Riviere, a lot turns on the patient's fantasy of being seduced by a black man. It is worth remembering that the "evidence" for these readings is itself phantasmal – as phantasmal perhaps as the idea of justice in a world governed by the distorting logics of sexual difference and racial inequality. Nonetheless, Riviere's patient's sexual fantasy is predicated on the belief that she can "defend herself by making him kiss her and make love to her (ultimately so that she can then deliver him over to justice)" (Hughes 1991: 93).

Echo seems to want something similar: a way to "de-liver" Grant's failed liver, to not waste it. Riviere's patient experiences her sexual desire through the prism of racial injustice: her pleasure comes from the sadistic identification of realizing she can indeed "deliver him over to justice." Echo attempts to stop her grief over Grant's death by raging at the university's racial and sexual injustices. In accusing the university, Echo activates her aggression which allows her to begin the long process of working through her mourning (she was mourning both Grant and her idealization of the university).

The uncomfortable structure of repetition which informs my account testifies to the tenacity of mimesis and mimicry for women. I can only hope that the continual exposure of that repetitive identification will eventually inspire new forms of identification. To that end, I hereby inscribe this analysis publicly with an acknowledgment of my own grief. I do miss my sessions with Echo; my reading of her words is an attempt to continue my conversation with her albeit in a public, rather than private, key.

Imagine my surprise when after a silence of one year, I received a final section, a continuation, of Echo's essay on Rena Grant's work. On a small note attached to the manuscript, Echo wrote: "Some final thoughts on Rena – and I suppose on *us*. The cure by love?" There was no signature.

VII

POST-SCRIPT TO ECHO'S TRANSCRIPT

After this essay was written I saw a note announcing another essay by Rena Grant soon to be published in **Lacanian Ink**. *I called and requested a copy before publication. The page proofs arrived: "Characterhysterics II: Repeating Oneself." It takes two to create hysteria: the model and the copy whose function is to obliterate the distinction between model and copy. Grant's essay is an uncanny reading of Robert Aldrich's 1962 film* **Whatever Happened to Baby Jane?** *starring Bette Davis and Joan Crawford. This essay develops her reading of womanliness and extends it to the film.*

In **Whatever Happened to Baby Jane?** *Bette Davis plays Jane Hudson, the child star who is never able to conquer her Oedipal complex. Desperately in love with Daddy, Jane, as an adult, falls for a man who is the perfectly perverse match for her. While Jane is the quintessential "daddy's girl," he is the quintessential "mommy's boy." Jane is impossible to like: she is an alcoholic, a thief, a sadist; she is caught in some childhood game she cannot win. She carries a doll of her likeness around and begs to be loved – all the while rejecting any overtures of kindness made to her. An aging Jane lives with her sister Blanche, a film star who, at the height of her career, was paralyzed in a car accident. The two women live alone in an old mansion and are visited only by their maid Elvira, and the accompanist Jane falls for. When neighbors attempt to visit Blanche, Jane turns them away.*

In an almost classical expression of the Lacanian mirror phase, the two sisters spend their lives vainly trying to find "the proper distance." As if obliquely commenting on the Papin sisters' spectacular murder, Aldrich is at pains to demonstrate that the domestic arrangement between the two sisters continually positions one as the handmaid of the other; Blanche has the money, but Jane has the mobility. Jane cooks and cleans and serves Blanche food; but the meals are dramas of sadism. But more than commenting on the strange psychosis of the Papin sisters, Aldrich's film also remarks the structure of the representation which brings that psychosis to view. The Papin sisters' murder of their bosses shocked France in part because of the way in which the actual drama of the maids' social relation became a mirror on the social for French intellectuals. Sartre, Beauvoir, Lacan, and Genet immortalized the sisters through a series of political, intellectual, psychic, and theatrical re-interpretations. In the United States women who are "mirrors" of social relations are film stars. Thus the sisters in Aldrich's meditation are not (un)dependable maids, but (in)dependent film stars. Rather than maids murdering their employers, in the film Jane kills the maid. But the structure of violence as the consequence of a failed sororal bond remains intact. Both pairs of sisters fail to find the proper distance. The proper distance in film, as against theatre or politico-economic arrangements, seems to involve most radically a question of perspective – literalized through camera angles. When it is impossible to distinguish the original film from its copy, and when the content of the film is about two sisters who are "paralyzed" by the memory of past performances, it is extremely difficult to know where the sisters' performances and "authentic" identities begin and end. In two brilliant scenes, Jane imitates her sister's voice on the telephone and the telephone auditor believes he is speaking to Blanche. But the film spectator can see the aural deception and thus has a different perspective on the "knowledge" being proffered by Jane.

Grant's reading of the film recasts the argument I am making here and accents several of its preoccupations. Grant reads Blanche and Jane in terms of hysterical and narcissistic identifications. She argues that the film demonstrates "the impossibility of the survival of the narcissistic woman; [and] the impossibility of the desires of two women being worked through in one movie" (Grant 1994: 83). At the end of the essay the editors have added: "To be continued in the next issue." Reading the line I shudder and remember Psalm 68, "And unto God the Lord belongeth the issues of death." In the future issue expect to see a new essay by the dead writer. As Barbara Johnson has noted, the voice of the dead, the voice that is published posthumously, gains its authority because it seems to issue from "the other side." On the side of the other, Rena Grant raises a question about what it would take for "the desires of two women to be worked through in one movie," in one essay, in one crumbling mansion, in one (bed)room.

Perhaps it is correct to emphasize that the impossibility of staging such a desire produces violence in and among women. Grant discusses Jane's murder of Elvira in this context. It is useful to recall that just as Riviere's patient uses the body of the black man as a cypher for her own sadism, so too does Jane use Elvira to express her rage and aggression towards her sister. In each case the white woman uses the black body as a means to escape guilt. Too "innocent" to have sexual desire for a black man, and too "nice" to kill her sister, Riviere's patient and Jane Hudson use black bodies to overcome guilt about their own bodies. Jane feels guilty because she can walk and dance and her sister cannot. She longs to stop moving and kills Elvira as a rehearsal because she cannot kill either Blanche or herself. Or at least not yet. Precisely because Jane has enough distance from Elvira she can kill her. Elvira's race and class position in relation to Jane make it impossible for Jane to confuse Elvira with her own ego-ideal or internal imago. This is one of the ways in which the psychic and political dimensions of racism are thoroughly entwined.

The aggression and violence between and among women is a complex response to a subtle but pervasive cultural misogyny. Since women are continually associated with the abject, with the hated, women must themselves develop an alternative system of value, of ethics, of love. Grant subtly insists that learning to love the unlovable would be the first step in such a project. She models what such a love would look like by loving Jane Hudson in her essay. The question posed by Grant's writing and by her life is a question about the limits we learn to put on love. Adrienne Rich, the great poet of women's love, stopped over these words: "I choose to love this time for once / with all my intelligence" (Rich 1978: 11). The speaker of the aptly titled poem, "Splittings," wants to abandon loving stupidly, one of the most consistent performances women have undertaken throughout the ages. Romantics argue that the greatest freedom that love offers us, finally, is the freedom from intelligence: and the liberation from logic, from proof, from the currency of the good wager is not something to abandon easily either. But the ability to abandon reason puts us in the realm of narcissistic identifications; more often than not white women in love form hysterical identifications. Often white women love using all their intelligence against their intelligence: arguing for a hopeless love requires deep imagination, spectacular logic. This is the structure of hysterical identification in mourning: the object is lost but cannot be entirely abandoned. Does love's glory depend precisely on its stupidity?

Grant refused to live a life in which she honored the single most powerful lesson offered to white girls: that they must learn, above all, to be lovable. Enshrined as the exemplar of the logic of the Oedipal complex on stage singing "Letter to Daddy," off stage Jane Hudson was enraged by the psychic and economic asymmetry of that same Oedipal complex. (Psychically she was a supplicant to the father; economically, she kept the father – and the family – eating.) For Jane, like many working women, the impossibility of that paradox produced somatic symptoms.

As an adult guzzling scotch, Jane plans her comeback. She rehearses singing and dancing the exact same routines that she did as a child; she forges Blanche's signature exactly in order to have exact copies made of her stage costumes. The pathos of the gesture of copying conceals the rage that it also produces. Like the Hollywood producers who flinch under the contract that requires them to make a film with Jane for each film they make with Blanche, the "legitimate" star, the spectator of Jane's private performance is soon enough disgusted. Jane is an embarrassment. A has-been. A lush. She is impossible. She cannot quite quit the stage and she cannot quite reclaim it. The well known off-screen rivalry between Joan Crawford and Bette Davis gives the on-screen competition between the sisters a supplemental edge of violence.

Much of the critical discussion of the film pivots around the sincerity of Blanche's "deathbed" confession. Lying on the sand wrapped in a blanket, looking as if she might seep into the grave, Blanche tells Jane that the accident that left Blanche paralyzed was not Jane's fault. She says she paralyzed herself.

Going further too, she says she is also responsible for Jane's "surpassing ugliness" (Grant 1994: 78). Jane, lost in her own reveries of the past, simply says, "You mean all this time we could have been friends?"

The question of what it might mean for women to be friends is a serious one. It must involve the repression of guilt – either a studiously performed repression or an "actual" one – in the end, the difference is immaterial. Grant reads Blanche's confession as an actual one. "[W]e assume throughout the movie that Blanche has been robbed of her career and paralyzed and has taken it nobly on account of what she describes as Jane's former youthful liveliness, but at the end, it becomes clear that it is Jane whose life has been ruined by her mistaken belief in her own guilt" (ibid.: 78). Grant takes Blanche's confession sincerely; she believes her. But I find Blanche's confession preposterous. It requires a large leap of faith to believe that she drove her car into Jane, missed, and, already paralyzed, dragged herself to the front of the car to make it look as if she had been hit by Jane. At the moment of her death, Blanche wants to give Jane a new life, a life without guilt. She tells Jane in effect: **I offer you the only thing I have left to give, precisely because it is not "mine" – your life. Live without mortifying guilt.** The status of Blanche's confession is, admittedly, densely ambiguous; for Blanche surely knows that Jane is guilty, if not of the accident that paralyzed Blanche, certainly of the murder that killed Elvira, the maid. Since so little of the communication between the sisters is direct, Blanche may be trying to forgive Jane for Elvira's murder at least as much as she is pardoning her for the accident. In placing herself as both the driver of the car and the one who was hit by the car, Blanche illustrates the doubling of her psychic position in relation to Jane. She understands that her confinement drove Jane mad, mad enough to murder Elvira. Jane killed Elvira because she could not kill Blanche. Just as Jane could neither leave the stage nor reclaim it, she could neither bear nor abandon Blanche. While Blanche was organically paralyzed, Jane was psychically crippled. The intensity of the sisters' identifications with each other made it impossible for one to make a move without the other. Thus when Blanche tells Jane that she herself drove the car that paralyzed her, she is trying to explain that she can see that the accident put Jane in a psychological wheelchair as confining as her own.

Jane's response to Blanche's confession, "You mean all this time we could have been friends?" returns us to my earlier question: **What would it take to invent another form of identification between women? One not read as confirming and conforming to the mutuality of "womanliness" at all? An identification in which resemblance was based not on physical or psychic overlaps but rather on uncertainty, doubt, the unfathomable? How might such a phantasmatically compelling identification be performed?** *Whatever Happened to Baby Jane?* presents one such identification.

For Grant the structure of identification between the two sisters can best be comprehended through technological repetitions and identifications, rather than *narrative ones. Noticing that the overhead long shot on the beach repeats the overhead shot in the bedroom when Blanche discovers the dead rat Jane has served her for lunch, Grant effectively underlines the point that the film asks us to see both women from a position that is, literally, impossible within the terms of cinematic realism – but they are the only terms that melodrama can employ. If we were on the beach, we could not see Jane from the position the camera does; if we were in the bedroom we could not see Blanche spinning, dancing really, in her wheelchair. It is this impossibility, the failure of ocular perspective to capture the social-psychic relation between Jane and Blanche that, in my view but not Grant's, makes it impossible to know also what happened to put Blanche in the wheelchair. The structure of their identification, in other words, cannot be seen from within that structure. The film must create an outside, a beyond, in order to display the complexity of the sisters' identification.*

Throughout the film, Jane longs to return to her earlier stardom, but she recognizes that she is beyond it even as she seeks to repeat it. That beyond – the accelerating motion of time and life – has made it necessary for Jane to find a way to still life. The meals she prepares for Blanche resemble nothing so much as those traditional still lives so obsessively captured by nineteenth-century painting: serving her sister a dead bird and a dead rat are assuredly sadistic gestures. But they are a kind of psychic painting in which the cook rehearses for the death of the one who eats what has been stilled, killed, and prepared for her. In this sense, Jane rehearses killing Blanche by killing "for" her. And this is what Blanche attempts to forgive in her confession on the beach. She sees that Jane's murder of Elvira is a form of address to Blanche, that she is the recipient of the gift of death.

Jane progressively paralyzes Blanche: she pulls the plug from the phone and from the household buzzer; she ties her up, tapes her mouth, suspends her from the traction pull above the bed. She is "drying" her model, preparing it for the final pose. Once Blanche's absolute stillness is assured, Jane can finally move. On the beach in front of the crowd, Jane moves beyond her well rehearsed choreography into a fluid jouissance, an improvised choreography whose gentle circles absorb the spectator's upsetting memory of Blanche's frantic spinning in her wheel chair. Dancing with such fluidity, Jane seems to inspire the camera itself to dance up and away from the scene it records. No longer substituting and standing in for the eye of any characters in the narrative, the camera approaches its own "beyond" and records something akin to "pure" sight. (Such "purity" is itself registered by the conventions of the "beyond": the long overhead shot is easily recuperated as a traditional view of "omniscience" – the eye of God in heaven.)

Pure jouissance, Jane's dance is (it does not "signify"– it is) an entry into the "beyond" of the pleasure principle. That Jane achieves this is remarkable. Looking like "nothing on earth" as Grant puts it, Jane Hudson dances toward a jouissance that critical interpretation, within its compass of rationality, can only label pathological. Without romanticizing psychoses, I nonetheless want to suggest that there is something heroic in Jane's dance. While Ismene refused to honor her bond to Antigone, Blanche and Jane do honor theirs to each other. What that decision produces is an intense melodrama, which is not the same as tragic theatre. Is melodrama "better" than tragedy? Perhaps not. Yet the excess and repetition of that form might hold something worth touching. Jane's dance, if only for a moment, brings into being a jouissance that transcends the killing stillness of womanliness as mimicry, masquerade, repeated disguise.[8]

VIII

A FRAGMENT, CONTINUED

When I read the final portion of Echo's transcript I was quite taken aback. The tone had changed. She was no longer questioning so intently. She had, it seemed to me, settled a few things. I felt confident she would not be tempted by suicide anymore. And yet nonetheless her analysis of Grant's reading was itself a template for her own unresolved psychic conflicts. Before turning to them, I would like to "confess" that the change in her tone prompted me to re-read my earlier writing about her. I was surprised to discover that in my discussion of her dream my own tone changes. I think I had been laboring under the idea that her mimicry of me was blocking the analytic work. While I remain convinced that was true, I now see that her mimicry of me, in and of itself, did not have to bring the analysis to an end. Interpreting her mimicry as her way of addressing and copying "me," I was blind to the activation of my own narcissism, my own narcissistic belief that I was the source of *the* "psychoanalytic utterance" spoken in the session. But I do not want to speculate here on the reasons for this. I believe it is more helpful to turn again to Echo's essay.

Echo cannot bring herself to believe Grant's interpretation of the film's final scene on the beach. It is obvious that both Grant and Echo use the film as a way of testing their hypotheses about themselves as women and both implicitly take Davis as a surrogate for Grant. Grant finds it necessary to believe that she is not guilty; that she suffered for a crime she never committed. In order for that exoneration to be grant-ed, however, another woman must admit that she crippled herself. Thus, a double psychic positioning is at work in Grant's reading of the film: Jane did not actually commit a crime, yet she nonetheless believed herself guilty – if only of not believing strongly enough in her own innocence, her own right to freedom.

Echo insists that Jane – and by implication Grant – has achieved something profoundly transcendental in her dance at the end of the film. Echo gives no attention to the ethical implications of her remarks about the beyond of jouissance. Her need to believe that Grant's life was not wasted motivates her reading of the end of Aldrich's melodrama. In my opinion, the excessive weight Echo accords to Jane's "achievement" at the end of the film expresses her own guilt about surviving after Grant's death. One of the consequences of survivor's guilt is a remarkable compulsion to romanticize and make heroic those who have not survived.

I am not competent to engage in film criticism and so I cannot really evaluate the quality of the two arguments in this regard. But there is an important aspect of Echo's case history that can be helpfully clarified in relation to the film. I have no way of knowing whether or not Echo saw *Whatever Happened to Baby Jane?* before she dreamt her dream of being switched at birth. But surely the dream itself is an elaboration of the narrative structure of the film: two women playing each other's part, miscast in one another's narratives. Bound together out of guilt and need, both women are embarrassed by their dependency and psychically alarmed by the task of breaking free. The women are able to recognize that their bond has created a dynamic in which one of them apparently must be made still in order for the other to give herself permission to move, to live. Perhaps Jane's tragedy is her blindness to the possibility of another way of identifying with her sister. It is from this perspective that Echo's haunting question must be addressed: *"does love's glory depend precisely on its stupidity?"*

What I most regret about my work with Echo is how thoroughly we concentrated on her writing. Her "speech" was already performed on the page and we suffered the illusion that she herself was "embodied" in that writing. I see now what a big mistake that was. In the mythological story of Echo, as a result of Juno's curse, Echo loses her ability to generate speech; she can only repeat what she hears. She cannot express her longing for Narcissus. Unable to give voice to her desire, Echo is killed by Narcissus. There may be a compressed theory of sexual difference at work in the myth: Narcissus loved what was added to himself, his reflection. He thinks it is form, body. Echo cannot give form to her love, she can only echo what he says. One of the most common anxieties of academic women I have treated is that they are lovable, valuable, important, only when they are producing work, echoing back what (and that) they have learned. This anxiety was at work in Riviere's patient's flirting performance which she took up immediately after delivering public lectures. While in the main I agree with Riviere's assessment of the causes of her patient's acting out, it may also be that Riviere's patient was allowing herself to be dumb, even idiotic, as a reward for her hard work.

Perhaps she was reassuring herself that she could be loved even if she never did another bit of work in her life. Riviere's patient hoped that the men in her audience would not take her intelligence as a strike against her. Among academic women, one would have thought, the question of intelligence would not have produced similar anxieties. But about this too I now see I was somewhat blind.

And perhaps my own blindness is a response to Echo's question, "does love's glory depend precisely on its stupidity?" I was unable, or perhaps unwilling, to press Echo about her cathexis with Rena Grant. I suspect I feared that it echoed a bit too loudly the cathetic bond between Echo and myself, a bond I came to believe was choking her "real" ability to speak to me. But perhaps for both Narcissus and me the true problem stemmed from our inability to distinguish between the context of the utterance and its source and motivation. Mistaking content for source, we risk losing the love within the echo. Both my patient and her namesake wanted to be fully introjected before they were lost or mourned. Knowing full well that such introjection was impossible, Echo sometimes attempted *to be* the "something in common" that she knew others wanted. And when she echoed my own language, perhaps I was somehow threatened by precisely that commonality in a room in which I was paid to cure her, *to be* something other than her equal, her sister, her self. The theory of the transference and the counter-transference that I learned in my clinical training has a certain repression built into its structure. The homosexual attachments that develop between the analyst and the analysand have been discussed in relation to men, but the discussion about women remains in an embryonic stage. One reason for writing this essay, and using Echo's transcript so liberally, is to prompt further discussion of this important and neglected area of our practice.

IX

POST-FACE, A RETURN TO THE COMPOSER OF THE SET UP

I was reading Freud and thinking about Hopkins while thirty-six women in Las Vegas, Nevada found themselves in a hotel hallway where drunk, leering military officers mauled their breasts and groped their genitals. The powerful public humiliation at the heart of this misogyny, a misogyny expressed sexually and in front of an audience, is based on identification, crude resemblance. Like me, the Tailhook victims have female bodies – breasts, hips, vaginas, soft skin. In moving from my name, to my institutional affiliates, to my sexualized body, my identifications become progressively hysterical, and as my drive to live overwhelms the death drive, my identifications also move from whole objects to partial ones. To put it slightly differently, my identifications, hysterical and narcissistic, move from the logic of metaphor to the logic of metonomy.[9]

White women's masquerade of sexual innocence and racial benignity is constantly performed in relation to the whole, to the Symbolic whose foundation is determined by the simultaneous inclusion and exclusion of white women. White women's relation to the Symbolic is riven with ambivalence. Patriarchal institutions, from the university to the military, encourage white women's identifications with them to become hysterical rather than narcissistic. When women form hysterical identifications and then lose them they retain the object-cathexis through an introjection of a partial object. Then they have a difficult time abandoning that partial object because it has become part of them. Narcissistic identifications can be abandoned – although not easily – because the object remains whole, not partial, and its loss activates the aggressivity of the ego. Hysterical identifications limit white women's ability to convert their mourning into militancy.

The political efficacy of some women's grief may involve the public performance of a layered and intimate voice tuned to the repetitious structure of that grief. Theatrical and literary performances, in their rhythmic dwelling on repetitions and citations, may be capable of rewriting the unhappy story of hysterical or narcissistic identifications between women. But such a rewriting must begin with an imitative, repetitious display of the symptom itself: for the cure by analysis must be accompanied by the cure by love. And love is, among other things, the performance of belief in repetition – that the beloved will return, that you each will come again.

The imitation and mimicry at the heart of repetition is motivated by the desire to retouch, revise, re-interpret how one has lost, is lost. Critical writing, with its citations, quotations, allusiveness, and intertextual resonance is a field of grief and longing. Exposing the logic of partial objects, like my high school nun's lesson about Hopkins' poem anatomizing partial souls, might enact a different relation to the creative cure, the cure by love. Re-covering the partiality (in both senses) of the identification with the partial object might allow for a different form of transference. I hope it may go some way toward thinking a psychoanalysis of grief responsive to sexual and racial difference. In the current climate, which D.A. Miller has called "morbidity culture," this is an enormously complex and urgent task. Here I can only write the words I remember I want to hear again now that their authors have stopped writing and speaking. My grief is here with me as I sit down in the quiet of my study and quote and write about Rena, Riviere, Freud, and Hopkins himself:

Ah! as the heart grows older
It will come to such sights colder
By and by, nor spare a sigh
And yet you *will* weep and know why.
Though worlds of wanwood leafmeal lie;
Now no matter, child, the name:
Sorrow's springs are the same.

I no longer believe that "sorrow's springs are the same" and I've long ago lost touch with the nun who first taught me Hopkins' lines. What is the same is that "Rena Grant is dead." In telegrams, letters, the notes to critical essays. I can still hear her voice, with my partial ear, Echo.

APPENDIX A

TRANSCRIPT FROM ECHO'S ESSAY

"Let Daddy Do It For You" returns to Joan Riviere's "Womanliness as a Masquerade" essay, first published in 1929. [...] Riviere, who was a patient of both Freud and his biographer, Ernest Jones, also became one of Freud's English translators. Riviere's relation with psychoanalysis is bizarre: she was badly analyzed by Jones between 1915–21 (with a year off because she had tuberculosis). Jones botched the counter-transference and in January 1921 sent Freud a letter asking him to continue the analysis; in the same letter he mentioned she was a translator. Freud agreed to analyze her, but his counter-transference was explicitly based on his dream of how she might be able to help him, that is, how she might aid in the reproduction and dissemination of his work. After analyzing her briefly, Freud wrote to Jones in May 1922 to say she would be a great help to their work – "[she] is a real power and can be put to work by a slight expenditure of kindness and recognition" (11 May 1922; quoted in Hughes 1991). Freud invited her to become a member of the Glossary Committee of the International Psychoanalytic Society – the other members were Freud, Jones, Anna Freud, and James and Alix Strachey.* (Riviere had never gone to University.) This committee defined how the technical words of psychoanalysis were to be translated – ego, id, cathexis, and so on. As well as translating, Riviere wrote many articles herself, saw patients, and helped spread the work of Melanie Klein. She translated "Mourning and Melancholia" into English for the first time in 1925.

---

*Although Echo seems to think this was a form of exploitation, I happen to know that Riviere herself was delighted to serve on the Glossary Committee. The only awkwardness she felt was in relation to Jones, with whom she had an unsuccessful transference. And when she first met Freud I suspect she suggested to him that she was interested in becoming an analyst, as so many of Freud's patients were. (Doctor's note.)

NOTES

1 Lacan himself proposes that this originary grief is the engine that drives the Symbolic itself. Whereas most of Western culture assumes that grief is motivated by death, Lacan suggests that it is motivated by the acquisition of sight and speech, a dual inheritance offered as compensation for the loss of *jouissance* that occurs when we enter the Symbolic. Such a theory correctly reflects the triple consequences of postlapsarian Being as outlined in *Genesis*: the unavoidability of Original Sin; the degradation from divine vision into "mere" sight – "The eyes of both them were opened"; and the exile from Paradise. While much attention has been given to the ways in which Judaism informs Freud's work, less attention has been given to the striking ways in which Christianity (more particularly French Catholicism) informs Lacan's. For a brief discussion see Clément (1983). It is more than instructive to read Lacan's "The Mirror Stage" and *Genesis* together.

2 Because women are made to be so aware of their bodies, physical mimicry operates in both narcissistic and hysterical identifications outlined by Freud.

3 Freud argues that grief taps psychic formulations of identification which are either hysterical or narcissistic. Since Freud's definition of hysteria developed from his treatment of women, and his understanding of narcissism was derived largely from case studies and theories of homosexuality, his concept of grief is itself based on a dual notion of female and "aberrant" sexuality. But since female sexuality was, within Freudian theory, something of an aberrant terrain anyway, one wonders if Freud's identification with homosexuality and female sexuality is hysterical or narcissistic.

4 The singularity of "the cure by love" is set against "a cure" that psychoanalysis might be able to perform – one curative route among many.

5 And on my own counter-transference with her. She had something to teach me but it is only now that I feel ready to learn it.

6 By "obligated to die" I mean to say she felt the logic of mimesis more acutely than almost anyone I've ever encountered. She was, therefore, extremely fearful of it.

7 I am skipping quite a long section of Echo's essay here which is not relevant to the analysis at hand. I transcribe the most important part of it in Appendix A.

8 Lynda Hart (1994) has described this passage into the beyond; see especially her chapter, "Surpassing the Word: Aileen Wournos."

9 As Jean Laplanche has brilliantly demonstrated, the elaboration of sexual identity proceeds only after the self-preservation drive emerges from its instinctual function:

> "The two essential phases here are a *metaphorization of the aim*, which brings us from the ingestion of food, at the level of self-preservation, to fantasmatic incorporation and introjection as actual psychical processes, this time at the level of the drive – and, on the other hand, what might be termed ... a *metonymization of the object*, which substituting for milk what is directly contiguous to it (the breast) introduces that hiatus which allows us to say without contradiction that "finding the object is refinding it," since the rediscovered object is in fact not the lost one, but its metonym".
>
> (Laplanche 1976: 137)

8

Infected eyes: Dying Man With A Movie Camera, *Silverlake Life: The View from Here*

Because I cannot now love you body to body I will try to love you in words. Hand to eye, my fingers playing lightly across your closed eyes, tongue to ear. Can you still hear my voice there? Sliding across the screens we dreamt we'd make our different dreams live on, I pause and feel the depth of the screen that keeps my body here and yours there. When we made our plans, the screen was flat. But you went right through yours (I saw you leach under the silver light) and now all my computer screens, smoke screens, are open orifices and I am like Alice again falling through.

You used to say girls didn't understand the allure of holes. You were sometimes wrong.

We know something about slipping in and out of cells, animate and still. Like Gretel I want to map my trip into the dense forest of you, dropping these words so I can get back out. But I've read her story (so many stories now) and you taught me fairy tales are forced to be tragedies to keep us from wanting to be fairies. Words and pictures, smoke and scotch, me and you, here and there, then and now, how I want to be with you still, frame by frame, hand over hand, word by word. Burrowing into the hole you thought I was blind to, sliding out, I now know that the architecture of the screen that holds our bodies is never ever flat. Take one.

PURPOSE

To rethink our own onto-theological relation to dying; more specifically, to our own deaths. Such thinking is speculation in the key of grief; it requires a passion to know our relation to loss more intimately, more rigorously. I am calling this thinking "performative" because it enacts the difficult force of a grief which simultaneously mourns the lost object and ourselves. Inside and Outside. We can perhaps touch the architecture of this blind grief by rehearsing the psychic substitutions at the heart of cinematic and sexual identifications.

PROPOSITION

Let's suppose that lesbians and gay men in the contemporary United States have a particularly potent relation to grief. Exiled from the Law of the Social upon which heterosexuality is based, many gay men and lesbians may have introjected the passionate hatred of mainstream homophobia and taken up an embattled, aggressive, and complex relation to the death drive. The aggressiveness of this relation may make it possible for us to survive our (first) deaths. While we wait for the next, we perform queer acts.

CASE STUDY

The film *Silverlake Life: The View From Here* (1993) exposes what is at issue, ontologically, politically, aesthetically, and affectively, in the dying brought home to us by AIDS. For those of us who have survived our own deaths, there is something at once compelling and (re)traumatizing about watching the other die. This is one of the things that the film makes possible, and one of the things upon which the film insists.

EXPOSITION

Tom Joslin died of AIDS on July 1, 1991. Mark Massi, his lover of twenty-two years, was with him when he died. Eleven months later Mark Massi died of AIDS.

Shortly after his diagnosis, Joslin began a video diary and plotted a film that would document his life and death. Intended in part as a love letter to Massi, and in part as a political statement about the impact of AIDS on the material, familial, and cultural body, the film is also a thanatography, a study in dying.[1] After the deaths of Joslin and Massi, their friend, Peter Friedman, a former film student of Joslin's, edited over forty hours of video into the two-hour film, *Silverlake Life: The View from Here.*

The view is grim. Formerly routine trips to the supermarket are physical endurance tests requiring between aisle rests in the car. Family dynamics are psychically grueling, fittingly nuclear. Eating is a game of conning the body into keeping something in. Taking medicine is a discipline that demands vigilant attention every thirty minutes, around the clock, day in and day out. And yet, despite that vigilance, the end result is the same: dead, too fast, too painfully, too young.[2]

Silverlake Life accomplishes several important political tasks. Reversing the mainstream cultural imperative that constructs AIDS as shameful, humiliating, and obscene, the film gives the dwindling materiality of the AIDS body an awesome ocular weight. It is impossible to look away from Joslin's body as it lives its dying. *Silverlake Life* renders Joslin's consciousness about his death palpable, factual and formal. Positioned as a witness to the return of the culturally repressed body, the spectator watches a film that eventually is not visibly, materially, "there." The film insists that the spectator look at a body, a phantasmal body that cannot be, and *therefore* is not, screened. (The spectator is asked to look at a body that cannot Be – a phantasmal celluloid body that can be generated in film but perhaps not in actuality.) Joslin's screened body becomes a means to expose the spectator's screen memory of his or her own encounter (in the temporal phantasm in which past and future are one) with death.

We know people die. Most of us have already been a witness, sometimes eager, sometimes reluctant, to someone else's death. The uncanniness of the encounter staged in *Silverlake Life*, however, derives from the fact that it occurs across, through, and on the body of the film. Meeting within the luminous space of the filmed image, Joslin and the spectator engage in a transference/counter-transference dynamic that transforms the film from a documentary into a new manifesto for a politically motivated talking cure.

Joslin's insistence on finding an image, creating a record, chronicling his night sweats, exposing his lesions and measuring his weight loss, repeats the insistent search for a record, a form of learning the body's traumas, that led to the invention of psychoanalysis. Anna O. and Breuer, after coming to understand that bodily trauma required a temporal order, "invented" psychoanalysis as the way to give time to the body. Similarly, Joslin comes to believe that making *Silverlake Life: The View from Here* will not only "capture" his life on film but it will fashion and prepare an ending, a way for him to leave his life. Like psychoanalysis, Joslin's film gives time to his body. Transferring his life to film, Joslin renders his body a body of film. This body can be edited, replotted, revised. Near the end of the film, at the memorial service, a large still photograph of Joslin sits near the altar, in place of a coffin. As his film continues, he is captured in this static print as friends and spectators remember him and weep in waves of grief.

The transfer Joslin undertakes from life to film generates and guides the spectator's parallel transference: the viewer's focus moves from the body of Joslin to a body the film can gesture toward but cannot actually project. In the luminous light of Joslin's and Massi's mourning is the outline of an earlier grief – the one to which we fear we will be returned in the future.

In the only scene in which Joslin and Massi participate in the formal talking cure, the analyst asks them to describe (what else?) how they are feeling. Massi describes his frustration with Joslin's lack of interest in taking his medicine and Joslin says that he does not feel "desperate" about taking his medicine. All of his desperation, he says, is reserved for making *Silverlake Life*. The making of the film, rather than the taking of his pills, is the way to enhance, if not prolong, his life. Even if the making of *Silverlake Life* is a kind of talking cure, the cure is "too late" for the bodies of Joslin and Massi. Death cannot be avoided. But perhaps the spectator's encounter with Joslin's death can effect a transference beyond the usual notions of the limit of the body's time. Filmmaking is not a homeopathic "cure" for AIDS. But at least in this instance it is an empathetic interrogation of what it is to die, and by extension, of what it is to witness death.

Silverlake Life resolutely and imaginatively re-examines the link between the temporality of death and the temporality of cinema.[3] In that re-examination, death and cinema become, bizarrely, comforting bedfellows.

Theories of photography, and especially those proposed by Susan Sontag and Roland Barthes, have emphasized the link between death and the still image captured by the photographic camera. Surprisingly, however, theories of cinema have been reluctant to link the moving image to death, presumably because death, like photography, stops the body, arresting its movement through time.[4] *Silverlake Life* suggests that this link between photography and death might be misleading. The film suggests that time stops without a living, moving body, but that the body itself does not stop moving; cinema is one place where the still-moving body leaves a trace. For this reason, it might make sense to think of a cinema for the dead. Such a cinema has a specifically curative appeal in relation to mourning. For if humans come to grief over the impossibility of stilling death, arresting its progress as it envelopes the body, a cinema for the dead allows us to imagine that precisely because death is unstillable we will not be separated from it. If one of the things we grieve over is the end signified by death, a cinema for the dead reveals that such an end keeps moving, and does not end. *Silverlake Life* reminds us that we still have no idea what death "is" – what Being the being of death comprises – but the film wagers that the dead body might well have some movement in it. The focus of the film is on cinematic time. The "theory" of time proposed by *Silverlake Life* is one that raises a general question about the status and function of art as memorial.

I want to emphasize that the remarks I am making here refer only to portrait photography and to the filmic documentary. I am not speaking of Hollywood cinema or photographic enterprises that refuse the human subject. I am, in this sense, interested in the implicit anthropomorphic longing that haunts mimetic art. The particular grief that portrait photography exposes – *anticipated* grief, as in *Silverlake Life* – is inherited from painting, the origin of which is described by Pliny the Elder. The story goes like this: Butades, a Corinthian potter, had a daughter (whom Pliny does not name but commentators refer to as Dibutades) who was in love with a sailor. One night, after he told her he would be going on a voyage, she drew in outline the silhouette of his face thrown by a lamp on the wall above her bed. Knowing how much she would miss her sailor in the future, Dibutades, grief-stricken, began to miss him even before he left. However, his image, the outline of his profile, would keep her grief at bay – for through his image, he would remain with her. (Butades, a remarkably friendly father for this type of tale, sculpted a bas-relief on this outline which is said to have been preserved in the Shrine of the Nymphs until the destruction of Corinth by Mummius.) But Dibutades' drawing held more than a profile. What she was tracing, as clearly as she was tracing the sailor's nose and chin, was the hook and cleft of her own longing to stop time, to hold it back, so she might hold him longer. The pressure of that desire left an impression on the wall, which stood long after both Dibutades and her sailor ceased to see.[5]

What is preserved in the still image, and the "instamatic" photograph in particular, is the compression of the present and the resistance to releasing the moment into the past without securing its return. (The unconscious functions in a similar but less literal way.) The photograph serves both to "conjure" the moment, the scene in which the photograph was taken, and to take the moment out of time – to render it the subject of new narratives, to give it a new temporal logic, a new causal relation to the autobiographical, in the largest sense of that term.

Cinema, as against still photography, has a more complex relation to narrative and causality. Projected, seen, and made visible across time, cinematic time occupies two distinct temporal fields: diegetic time and the time of the film's projection. Moreover, the technological possibilities of the movie camera, especially those of reverse, slow, and accelerated motion, reveal a view of time that are optical and psychic possibilities, but, as far as we can tell, not actual ones. Thus cinematic time forces us to wonder what we actually mean by actuality, just as psychoanalysis forces us to wonder what we actually mean by reality.

The uncanny achievement of *Silverlake Life* is the creation of a cinema for the dead.[6] What the film suggests is that the cinema for the dead contains images of the past that flow and unfurl in the vast expanse of a time that no longer moves. The films of one's life no longer run forward or backward: all the images are off their reels. Infinity is the slow shifting of a lifetime's record of film, shot at twenty-four frames per second, into an endless number of sequences with sound synch, off synch, voice-overs, in a countless number of sequences, montages, collages, whose end cannot ever host "us" because we can never arrive there, even in death. And that, in an odd way, is terribly consoling.

THE FORMAL PAPER

My title alludes to Dziga Vertov's 1929 masterpiece, *The Man with a Movie Camera*. Among the first great city documentaries, Vertov's film celebrates the vital motion of the bustling, productive city. For Vertov, the movie camera is the instrument, par excellence, with which to record the energy of motion itself – slow, fast, reverse, athletic, industrial, mechanical. In her impassioned reading of Vertov's filmmaking, Annette Michelson explores his extensive use of reverse motion in *The Man* in terms of a new epistemological achievement: reverse motion renders causality visible (Michelson 1972). Vertov reverses time by playing action – motion – backwards. Thus we see an image of a train entering the station, and then immediately thereafter we see the cameraman and the camera on the track shooting the image – not the simple reverse motion which would show the train pulling out of the station, but the reversal of the order of composition. First we see the composition of the shot fully manifest (in other words we see the completed image first), and then we see the past – the process of staging the shot that preceded the image in time, the past that made the shot come into being. The first shot we see, we realize retrospectively is in the past of our viewing and in the future of the process of composition that Vertov methodically exposes to our view as well.

Vertov's composition helps us see that a fundamental drive of moving photography is to create a cinematic memory. The very "presentness" of the current image, the visual field that fills the screen, threatens to become dislodged from the previous image. Hollywood cinema has dealt with this problem by using narrative cinema, and especially "genre" pictures, to keep spectators remembering. Vertov, and Joslin after him, discover that the problem of cinematic memory (a problem of time) instigates the production of an architectural interiority within the screen itself (a resolution in space). Behind the image of the train that the spectator sees is a previously positioned camera, and behind that, another previously positioned camera. Behind the present image then, a past, and behind that, another past. The *mise-en-abyme* of spatial and temporal regression that Vertov exposes leads to a dizzying transfer between time and space more generally. As the spectator sees the dimensions of the present image's composition (a camera observed by a camera one cannot see in a spatial field that frames the shot's composition), the "flatness" of the screen becomes illusory. In creating architectural depth for the screen, Vertov maps the interiority of what seems to be a flat surface. This is the lesson Joslin learns from Vertov. But as we shall see, Joslin's map takes him inside his body, more specifically, his eye. A bizarre form of cinematic autopsy, Joslin's exposure of his injured eye returns us to the etymological roots of autopsy – to see for oneself. *Perhaps*

the eye's deepest desire is to see its own stillness. Just as we want to be
loved "for" ourselves and not for what we do, so too does the eye long to
be loved, and to love itself, for being, rather than seeing. In Silverlake Life,
Joslin's eye enters a field in which it remains in touch with Being long after
it ceases to be.

Vertov's complex meditation on the nature of causality, Michelson argues, transforms Vertov from a magician in the tradition of the Lumière brothers into an epistemologist. This transformation, Michelson maintains, was decisive for the future of cinema. Vertov was able "to recognize the privileged character of the medium as being in itself the promise of an incomparable, an unhoped for, grasp upon the nature of causality" (Michelson 1972: 66–7). The movie camera can manipulate time: it slows time down, speeds it up, and perhaps most spectacularly, reverses the sequential, forward direction of time. In the age of AIDS "an incomparable, an unhoped for, grasp upon the nature of causality" is of more than cinematic interest.

Our emphasis on causality in relation to AIDS is itself "a symptom" of the virus. The announcement of the disease contains within it the question of cause: How and when was I infected? The temporal index is especially crucial because one wants to measure the duration of the virus's incubation against a projection of its triumph. To take one typical example of the link between cause and diagnosis, Harold Brodkey begins his essay, "To My Readers", with this: "I have AIDS. I am surprised that I do. I have not been exposed since the nineteen-seventies, which is to say that my experiences, my adventures in homosexuality took place largely in the nineteen-sixties, and since then I relied on time and abstinence to indicate my degree of freedom from infection and to protect others and myself" (Brodkey 1993: 80). The moment of infection revises the acts that comprise one's (sexual) history. Under the new interpretation of infection, those acts may become newly dangerous as they wake from the slumber of a forgotten history, forgotten sex. A positive diagnosis necessitates that images of the past be re-developed. Was that body there or there? Did we shower or were those tears I remember? Did we meet in the early part of that year or the latter?

Embedded within *Silverlake Life* is an interrogation of causality. This interrogation includes questions routinely associated with "the gay lifestyle" – "What causes homosexuality?" and "What causes AIDS?" Remarkably, the film also broaches questions about the body's time that upset the causal logic according to which "living" and "dying" are rendered separate states of being. Temporality constructs a causality that is apparently precise in regard to life and death: the body lives before it dies. The living body is healthy; without health it dies. In terms of terminal illness, death happens when the illness within the body surmounts the health within the body. (The "cause" of death is insufficient health.) This conclusion seems rather obvious. But the epis-temology of cinema suggests another way of thinking about causality. Cinematic "documentation" appeals to us because it seems to give us another chance, another way to order our time. The reversal of time is made apparent through the visual reversal of action, of motion. What makes time's "negative" visible is reversed action. Within the epistemology of cinema it may well be that we die more than once; perhaps we do indeed survive our deaths. Perhaps dying happens not at the singular end of living, but, if not frequently, more than once. And perhaps this is why we like to go to the cinema: if we can reproject the film, maybe we can play the films of our dead and of our death over and over again.

If still photography takes moments out of time, movie cameras take histories. Part of the allure of the movie camera, as against the still photograph, is that it makes visually evident the possibilities of reversing time, of having history back. For Vertov in 1929, those possi-bilities were embraced with exuberant joy. For Joslin in the late 1980s, these possibilities are embraced with tentative hope. Employing cinema as a way to grieve and to confront the physical and psychic limits of dying, Joslin challenges cinema to give time, his time, to the living. In this transference, Joslin also allows us to sense the supplement – the residue of the past that awaits us as we sink into projected scenarios of our own deaths.

Cinema promises a giddy power; it allows time itself to be edited, cut, replayed. For *Silverlake Life*, as for Vertov's masterpiece, much of the art of the film is its editing. Friedman edited images Joslin and Massi created. Joslin, however, also wrote a script for the film that contained material Joslin was never able to shoot. Massi, moreover, filmed Joslin after he died. He also recorded the funeral and the day that Joslin's ashes "came home." Friedman, in turn, filmed Massi five months after Joslin's death, and turned the forty hours of footage into a two-hour film. In an interview conducted by the Public Broadcasting Corporation, Friedman emphasized that his editing style differs from Joslin's. No doubt, part of what he is mourning through his editing is the loss of Joslin's. But by looking at, manipulating and editing Joslin's images, Friedman renders them no longer, strictly speaking, "his." It is a triple seeing – Friedman's view of Joslin's and Massi's images – that we see. The formal transfer-ence from Joslin's style to Friedman's rehearses the psychic transference at the heart of the film in which the image of Joslin's body, as it approaches death, becomes at once opaque and dense with images that do not "originate" with Joslin's shots. These other images are the specta-tor's own projections of other bodies that are not, achingly not, there.

Friedman's editing task required that he look at an immense amount of footage and then carefully organize – and repeatedly look back and forth across – the history Joslin had recorded. This formal and technical process leaves its most telling trace in Friedman's use of reverse motion. In the double look of reverse motion, cinema promises us a chance to revise that which has passed. Vertov defined his own filmic ambition as an effort

> to film, in slow motion, that which has been, owing to the manner in which it is perceived in natural speed, not absolutely unseen, but missed by sight, subject to oversight. An attempt to approach slowly and calmly that original intensity which is not given in appearance, but from which things and processes have nonetheless in turn derived.
>
> (Vertov quoted in Michelson 1972: xix)

The point of such a slow methodical looking is to return us, as the approach of death often does, to the "original intensity" of the everyday. The things that are routine and assumed – eating, sleeping, going to the grocery store – are, from the heightened point of view shared by the movie camera and the dying, returned to their original intensity. The desire to look again is such a compulsion that Joslin suggests that it, like the blink reflex, might continue after death. Looking again, the intensity of the thing returns even more fully than when it originally appeared to our distracted eyes. It may well be that the movie camera's greatest technological achievement is that it can ease our dying. It allows us to see what our busy vital eyes are too blind to see, and what our closing eyes most fear losing as they cease to see.

The affinity between slow motion and reverse motion is more than technical. In *Silverlake Life*, the emphasis is on reverse motion. Michelson likens reverse motion to an aspect of classical rhetoric: "The figure of speech known in classical rhetoric as hysteron proteron, that figure by which what should come last is put first, positioning or arranging things in reverse of their natural order" (Michelson 1972: 67). This device is employed throughout *Silverlake Life*. The film opens with Massi on the couch talking to Friedman about Joslin's death. Initiating the story "on the couch," the film underlines the connection between psychoanalysis and editing: two different methods for examining the past, for revising the temporal, causal structure of one's autobiography. (Perhaps the camera's method leads to autopsy, seeing from the inside, while the talking cure leads to psyche-soul-reading.) Friedman's conversation with Massi on the couch was the last to be shot and the first to be seen (of the footage this film projects). But unlike the traditional use of cinematic flashback, the images are not simply shown in reverse chronological order. Rather, the "end" is given in the beginning of a film that goes on to discover ever earlier beginnings and later endings. Enfolded within *Silverlake Life* are clips from the beginning and the ending of one of Joslin's early films, *Blackstar* (the title letters are themselves written in reverse order, in a mirror – BLACK STAR, created about fifteen years before *Silverlake Life*. But within this "original" documentary of Joslin and Massi's love, there is another "original." Enfolded within *Blackstar* is a sequence of home movies created about twenty years before *Blackstar*. Behind the past, there is another past that the projection of the "first" past allows us to glimpse. Joslin's screen will hold his memories, even if they can only be other screen memories.

Thus the film illustrates a kind of perpetual unfolding of the past within the past (what French gives us in the pluperfect). As the narrative telos of the film moves closer and closer to Joslin's death, the film itself expands and stretches toward a fuller embrace of the past. The future that death signifies – "the void" as Joslin calls it – reveals the endlessness of the (filmic) past. That which has been seen in the past returns as the end begins to end. That "ending" is itself re-seen by the camera and then revised again by the editor, usually many times. The end of a filmmaker's life is not the end of his film. In the transference enacted across the body of the film, the making of the film, like the making of the memory of the filmmaker's life, continues in the unfolding present. For that continuity to continue, the filmmaker's filmic body, the film itself, must be replayed, revised, reprojected. In psychoanalytic transference, the analyst stands in for the subject with whom one is engaged; the analysis stages the analysand's confrontation with the subject who is not there. In *Silverlake Life*, Joslin's dying stages the spectator's confrontation with the deaths he or she wants to repress – the spectator's own, and/or the memories and anticipations of the deaths of our beloveds. Just as the transferential relation in the psychoanalytic encounter scrambles time so that the analysand is living in both a new past and a repetitive present, so too does *Silverlake Life* both revise the past and amplify the dull beating declension wrought by the AIDS crisis: he died, she is dying, they will die.

The spectator of *Silverlake Life* must create a narrative chronology out of the temporally scrambled shots. That chronology is in turn elaborated through a pre-existing narrative of "illness" and "health" which is aggressively teleological in relation to terminal diseases. We watch the life of Joslin unfold through our own lens of "terminal illness" – we expect building clouds, darker skies, and then the final surrender. We see Joslin's first tape, in which he announces with great happiness that he is about to embark on the diary, and then we see his emaciated profile as the title sequence rolls. In the image Joslin's first tape records he appears robust, happy, full of life. That vibrancy is registered retrospectively: he appears vibrant because the next image shows him weak and thin. Like the disease it documents, *Silverlake Life* barrages the viewer with highs and lows, with upswings and depleting views. As the temporal discrepancies continue, the notion that death is a straight turn off the road marked "health" is undercut, and the logic of causality begins to crack.

After his death, Massi tries to close Joslin's eyes. But, as he tells Friedman in the first moments of the film, Joslin's eyes pop open again. After life has left him, his muscular reflex to look remains. Massi tells Friedman how surprised he was to discover that death is not "like it is in the movies." This movie tries to make death appear the way it does in life.

Massi explains to Friedman that the most difficult thing about Joslin's death is that he can no longer touch him. The celluloid body that Joslin and Massi share makes it possible for the spectator to see Massi and Joslin touch, but that of course is not the same thing. Christian Metz: "Most of all, a film cannot be touched, cannot be carried and handled: although the actual reels can, the projected film cannot" (Metz 1985: 88).

Joslin's emaciated body, empty of light and a/void/ing movement, forces us to ask: What is death? What is its Being? Is the death of the other the only death we can see? And in that seeing do we become, necessarily, blind to our own death? Is Joslin's death the cipher for the death we cannot see? The one we cannot live to tell, to film, to watch?

INTO THE WOODS

Forever failing to watch my own death, I watch his. But as I watch him approach and fall away from death, I see the bodies of others, bodies outside the frame of his film (the film that is truly "theirs"). I see bodies from my own past hover at the phantasmal edge of the frame. Is there a border to this projected light? I cannot, you cannot, make it out (alive). Other bodies I have watched die – bodies that have escaped the celluloid coffin, tiny frames stuffed with Joslin's and Massi's lives – appear on the border of the film's frame. The transfer the film enacts is a transfer across the particular bodies shown on the film to the bodies we project in the intimate cinema of our own phantasmal past and future, the film we save for our own dead/th. These revenant bodies have seeped under the surface of the screen, leached across the surface of the film's translucent skin. These intimate images live still in some interior chamber, deeper than a corporeal orifice, a crypt whose key the conscious mind cannot quite grasp.

In this sense we can see that the film called *Silverlake Life* is a prompt that enables us to enter an interior cinema that projects our own living and dying. The specters we project in our own interior cinema haunt us unpredictably. They refuse to be narrated, and saying their names does not always summon them. (Heidegger: "The essential relation between death and language flashes up before us, but remains still unthought" (quoted in Derrida 1993: 35).) Such specters remain, in their remains, unpredictable, unthought, uninterpreted signs of a past whose end we cannot reach.

Of course it is her body I conjure when I look at his. Way beyond thin, skin the color of betacarotene, bright orange in the palms and at the feet. Anorexic. I woke her early as she requested. As I walked toward the door of the room, I watched her, in the mirror at the edge of the door, rise. Her hips stuck out; her knees looked like the joints on Balinese shadow puppets. I continued walking toward the door, my eye watching her in the mirror. ("The torsion of a retrospective anticipation that introduces the untimely moment and the posthumous in the most alive of the present living thing, the rearview mirror of a waiting-for-death, at every moment" (Derrida 1993: 55).) Watching and waiting, my hand now reaching for the doorknob and then you, I mean she – when narrating the cinema of the dead it is difficult to know to whom one is addressing the narration – she fell to the floor. (Like Anna O. she fainted – but it was me looking in the mirror this time, not her.) I turned back and gently lifted her. I was a paleontologist with my specimens; I was a chef with his carcass; I was carrying your bones ("Son of Man, can these bones live?") I was shocked by your lack of body, lying there between the booming pressure of my two hands. I lay you in the bed. I put my sweating fingers, the two main digits, the index and the middle finger of my right hand, against the vein in your neck. The jugular vein. I heard a pulse. I was stunned, amazed, bewildered, relieved. I left you there in the bed, sheets off, skin exposed. I went to the freezer and retrieved a can of frozen orange juice concentrate, the big size that makes a gallon. I returned to the room. I pressed the can against your wrists, first your right, then your left. I then applied it to your neck, then to your forehead. Gradually, you returned to consciousness. The light broke the grey pallor first at the mouth; it rose slowly and settled at last in your eyes. You blinked twice. "Are you OK?" "Sure, just a little hot." I left the door open when I left.

She is there with me as I watch Joslin's body fade. I fear this body, this body that is not my own, the way the body I look at on the screen, makes me see her body (only) through the screen of his. I see it again, even though I know, deeply I know, she is not here. As the body of the other collapses in on itself and reveals the cities of veins, the electric wires of hair, the cavity in which the eye blinks its dwindling lashes, I see an other body. I cannot look and yet I do: I look but I see something that is not visible.

Do I fantasize her body at the moment of Joslin's death – a moment of panic – because I eroticize women's bodies? Perhaps. But perhaps the fantasy is *released* by the film. Perhaps the disappearance of Joslin's body makes room for a different apprehension of her body – an apprehension that signals a specific form of lesbian interpellation, a way of addressing implicitly and explicitly those who don't appear in the visual field of the cultural imaginary.

Within the logic of reciprocity which informs our psychic architecture, her body must be in some senses phantasmatic because my own is. I cannot write my body any more than I can touch her now. In that missing there is a space, a blank, a stage, a scene, in which I attempt to re-member her and thereby perhaps find a way to get a hand/le on myself. "Take yourself in hand." Writing is one of the stages in this attempt: handwriting is a performance of putting oneself in hand. Writing is especially acute when she is not at hand – hence the history of the muse's music. The film, that writing in light, plays on and on above my fumbling, stumbling hands. I watch Tom disappear in the hollow space of my grief. He does not look back. He looks at an other Mark.

As Judith Halberstam has pointed out, *Silverlake Life* eschews shot/counter-shot. The expected illusion of a reciprocal gaze that most cinema perpetuates is withheld here. The shot/counter-shot that is the primary grammar of documentary, "literally marks the presence of life, of a view from 'here,' that is responded to from 'there.' . . . The view from here disappears until there is quite simply no view" (Halberstam 1995: 18). The claustrophobia of this shrinking vision, the failure to have one's deepest gaze returned, is at once startling to see on film and, for many lesbians, also startlingly comforting. Insofar as *Silverlake Life* documents the inability to be seen, to have a queer gaze returned, it comes close to creating a space for lesbian interpellation. (I mean a space *for* rather than the space itself. Such a spatial architecture remains, still, beyond the frames of our very best cameras.) This "space for" acknowledges the impossibility of creating a camera capable of documenting the groping for a body that can never be confirmed by sight. It imagines the development of a phantasmatic camera, an MRI of the psychic skeleton of our persistent desire, a desire that overpowers the virus that contaminates the frames we impose on the world that seduces and repels our restless eyes. While such a camera has not yet come into existence, I have nonetheless seen it and operated it. It is a fantastic thing. But I have not yet been able to lend it to anyone else and so far I have not been able to translate the negatives into prints I can press into your hand. My own left hand dangling empty at my side, I press the fingers of my right hand on the keys, trying to measure the hole I find myself in. Bigger now than Alice's.

THE MAP

According to Walter Benjamin, the materialist historian grabs hold of a memory as it "flashes up" at a moment of danger (Benjamin 1969: 255). Including the memory of Heidegger's dangerous sentence: "The essential relation between death and language flashes up before us, but remains still unthought" – dimly remembered, but not interpreted. The memory illuminates the dangerous event but not in a causal or linear manner. The memory softens the danger of danger. It reminds us that we may survive. By "possessing" the memory, however insecurely, we witness our own survival. The danger, the blow that ends our previous way of being, can be survived – but at a cost. The work of mourning begins long before the physical death of the other.

Joslin invites the viewer to become a historian in Benjamin's sense. In the excerpt from *Blackstar*, he asks his mother if she remembers when he first told her that he was gay. "I certainly do," she replies, naming the time and place in which he made the revelation. She recalls the orange carpet she stood on and the exact moment when she asked for a chair. The moment of danger is remembered as if it were recorded on film, a carefully preserved sequence of images whose vibrancy and exactitude remains intact. She may not remember what his words were exactly, they may have been too dangerous, but she remembers the orange carpet. The dividing line between the "before" and "after" of his revelation is decisive. And just as she crossed the line once and survived, as he approaches the dividing line between life and death, he returns her (and us) to that initial crossing. *Silverlake Life* returns to the (filmed) past, the original revelation of his homosexuality recorded in *Blackstar*, a revelation that his family survived, to assure them that they can survive his death as well – the death he records in *Silverlake Life*.

Hysteron proteron: the time is out of joint. Time and utterance won't jive: the tracks on which the words should run smoothly are cracked. The bed on which time should lie calmly is a wrack of night sweats. Proteron, prototype, primary: and the first shall be first. Hysteron, hysteria, history. The death of a man one hardly knows is announced at the start: Hysteron proteron, the cart before the horse, the death known before the beginning (of the film) of his life. Hystero, "to be behind, to come later than, to lag behind, to be inferior to, to be lacking in, to come to grief, to be in arrears, to be in debt, to be indebted" (Rand 1986: 56). Indebted, we come to grief – but in arrears to what? To the proteron, the first. Hysteron, hystera. Hysteria. Hystera for the womb, the latter or "upper" part of the reproductive system; hysteria, wandering womb diseases. Wandering wombs breed wandering words. Time's body will not cohere. The body of the sentence is inverted: the invert's body speaks the language of inversion. The *Oxford English Dictionary* defines hysteron proteron as an "inversion of the natural or logical order; as by placing the conclusion before the premises." Time's order is what is reversed, revised, inverted in *Silverlake Life*. The inversion of action makes visible time's reversibility – if only in cinema (and certain forms of chemistry and physics). The events that we plot so carefully on a graph of time can be re-ordered. Hystera. Hysteria. History.

The life of someone whose existence has somewhat preceded our own encloses within its particularity the very tension of History, its division. History is hysterical: it is constituted only if we consider it, only if we look at it – and in order to look at it we must be excluded from it.

(Barthes 1981: 65)

Death may guarantee us this exclusion; no longer in our intimate film or shooting it, we lie down and it fills the screens which enshroud our bodies.

The looking solicited by *Silverlake Life* is a hysterical looking – not a calm, objective, "exclusive" and excluding look. Joslin asks us to consider his history not from outside his life, but from the inner intimacy promised by the video diary. The "objective" look is the look of science, and of the doctor; the filmmakers prefer the look of the hysterical patient. Joslin wants to suggest that dying, like living, is an "is" – its Being fills the present. Dying is not in the future; death is not in the past. Dying is. And this is a film that shows us how long that "is" is, how many shapes and colors and emotions live and die in it, who comes to hold its hand, who stays away out of fear, shyness, hunger. Furthermore, within the cinema, living can occur after dying, can continue after dying. Therefore, dying as an act, a performative under-taking, consists of – *is* – the marking and mapping of the border between living and dying.

Silverlake Life asks how the body's health and death are defined. How are the spatio-temporal marks of location "given" to the body and how do those marks in turn give the body up? Throughout the film, voice-overs announce the date, the location, the hour and space of the images that unfurl across the screen. Without these indexical notes, it would be impossible to know the location – physical, psychical, philosophical, temporal, spatial – of the images embodied in the celluloid.

To die might be the decision to say "here, now," to pick the moment to leave, or, following the Derrida of *Aporias*, the moment to arrive. Such a decision would involve biological, psychic, political, and emotional readings, active performative readings, of the present tense. In *Silverlake Life*, Tom Joslin does not try to outlast death (not only would such a contest be doomed, it would also fail to question the causal bridge between life and death), but he does inter-rogate its borders. Just as the shots in the film require voice-overs describing where they occur in space and time, so too does the body's final act require a verdict, a sentence that can pronounce its last word. Not a verdict of "life or death," but a verdict that holds a body in its living dying, an interpretation that indicates the limit, the edge of comprehension.[7] Perhaps beyond that limit lies not a silent death, but

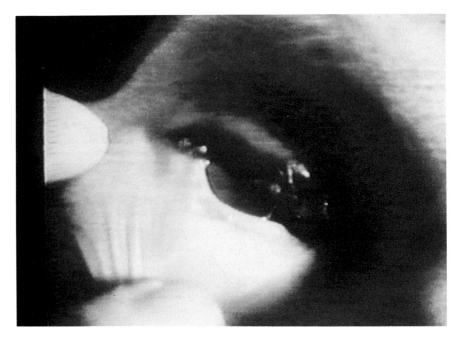

Figure 9   Film still (by Carolyn Shapiro) from Joslin's *Silverlake Life*.

another series of images yet to be joined to interpretation, yet to be narrated.

The most riveting moment in *Silverlake Life* occurs near the end. Joslin is in bed, as he has been for several months. He is impassive. Mark is holding the camera, and he zooms in on Joslin's right eye (see Figure 9). It is swollen with a lesion caused by Kaposi's Sarcoma. Mark brings the camera in close to Tom's eye and tenderly lifts the lid. He is explaining to us how painful the eye is for Joslin. The eye is full of pus and ooze. Joslin is silent while Massi continues. He succeeds in opening Joslin's wounded eye. Moving across his face, Massi then shows us Joslin's other eye which Massi declares perfectly fine. This eye, woundless, looks more vulnerable, less protected, almost naked. The eye gazes in an out-of-focus way at something whose interiority – or perhaps immense exteriority –– can no longer be linked to our gaze. At the limit of the body, at the limit of the unwounded eye, the camera points to a way of seeing that we may be able to comprehend, if not perform. It is this vanishing, the dissolution of vision itself, that *Silverlake Life*, uncannily and against all logic, achieves. Dissolving vision, this film composed of seen images, achieves an image against the logic of film itself. It escapes its own terms and sends the spectator into a cinema of his or her own imaginary.[8] It sends the spectator to her eye's autopsy and she sees for herself the still orbit of her own eye.

Joslin's eyes, one swollen and wounded, the other "perfectly fine," see things that the camera cannot. The camera can record him seeing, but not what he sees. The isolation experienced by the spectator at this moment is intense – indeed, it is the "moment of danger" that flashes up and leads the spectator's eye off the screen itself into the intimate cinema of her own dead/th. This burrowing off is also a burrowing in, as if we might ourselves slip under Tom's open lid, slide under the screen, under the skin of the suffering body we can see but cannot comfort or console.

Near the beginning of the film, an image of the interior of an MRI (Magnetic Resonance Imaging) camera fills the screen. Then we see the X-ray image of the interior of a body that the MRI camera captured. It is as if Joslin has taken his camera inside the supercamera that records the interior spaces of his body. The next shot shows Joslin (not holding a camera) strapped to the MRI table; he submits to the camera's full embrace of his body. When the MRI is done, Joslin gets up off the table and walks calmly to a camera set on a tripod; another camera records him disassembling the camera on the tripod. Behind each camera, another camera. Like Vertov, Joslin is both magician and epistemologist, to use Michelson's terms. But unlike his precursor, Joslin is not celebrating and authenticating the logic of causality: he is challenging it, exposing its blindness.

The MRI camera can provide an interior image of the body; Joslin's camera for the most part is content to stay on the surface of that body. Surveying the changing colors of the Kaposi's Sarcoma lesions across Massi's back, zooming in on the doctor's hands as he grinds Massi's medication, strolling over the books and photographs in their apartment: much of *Silverlake Life* is content to record the rituals and objects of everyday life. But when Massi opens up Joslin's body, lifts the lid that keeps the light out, the film approaches one of its several ends.

In the next sequence of images, Joslin lies in the same position on the bed and Massi, in voice-over, announces that it is "the first of July and Tom has just died." Without the voice-over, the spectator would not know that the image of Joslin on the screen is an image of Joslin after he has died. In this sense it is literally an after-image; for what the viewer retains on the retina is the previous image of Tom alive lying in bed in the same position.

Science tells Joslin he will die. Filmmaking promises him he will be preserved on film – walking, talking, eating, sleeping. He will become a filmic body. ("I'm desperate to make *Silverlake Life*. Not to take my pills.") The film presents two narratives with different temporalities: cinematic narrative, which contains a finite number of events that can be projected either in a forward motion (in synch with linear time) or in reverse motion (which runs time "backwards"). The spectator reads this temporality as a truth specific to the culture of cinema, a culture he or she can visit but cannot fully inhabit. The spectator is prevented from inhabiting cinema by a previous belief, a higher faith one might say, in the "truth" of the narrative logic of scientific biology. Biological narrative operates in a non-cinematic temporality, one that only moves forward.

Within the temporalities of biology and cinema Joslin's body comes to an end, or at least to an end of what we can know about it. "Dying is neither entirely natural (biological) nor cultural" (Derrida 1993: 42). It is an act, a performative undertaking, that requires interpretation. The technologies of death, from terrorist death squads to "merciful" suicide machines, are interpretive machines that suture the gap between biological and cultural definitions of death. Joslin suggests that cinema is one of the sweetest, most comforting machines to assist us with this editing.

Psychoanalysis, born at the same moment as cinema, allows us to see that there is a psychic "working through" of these two different definitions of death. Psychoanalysis is a performance of mourning. The witness to the death of the other must interpret and come to accept the other's death through a process of introjection and evacuation. In successful (non-melancholic) mourning, a transference occurs between the one who grieves and the one who died. Simultaneously newly cathected and given up, the libidinal investment in the dead is trans-formed until the dead inhabits a new psychic location. In undergoing this *moving*, the dead person alters the psychic terrain of the witness. This transference takes time: one might call the movement of this time the temporality of grief. After Joslin's death, Massi's counselor sends him a book entitled *How To Survive the Loss of Love*. In it, a zig-zag chart illustrates the forward and backward emotional and psychic measurements of grief along the y axis; the x axis charts time's forward advance.

Whatever else the work of mourning requires, it demands time. It has always struck me as odd that cultural monuments to the dead, public attempts to acknowledge grief, usually take the form of sculp-ture. It would seem more sensible to use temporal forms – such as film and music – to commemorate those who are no longer with us. Sculptural monuments tend to re-member the dead by turning the work of mourning into an object that stands in for the long process of working through. Temporal art forms such as music and cinema are able to perform the working through of mourning in the work itself. But perhaps because music finally reminds us of the limitless sound-scape of silence, and because cinematic projectors eventually burn out, reminding us that our images are an intricate physics of immaterialized light, such art forms might lead us to believe that like the dead who have reached the end of life we will reach an end to grief. Public sculptures in their very solidity and monumentality suggest the weight and scope of mourning. However, they sometimes also suggest that grief is there like a clear knife piercing the heart, cleaving us in two. The work of mourning is never clear, never complete, never solid.

And yet some of us do sometimes let go and release our grip on the killing work of mourning. Sculpture, precisely because it can be touched, unlike music or cinema, gives the viewer something that is perhaps even more important than time – sculpture is embodied form. And perhaps that solidity provides a form of comfort that the abstractions of music and cinema cannot.

I do not believe there is an end of grief. But working through grief sometimes gives us a way to let the dead be as dead. The work is hard because we must kill our desire to make them live and killing our desire often feels as if we are effectively killing them (again). This is why aggression, as Crimp reminded us in "Mourning and Militancy," is so crucial to psychic health.

Silverlake Life suggests that "in the end" there is always another return. After his death, Massi tells Friedman that Joslin came back and visited him in the house several times. Perhaps he did. Or perhaps Massi's own intimate cinema began after Joslin's stopped and what he saw was Joslin in their house in a pose he hadn't noticed before. The film we see is one record of Joslin coming back; it suggests that it may be possible to document the temporal unboundedness of death itself.

Comforting stories to put myself to sleep. Who knows if they are true? Who can know what happens after death? The cart before the horse. Hysteron proteron "is sometimes difficult to detect – as in the sequence of a locomotive moving either so quickly or slowly that we deduce its inversion from other elements in the image – from the movement of human figures at the periphery of the screen" (Michelson 1972: 70). As we watch Tom's "perfectly fine" eye stare blankly into the camera five days before his death it is impossible to tell if he is in our time or a new time. It is impossible to say if his eye is moving so slowly or so quickly that we cannot discern its orbit. Unable to track the perspective of Tom's eye, we also lose, if only for a moment, the lines of time itself. Freed for an instant from time's measure, we fall into the void of an unseeing eye. Blinded for a second, we are also free; we escape, if only for a second, the compulsion to remember, to record what we see.

This is the freedom that lies on the other side of the eye's external cinematic gaze. Joslin and Massi configure Joslin's eye as an orifice, a bodily orifice, that a lover can enter. As the camera moves its lens into

Joslin's eye, the spectator sees – in a flash – her own interior cinema. The screen gains an interiority that allows the spectator to convert the film's manifest images into her own imaginary. *Silverlake Life* points to a cinema of inversion, a queer cinema of the spectator that the external camera can not see. *Silverlake Life* looks into what we can never see: the love that survives the end of our ability to feel or witness it. This is the love that we project in order to live our many deaths. Falling into this loving *screen*, we are like bats wildly beating, hoping to be ensnared in night's blessed blindness long enough to lie still.

As Massi shoots the images of Joslin's dead body, he sobs. Continuing to address Joslin as if he could hear his speech, Massi promises Joslin that he and their friends will complete *Silverlake Life*. The promise to the other at the moment of death is always the promise not to forget. *Silverlake Life* is the fruit of that promise.

Constructed as a transference/counter-transference, the promise of the film eventually passes from Massi to Friedman. After Massi's death, Friedman selected this material. Knowing that there are still thirty-eight hours of tape, one begins to understand again that the encounter with the other is always one that is limited by the temporal frame of its occurrence. The remarkable thing about the composition of the "video diary" is how many lives are left on the cutting-room floor. The living dying we see onscreen is just one version of that living dying. The limit of the gaze, the end point of what we can know about Joslin, is underscored by Massi's record of Joslin's open eyes, captivated by a different image, in a different time than the ones the camera can record. Staring off time (in a manner analogous to staring off frame, but in a temporal rather than spatial key), Joslin creates a space for the spectator to view the lives of the dying who are not physically there. The spectator begins to feel the weight of all the other Toms and Marks, Danitras and Catherines, whose lives and deaths are not projected in the silver light of *Silverlake Life*. Watching the sliver of Tom's eye swell in the silver light of the cinema screen, we feel a strange transference take place. Underneath Joslin's swollen eye are cities of forgotten bodies, strangely summoned, strangely palpable in their heavy absence in the unfurling light of the film's projection. Summoning a cinema it cannot film, a body it cannot touch, *Silverlake Life* undoes the logic of film's insistent visuality. In its place, *Silverlake Life* offers viewers memories of bodies they would still love to touch. Memories are not bodies yet as they form they might help us grip our grief.

so yes please do stay in touch

NOTES

1 "Thanatography" is described and explored in Dubois (1983).
2 For a discussion of why "man – and not the animal – always dies before his time," see Derrida (1993: 4).
3 I shall refer to diegetic time in *Silverlake Life* as "cinematic." Although the film was shot on video, Friedman transferred the video to film (as per Joslin's instructions). I am satisfied that everything I say here about the temporality of cinema applies equally well to this video, although perhaps not to all videos. It must be noted, however, that video is a much more intimate and personal form of memory-making than cinema, in part because it is hand-held and ever ready. See Ulmer (1989) for a brilliant rendering of the epistemological claims made possible by video.
4 For an important exception to this claim see Jackson (1994).
5 The best treatment of the history of the origin of painting is Robert Rosenblum's (1957).
6 This "cinema for the dead" also has something to say about the alleged passivity of spectatorship. This will be discussed below.
7 These comments are especially indebted to Derrida's much more rigorous investigation of the border between life and death in *Aporias* (1993: 43-52).
8 Parveen Adams' brilliant essay (1994), "Father, Can't You See I'm Filming?," connects the psychoanalysis of perversion to Michael Powell's film, *Peeping Tom*. Adams' astute reading of the blind mother's relationship to the camera makes the point I am making here about *Silverlake Life*'s dissolution of vision seem perhaps a bit obvious. But perhaps it also suggests something queer about the way in which these two films use blindness as a way to establish a "perverse" spectatorial space.

Bibliography

Adams, Parveen, "Father, Can't You See I'm Filming?," in *Supposing the Subject*, ed. Joan Copjec (New York and London: Verso, 1994).

Adorno, Theodor, *Minima Moralia: Reflections from Damaged Life*, trans. E.F.N. Jephcott (London: New Left Books, 1974).

Anzieu, Didier, *The Skin Ego*, trans. Chris Turner (New Haven, Conn.: Yale University Press, 1989).

Appleyard, Bryan, "The Globe Cast as Political Football," *The Times* (London), 26 September 1984.

Aquinas, Thomas, "The Resurrection of the Lord," trans. and edited by C. Thomas Moore O.P., *Summa Theologica*, vol. 55 (New York and London: Blackfriars; with McGraw-Hill, and Eyre & Spottiswoode, 1976).

Babcock, Barbara Allen et al., "Judge Clarence Thomas' View on the Fundamental Right to Privacy: A Report to the Senate Judiciary Committee," *Court of Appeal* (1992): 255–68.

Barthes, Roland, *Camera Lucida*, trans. Richard Howard (New York: Hill & Wang, 1981).

Benjamin, Walter, *Illuminations: Essays and Reflections*, trans. Harry Zohn; edited with an introduction by Hannah Arendt (New York: Schoken, 1969).

Bersani, Leo, "Is the Rectum a Grave?," *October* 43, Winter (1987): 197–222.

—— *The Culture of Redemption* (Cambridge and London: Harvard University Press, 1990).

Biddle, Martin, "The Rose Reviewed: a comedy (?) of errors," *Antiquity* 63, no. 241 (1989): 753–60.

Billen, Andrew, "Arts Council Criticizes 'Gay' Clause," *The Times* (London), 23 January 1988.

Billington, Michael, "An American in London Plans a Restored Globe Theater," *New York Times*, 9 July 1987; C17.

Blais, Joline, "Perverted Plots: Rewriting Hysteria in Jean Rhys and Marguerite Duras," *unpublished manuscript* (1995).

Blanchot, Maurice, *The Writing of the Disaster*, trans. Ann Smock (Lincoln: University of Nebraska Press, 1986).

Bowlby, Rachel, "The Happy Event," *Paragraph* 14.1, March (1991): 10–19.

Brennan, Teresa, *The Interpretation of the Flesh* (New York and London: Routledge, 1992).

Brock, David, *The Real Anita Hill: The Untold Story* (New York: The Free Press/Macmillan, 1993).

Brodkey, Harold, "To My Readers," *New Yorker*, June 1993: 80–2.

Bronfen, Elisabeth, *Over Her Dead Body* (Manchester: Manchester University Press, 1992).

Bryson, Norman, "The Gaze in the Expanded Field," in *Vision and Visuality (no.2)*, ed. Hal Foster (Seattle: Bay Press, 1988): 87–113.

Buckborough, Anne L., "Family Law: Recent Developments in the Law of Marital Rape," in *Annual Survey of American Law*, Book 1 (New York, London, Rome: Oceana Publications, Inc., 1989): 343–70.

Butler, Judith, *Bodies That Matter* (New York and London: Routledge, 1994).

Caruth, Cathy, (ed.) *Trauma: Explorations in Memory* (Baltimore and London: The Johns Hopkins University Press, 1994).

Case, Sue-Ellen, "Towards a Butch-Femme Aesthetic," in *Making a Spectacle: Femenist Essays on Contemporary Women's Theatre*, ed. Lynda Hart (Ann Arbor: University of Michigan Press, 1989): 282–99.

Celan, Paul, *Breathturn*, trans. Pierre Joris (Los Angeles: Sun and Moon Press, 1995).

Cerassano, S. P., "Raising a Playhouse from the Dust," *Shakespeare Quarterly* 40, no. 4 (1989): 483–90.

Certeau, Michel de, *The Writing of History*, trans. Tom Conley (New York: Columbia University Press, 1988).

Chippendale, C., "Editorial," *Antiquity* 63, 240 (1989): 411–13.

Chrisman, Robert, and Allen, Robert L., (eds) *Court of Appeal: The Black Community Speaks Out on the Racial and Sexual Politics of Thomas vs. Hill* (New York: Ballantine Books, 1992).

Clement, Catherine, *The Lives and Legends of Jacques Lacan*, trans. Arthur Goldhammer (New York: Columbia University Press, 1983).

Cornell, Drucilla, *The Philosophy of the Limit* (New York and London: Routledge, 1993).

Cranefield, Paul, "Josef Breuer's Evaluation of his Contribution to Psychoanalysis," *The International Journal of Psychoanalysis* 39, September–October 1958, part V (1958): 319–22.

Crenshaw, Kimberle, "Whose Story Is It, Anyway? Feminist and Antiracist Appropriations of Anita Hill," in *Race-ing Justice, En-gender-ing Power: Essays on Anita Hill, Clarence Thomas, and the Construction of Social Reality*, ed. Toni Morrison (New York: Pantheon, 1992): 402–40.

Crimp, Douglas, "Mourning and Militancy," *October* 52, Winter (1989): 3–18.

Croce, Arlene, "The Spelling of Agon," *The New Yorker*, 12 July 1993.

Davis, Natalie Zemon, and Starn, Randolph (eds) *'Memory and Counter-Memory' a special issue of Representations* 26, Spring (1989).

—— "Introduction," in *Representations* (Special issue: *Memory and Counter-memory*), Spring (1989), 26: 1-6.

Derrida, Jacques, *Aporias*, trans. Thomas Dutoit (Stanford, Calif: Stanford University Press, 1993).

Diamond, Elin, "Mimesis, Mimicry and the True Real," in *Acting Out: Feminist Performances*, eds Lynda Hart and Peggy Phelan (Ann Arbor: University of Michigan Press, 1993): 363–82.

Doane, Mary Ann, *The Desire to Desire: the Women's Film of the 1940s* (Bloomington: Indiana University Press, 1987).

Drakakis, John, "Theatre, Ideology, and Institution: Shakespeare and the Road-sweepers," in *The Shakespeare Myth*, ed. Graham Holderness (Manchester: Manchester University Press, 1988): 24–41.

Dubois, Philippe, *L'acte photographique* (Paris and Brussels: Nathan & Labor, 1983).

Eccles, Christine, *The Rose Theatre* (London and New York: Nick Hern/ Routledge, 1990).

Edgerton, Samuel Y. Jr., *The Renaissance Rediscovery of Linear Perspective* (New York: Harper & Row, 1975).

Edinger, Dora, *Bertha Pappenheim: Freud's Anna O.* (Congregation Solel: Highland Park, Illinois, 1968).

Elson, John, "When Reporters Make News," *Time*, 28 October 1991: 30.

Foakes, R.A., "The Discovery of the Rose: Some Implications," *Shakespeare Survey* 43 (1991): 141–8.

Foucault, Michel, *The Order of Things: An Archaelogy of the Human Sciences* (New York: Vintage Books/Random House, Inc., 1970).

Fraser, Nancy, "Sex, Lies, and the Public Sphere: Some Reflections on the Confirmation of Clarence Thomas," *Critical Inquiry* 18 (1992): 595–612.

Freeman, Lucy, *The Story of Anna O.* (New York: Walker & Co., 1972).

Freud , Sigmund, "'Civilized' Sexual Morality and Modern Nervous Illness," in *The Standard Edition of the Complete Works of Sigmund Freud*, Vol. 9 (London: Hogarth Press, 1906–1908).

—— "On Narcissism," in *Standard Edition* (14) (London: Hogarth Press, 1914): 67–104.

—— "Mourning and Melancholia," in *Standard Edition* (14) (London: Hogarth Press, 1917): 239–58.

—— "From the History of an Infantile Neurosis," in *Standard Edition* (17) (London: Hogarth Press, 1918).

—— "Constructions in Analysis," in *Standard Edition* (23) (London: Hogarth Press, 1937): 259.

—— *The Interpretation of Dreams*, trans. James Strachey (New York: Basic Books, 1955).

—— *Three Essays on the Theory of Sexuality*, trans. James Strachey (New York: Basic Books, 1962).

—— *The Complete Letters of Sigmund Freud to Wilhelm Fliess: 1887–1904*, trans. and ed. Jeffrey Moussaieff Masson (Cambridge: Harvard University Press, 1985).

—— "Psychoanalytic Notes on an Autobiographical Account of a Case of Paranoia (Dementia Paranoides)," in *Standard Edition* (12): 1–82 (London: Hogarth Press).

Freud , Sigmund, and Breuer, Josef, "Studies on Hysteria," in *The Standard Edition of the Complete Psychological Works of Sigmund Freud*, ed. James Strachey, Vol. 2 (London: Hogarth Press, 1895).

Fried, Michael, *Realism, Writing, Disfiguration: On Thomas Eakins and Stephen Crane* (Chicago and London: University of Chicago Press, 1987).

Friedlaender, Walter, *Caravaggio Studies* (Princeton: Princeton University Press, 1955).

Fuss, Diana, "Freud's Fallen Women: Identification, Desire, and 'A Case of Homosexuality in a Woman'," *The Yale Journal of Criticism* 6, 1, Spring (1993): 1–23.

Getler, Michael, "Year-old British coal strike ends in confusion," *Washington Post*, 6 March 1985: A1.

Grant, Rena, "Let Daddy Do It For You," *Lacanian Ink* 3, Fall (1992): 55–65.

—— "Characterhysterics II: Repeating Oneself," *Lacanian Ink* 8, Spring (1994): 72–83.

"Group Letter defending McKellen," Letter to the editor, *The Guardian* (9 January 1991).

Gurr, Andrew, "The Glory of the Globe," *Times Literary Supplement*, 18 October 1991: 5–6.

Halberstam, Judith, "Queer Documentary: The View From Here," unpublished manuscript, University of California–San Diego (1995).

Hart, Lynda, "Identity and Seduction: Lesbians In the Mainstream," in *Acting Out: Feminist Performances*, ed. Lynda Hart and Peggy Phelan (Ann Arbor: University of Michigan Press, 1993): 119–40.

—— *Fatal Women: Lesbian Sexuality and the Mark of Aggression* (Princeton: Princeton University Press, 1994).

Hart, Lynda, and Phelan, Peggy, (eds) *Acting Out: Feminist Performances* (Ann Arbor: University of Michigan Press, 1993).

—— "Queerer Than Thou: Being and Deb Margolin," *Theatre Journal* 47 (1995): 269–82.

Hayes, Arthur S., "Courts Concede the Sexes Think in Unlike Ways," *Wall Street Journal*, 28 May 1991: B1.

Heidegger, Martin, *On the Way to Language*, trans. Peter D. Hertz (San Francisco: Harper & Row, 1971).

Hibbard, Howard, *Caravaggio* (New York: Harper & Row, 1983).

Hickey, David, "Nothing Like the Son: On Robert Mapplethorpe's X Portfolio," in *The Invisible Dragon: Four Essays on Beauty* (Los Angeles: Artissues.Press, 1993): 27–37.

Higginbotham, A. Leon Jr., "Race, Sex, Education and Missouri Jurisprudence: *Shelley v. Kraemer* in a Historical Perspective," *Washington University Law Quarterly* 67, no. 3 (1989): 674–708.

Hirschmuller, Albrecht, *The Life and Work of Josef Breuer: Physiology and Psychoanalysis* (New York and London: New York University Press, 1989).

Hollander, Anne, *Moving Pictures* (New York: Knopf, 1989).

Hollier, Denis, *Against Architecture: The Writings of Georges Bataille*, trans. Betsy Wing (Cambridge and London: The MIT Press, 1989).

Hopkins, Gerard Manley, "Spring and Fall," in *The Poems of Gerard Manley Hopkins*, ed. W.H. Gardner and N.H. MacKenzie (London and New York: Oxford University Press, 1970).

Hughes, Athol, (ed.) *The Inner World and Joan Riviere: Collected Papers 1920–1958* (London and New York: Karnac Books (The Melanie Klein Trust), 1991).

Hunt, Albert, "Tales of Ignominy, Beyond Thomas and Hill," *Wall Street Journal*, 17 October 1991.

Index on Censorship (London: Writers and Scholars International, September 1988).

Irigaray, Luce, *An Ethics of Sexual Difference*, trans. Carolyn Burke and Gillian C. Gill (Ithaca: Cornell University Press, 1993).

Jones, Ernest, *Sigmund Freud: Life and Work*, vol.1 (London: Hogarth Press, 1954).

Joyce, James, *The Dubliners* (New York: Penguin Books, 1967).

Kaplan, Marion A., *The Jewish Feminist Movement in Germany: The Campaigns of the Judischer Frauenbund, 1904–1938* (Westport, Conn.: Greenwood Press, 1979).

Kohler, Richard, "Excavating Henslowe's Rose," *Shakespeare Quarterly* 40, no. 4 (1989): 475–82.

Kolbert, Elizabeth, "Most in National Survey Say Judge is More Believable," *New York Times*, 15 October 1991: A1.

Koon, Stacey, L.A.P.D. with Robert Deitz, *Presumed Guilty: The Tragedy of the Rodney King Affair* (Washington, D.C.: Regnery Gateway, 1992).

Koppleman, Andrew, "The Miscegenation Analogy: Sodomy Law as Sex Discrimination," *The Yale Law Journal* 98, no. 1 (1988): 145–64.

Kurtz, Howard, "The Legal Reporter's Full Court Press," *Washington Post*, 10 October 1991: D1, D6.

Lacan, Jacques, *The Four Fundamental Concepts of Psycho-Analysis*, ed. Jacques-Alain Miller, trans. Alan Sheridan (New York and London: W.W. Norton & Co., 1978).

—— *The Seminar of Jacques Lacan, Book II: The Ego in Freud's Theory and in the Technique of Psychoanalysis*, ed. Jacques-Alain Miller, trans. Sylvana Tomaselli (New York: W.W. Norton & Co., 1988).

—— *The Seminar of Jacques Lacan, Book I: Freud's Papers on Technique, 1953–54*, ed. Jacques-Alain Miller, trans. John Forrester (New York and London: W.W. Norton & Co., 1991).

—— *The Seminar of Jacques Lacan, Book VII: The Ethics of Psychoanalysis, 1959–1960*, ed. Jacques-Alain Miller, trans. Dennis Porter (New York and London: W.W. Norton & Co., 1992).

Lacour, Claudia Brodsky, "Doing Things With Words: 'Racism' as Speech Act and the Undoing of Justice," in *Race-ing Justice, En-gender-ing Power: Essays on Anita Hill, Clarence Thomas, and the Construction of Social Reality*, ed. Toni Morrison (New York: Pantheon, 1992): 127–58.

Lane, Christopher, "'The Delirium of Interpretation': Writing the Papin Affair," *Differences* 5, no. 2 (1993): 24–61.

Laplanche, Jean, *Life and Death in Psychoanalysis*, trans. Jeffrey Mehlman (Baltimore and London: The Johns Hopkins University Press, 1976).

Levine, Laura, *Men in Women's Clothing* (New York: Cambridge University Press, 1994).

McLaurin, Melton A., *Celia, a Slave* (Athens and London: University of Georgia Press, 1991).

Malmo, Jane, *The Melancholy of Anatomy: Violence, Law and Subjectivity in the Renaissance Theatres of the Body*, forthcoming.

Marcus, Steven, *Freud and the Culture of Psychoanalysis: Studies in the Transition from Victorian Humanism to Modernity* (Boston: G. Allen & Unwin, 1984).

Masson, Jeffrey Moussaieff, *The Assault on Truth: Freud's Suppression of the Seduction Theory* (New York: HarperCollins, 1992).

Merleau-Ponty, Jacques, *The Visible and Invisible*, ed. Claude Lefort, trans. Alphonso Lingis, Northwestern University Studies in Phenomenology and Existential Philosophy (Evanston: Northwestern University Press, 1968).

Metz, Christian, "Photography and Fetish," *October* 34, Fall (1985): 81–90.

Michelson, Annette, "*The Man with the Movie Camera*: From Magician to Epistemologist," *Artforum*, March (1972): 60–72.

Miller, D. A., "The Late Jane Austen," *Raritan*, Summer (1990): 55–79.

Minow, Martha, *Making All the Difference: Inclusion, Exclusion and American Law* (lthaca: Cornell University Press, 1990).

Moore, Rachel, "Marketing Alterity," *Visual Anthropology Review* 8, no. 2 (1992): 16–26.

Morrison, Toni, (ed.) *Race-ing Justice, En-gender-ing Power: Essays on Anita Hill, Clarence Thomas, and the Construction of Social Reality* (New York: Pantheon, 1992).

Murray, Timothy, *Like a Film: Ideological Fantasy on Screen, Camera, and Canvas* (New York and London: Routledge, 1993).

Orgel, Stephen, *The Illusion of Power: Political Theater in the English Renaissance* (Berkeley and Los Angeles: University of California Press, 1975).

Orrell, John, "Nutshells at the Rose," *Theatre Research International*, 17, 1, Spring (1992): 8-15.

Orrell, John, and Gurr, Andrew, "What the Rose Can Tell Us," *Antiquity* 63, no. 239 (1989): 421–89.

Parris, Matthew, "Art of stealing the limelight," *The Times* (London), 16 May 1989: 17.

Pellizzi, Francesco, "Tombstone: Four Pieces and a Coda on the Idea of Burial," *Terrazzo* 4 (Spring 1990) 77: 92..

Perspecta, *The Yale Architecture Journal, 26, a special issue on "Theater, Theatricality, and Architecture"* (1990).

Phelan, Peggy, "Money Talks," *TDR* (T125) 34, no. 1 (1990): 4–15.
—— "Money Talks, Again," *TDR* (T131) 35, no. 3 (1991): 131–42.
—— *Unmarked* (New York and London: Routledge, 1993a).
—— "Radical Democracy and the Woman Question," *American Literary History*, Winter (1993b): 750–64.
Phelps, Timothy M., and Winternitz, Helen, *Capitol Games: Clarence Thomas, Anita Hill, and the Story of a Supreme Court Nomination* (New York: Hyperion, 1992).
Poirier, Richard, "Writing Off the Self," *Raritan*, Summer (1981): 107–33.
Rand, Richard, "Hysteron proteron, or 'Woman First'," *Oxford Literary Review* 8, no. 1–2 (1986): 51–6.
Rauch, Kate Darby, "Interviews Find Different Take on the Hill–Thomas Controversy," *Washington Post*, 7 December 1992: A3.
Reed, Susan, and McElwaine, Sandra, "Full-Court Presser," *People*, 28 October 1991: 55–6.
Representations 30, A special issue on "Law and the Order of Culture", Spring (1990).
Rich, Adrienne, "Splittings," in *The Dream of A Common Language* (London and New York: W.W. Norton & Co., 1978): 10–11.
Ridley, Nicholas, "Interview," *The Spectator*, 14 July 1990.
Riviere, Joan, "Womanliness as a Masquerade," *The International Journal of Psychoanalysis* 9 (1929): 303–13.
Robinson, Eugene, "British Court Rebuffs Move by Government to Shut Mines," *Washington Post*, 22 December 1992: A17.
Rose, Jacqueline, *Sexuality in the Field of Vision* (London: Verso, 1989).
Rosenblum, Robert, "The Origin of Painting: A Problem in the Iconography of Romantic Classicism," *Art Bulletin* 39, no. 1 (1957): 281–90.
Ross, Andrew, "The Private Parts of Justice," *Race-ing Justice, En-gender-ing Power: Essays on Anita Hill, Clarence Thomas and the Constructions of Social Reality*, ed. Toni Morrison (New York: Pantheon, 1992): 40–60.
Sedgwick, Eve Kosofsky, *Tendencies* (Durham, NC: Duke University Press, 1994).
Showalter, Elaine, "On Hysterical Narrative," *Narrative* 1, 1 January (1993), 24–35.
Sinfield, Alan, "Private Lives/Public Theater: Noel Coward and the Politics of Homosexual Representation," *Representations* 36, Fall (1991): 43–61.
Sontag, Susan, *On Photography* (New York: Farrar, Straus & Giroux, 1977).
Sophocles, *Antigone*, trans. Dudley Fitts and Robert Fitzgerald in *The Oedipus Cycle: an English version* (New York: Harcourt Brace Jovanovich, 1977): 185–238.
Souster, Mark, "Clash Over Wreath for Lord Olivier at the Rose," *The Times* (London), 14 July 1989: 1.
Stoddard, Tom, "*Bowers v. Hardwick*: Precedent by Personal Predilection," *University of Chicago Law Review* 54 (1987): 648–56.
Swales, Peter, "Freud, His Teacher and the Birth of Psychoanalysis," in *Freud: Appraisals and Reappraisals*, ed. Paul E. Stepansky (Hillsdale, NJ: The Analytic Press, 1986).
Tait, Simon, "Value of the Rose Theatre Site Highlighted in 1971," *The Times* (London), 17 May 1989: 1.
Tait, Simon, "Rose Theatre Could Attract 150,000 Visitors a Year," *The Times* (London), 5 June 1991.
Thomas, Kendall, "Beyond the Privacy Principle," *Columbia Law Review* 92, no. 6 (1992): 1431–516.
Tilley, Christopher, "Excavation as Theatre," *Antiquity* 63, no. 240 (1989): 430–5.
The Times (London), "Rose Theatre Site Wins a Breathing Space," 16 May 1989: 12–13.

Transcript from House of Commons Regarding Rose Theatre, *The Times* (London), 16 May 1989: 12–13.

Ulmer, Gregory, *Teletheory: Grammatology in the Age of Video* (New York: Routledge, 1989).

Vertov, Dziga, *Kino-Eye: The Writings of Dziga Vertov*, ed. Annette Michelson, trans. Kevin O'Brien (Berkeley: University of California Press, 1984).

Wainwright, G.J., "Saving the Rose," *Antiquity* 63, no. 240 (1989): 430–5.

Watney, Simon, *Policing Desire*, 2nd edn (Minneapolis: University of Minnesota Press, 1989).

White, Deborah Elise, "Studies on Hysteria: Case Histories and the Case Against History," *MLN (Modern Language Notes)* 104, no. 5 (1989): 1034–49.

Williams, Juan, "Open Season on Clarence Thomas," *Washington Post*, 10 October 1991: A23.

Williams, Patricia, *The Alchemy of Race and Rights: Diary of a Law Professor* (Cambridge, Mass. and London: Harvard University Press, 1991).

Wright, Lawrence, "Remembering Satan," *The New Yorker*, 17 May, 24 1993.

Young, Iris Marion, *Justice and the Politics of Difference* (Princeton: Princeton University Press, 1990).

Žižek, Slavoj, *Enjoy Your Symptom!* (New York and London: Routledge, 1992).

Index